THE VIRGIN
INTERNET

THE VIRGIN GUIDE TO THE INTERNET

VERSION 1.0

Simon Collin

First published in Great Britain in 1999 by
Virgin Publishing Ltd
Thames Wharf Studios
Rainville Road
London W6 9HA

Version 1.0 – December 1999

Designed and typeset by John and Orna Designs, London
Printed and bound by Mackays of Chatham plc

ISBN 0 7535 0405 7

A catalogue record for this book is available from the British Library.

//LET US HELP YOU TO GET THE BEST OF THE NET

'Try looking it up on the Internet.'

'Send me an email.'

'You can probably get that cheaper on the Internet.'

The Internet might just be the most important cultural revolution of our lifetimes. Yet it's managed to sneak up behind most of us and hit us over the head.

For years, it was the preserve of computer whizkids – almost impossible to set up, expensive to join and difficult to understand. Then manufacturers started to make computers that almost connect themselves, and the people who provide access to the Internet decided to do it for free. By the beginning of the twenty-first century, the Internet was a mass medium, just like television and radio – both of which, by the way, you can experience via the World Wide Web.

The Internet's still a technical marvel, and like all cutting edge technologies it can be a pain to set up and get started. So this book starts with some simple technical information and advice, which will save you time and hassle when buying and setting up your equipment. We cover all the basics of web browsing, email and chat, and will help you put things right if they go wrong.

But this guide isn't just for beginners. It's also for the millions of people who are overwhelmed or frustrated by the sheer size and complexity of what's out there. We've put together all the tips and tricks you need to make your time online more productive and enjoyable.

The core of this book is a list of the most useful, intriguing and amusing websites there are. The web is always changing, but all the Internet addresses in here are good springboards from which to start your explorations. They're kept up to date by their designers and provide pretty well what they promise.

Let this Virgin Guide be your guide to cyberspace.

Simon Collin, who compiled this guide, is a technology writer and net-obsessive who has worked for many of the leading computer magazines and has written over two dozen books about computing and the Internet.

The Internet is evolving so fast that, even though this book was correct at the time of going to press, there could be a few dud addresses or omissions. If you have any problems with anything in this book, send us an email at response@virgin-pub.co.uk. We'll make sure it's dealt with in the next edition.

//CONTENTS

1//WHAT IS THE INTERNET?

You're eager to get online and start exploring. You can, of course, just jump straight in and try out the directory of sites that we've compiled in the second half of this book. But it'll help if you have an idea of what the Internet is all about. Finding out how the Internet works doesn't take long and really isn't too complicated; for new users (who are called 'newbies' in the parlance of the Internet), it's such a different mind-set that it's well worth explaining everything clearly from the start.

This chapter will set out the foundations and give you an overview of the way everything fits together. In the next few chapters, you'll come rocketing up to speed on how to use the net to its best advantage.

//THE BIGGEST NETWORK ON THE PLANET

The Internet does all kinds of tricks. You can send messages over it, find out the local weather, check train timetables, ask questions about gardening, book a holiday, buy a car or read a book. There's nothing precise about the Internet and, because it's always changing and developing, it's hard to define exactly what it does.

Mind your language
The word 'Internet' is always capitalised. Lower-case 'internet' refers to something altogether smaller – such as a few office networks linked together. Feel free to call it the net but, for your own self-esteem, try and avoid calling it the information superhighway, unless you're a politician.

If we cannot really put our finger on what it does, we can at least tell you what it is. The Internet is just a way of linking a lot of computers together so that they can share information. The information is stored collectively on servers – computers that do nothing else but wait for requests for information and then supply it. A server can be a simple PC or a high-powered tower in a special room; you don't need to know since you only want to access the information it stores on its hard disk.

Each of these server computers has its own unique identity, called its IP (Internet protocol) address. This is a series of numbers that acts as a map-reference to help other computers find information. Every computer on the Internet speaks to every other computer in the same language, called TCP/IP, allowing each to process your requests and transfer information efficiently and easily.

The servers run special software that lets them deal with different types of request. Some servers only move electronic mail messages from sender to recipient, others are responsible for supplying files that can be downloaded and yet others only deliver web pages.

If you want to use the Internet and its vast collective store of information, you need to connect your computer to one of the servers. You do this using a specialist company called an Internet service provider (ISP). The link from your computer to the ISP is normally via a normal phone line – you'll need a modem that plugs into your computer and the phone. Once you're connected to the server at the ISP, you can jump to any of the other millions of servers on the Internet and see what information they offer.

In Chapter 2, we'll show how you to choose your new computer, modem and ISP and how to configure and link up to the Internet.

//THREE BASIC WAYS TO USE THE INTERNET

Once you are online, what will you find? You can use the Internet in three ways: first, use it as a library that has a vast store of information, which you can search and read. Second, use it to send messages to your friends and colleagues. Third, post messages in a public forum where they can be read by all. At the moment, if you want to use all of the features of the Internet, you'll need to use several different software tools. Here's a run-down of the various parts of the net, what they do and what you'll need to use them.

The World Wide Web (WWW or web)

The web is the fast-talking brash salesperson for the Internet. It's good-looking, packed with information (much of it unbelievable) and very easy to use. The web is a great way to present the information that's stored on the servers connected to the Internet.

The web consists of websites, millions of them, each being run by individuals or companies and most sites cover one particular subject. Each website is just a collection of individual web pages – think of it as a library (the web) with books (websites) that are full of web pages (the pages). The difference is, anyone can get published, all the books are linked together and there's a great index that lets you jump straight to any page. On the other hand, the cataloguing has been done pretty haphazardly – hence the importance of search engines (see page 53).

The clever bit about the web is called hyperlinking. Any web page can be linked to any other web page on any other website. If you've got a web page about gardening, you might include links that point to specialist web pages on shrubs, annuals, lawns and so on. A user clicks on a hotspot (that can be a bit of text or a picture) and jumps to the hyperlinked page. This following of links is one of the Internet's most fascinating and addictive aspects – you can wander around for hours and end up finding and reading something great that's totally unconnected to what you started with.

Presentation

Each website presents its information in very different ways. Some sites present information, advice or opinions in a magazine format, with text and pictures to browse; other sites let you type in a phrase to search a database for information; some sites let you order and pay for things.

There are literally millions of websites that cover every conceivable subject. There are sites with the latest news, weather, business, sport, education, jobs, cars, religion, ways to buy CDs, books or bikes, hobbies, games and an enormous stack of other subject matter, much of which is too weird to contemplate.

There's a lot of stuff out there, and for many people, when they talk about the Internet they mean the World Wide Web. But, it's just one part of the Internet experience – there's a lot more besides.

Electronic mail (email)

On a day-to-day basis, you'll soon find that the most useful part of the Internet is email. Email is the convenient, free, speedy version of the old postal service. You can send a plain letter – a message – to any other user on the Internet. It's just as easy to send a document, database, picture, video clip or sound file. Automatic systems can even send you a daily message with headlines or sports results, magazine articles or share prices.

In the same way that every server on the Internet has its own unique address, every person on the Internet has their own unique name, combining a user name (selected by you when you sign up for Internet service) and a server name (usually that of the Internet provider or perhaps your company's registered Internet name).

Each day, hundreds of millions of email messages are sent around the world. They are quick to create and delivery to any place normally takes under a minute. For the recipient, it can be very convenient: you can reply to messages in your time rather than have constant phone calls. And with a laptop, you can pick up and read your email messages from anywhere in the world.

Newsgroups, mailing lists and chat

The web and email are staid and slow in comparison to newsgroups, mailing lists and chat. Each allows users to air their views on any topic that's worth the effort – and plenty that's not.

Newsgroups work rather like a big pin-board; any user can pin up a message about a new topic or reply to an existing message. All the messages in a newsgroup are stored in public for a few days for anyone to read and comment on what's been said. There are over 60,000 newsgroups covering different topics that range from collecting Dinky toys to getting a job, from teaching to gardening. You can say or ask anything, get into an argument, get advice or just shout a lot.

Mailing lists are rather more sensible: if you're interested in the subject covered, subscribe by sending your email address. From now on, any subscriber can send a message to the list and it will be automatically distributed to the entire group. It's not an instant forum for chat, but a great way to distribute information.

Chat provides the most dynamic forum on the net. You can join a session and chat about anything to the other people who are there or use instant messaging to have a private chat with a friend or a stranger.

Extending the system of chat, you can make telephone calls over the Internet – either to a friend connected to the net or by dialling out to a real phone. With the right equipment, you can even see each other.

//A BRIEF HISTORY

For a true picture of the Internet, it's worth looking at the history and possible future of the net. It all started in 1964, at the height of the nuclear standoff between the United States and the Soviet Union, when a US think tank called the RAND group realised that one atomic bomb could totally wreck the US military computer network. It came up with an idea for a network of computers, each sharing the load while remaining totally independent. It was assumed that the network would be unreliable – so that if transmission of a message was interrupted by enemy action, the system would resend it or pass on the missing data until it was safely received. The other key points were that every computer within the network was equal (there was no one machine controlling things) and that messages and information could flow freely from one computer to another – it didn't matter which route it took, as long as it got to its destination somehow.

Birth of the network

Over the next few years, RAND and a couple of the top US universities – in particular, the Massachusetts Institute for Technology – worked hard on this concept. In 1968, the British National Physical Laboratory, in the perhaps unlikely setting of suburban Teddington, Middlesex, set up a network to test all these ideas. The US government then funded a far larger experiment named after its official funding body, the Pentagon's Advanced Research Projects Agency (ARPA).

By the end of 1969 there was an infant network linking a handful of supercomputers scattered in universities around the United States. This system was called ARPANET and the scientist Robert Kahn described much of the original architecture. Over the next few years, more computers (referred to as nodes) were added and soon a few dozen supercomputers were hooked up.

The idea behind the network was to share computer power, which in the pre-PC age was limited and very expensive indeed. However, in 1972, a simple program was developed to allow the operators of the computers on the network to exchange messages with other users of ARPANET over the network itself. To help organise the way this material was sent, a concept called a list was developed. This allowed little groups of users to redistribute a message to all members in the group. Email and mailing lists were born.

Through the 1970s, the larger US government research labs and communications giants (notably AT&T) started to develop their own networks to work in parallel with ARPANET. Most were purpose-built for a particular company, but a couple of these networks were just as freewheeling as the Internet. One, called BITNET, was used to link up universities. The other, USENET, was a way for users to exchange information. In the UK, the universities set up their own private network called JANET (Joint Academic Network).

Meanwhile, more computers from around the United States joined the ARPA network. It soon outgrew its own 'protocol' – the system used to package up the information, address it and send it around the network. A new protocol called TCP/IP (transmission control protocol/internet protocol) was developed by Kahn and another godfather of the Internet, Vincent Cerf. The first part (TCP) packaged the information into bundles or 'packets'; the second part (IP) was a method of addressing each packet so that it reached its correct destination. The great change to TCP/IP happened simultaneously across all the nodes on the Internet on 1 January 1983.

More people join in

TCP/IP was free to anyone who wanted to try it out, and the ARPA network was designed to be loose and easy to extend. So that's exactly what happened and, as the network expanded and grew, it soon became known as the Internet. By the end of 1983, the new Internet had 1,000 computers linked and online.

In the mid-1980s, the biggest labs and government centres for science (like NASA) stepped in and added their considerable computing weight to the Internet. The network had one big rule: it was strictly for educational purposes, and it was forbidden to use the Internet for profit and commerce.

As soon as the Internet was established as a unifying network standard, it was immediately used to build separate networks that grouped organisations with similar interests. The number of computers linked to the Internet (the combination of these individual networks) was beginning to grow and by 1988 there were 60,000 computers online.

Joining it all up

The early insular networks needed something to connect them all together. The catalyst was a US government organisation called the National Science Foundation, which had several very powerful supercomputers that it was willing to share with some of the universities. To do this, it set up a network called NSFnet that linked its own supercomputers and allowed universities access to the network. The backbone – the big communications link connecting these supercomputers – was only as powerful as one of today's 56Kbps modems.

Universities and organisations around the world soon latched on to NSFnet as a central hub that let them share resources and computing power. The NSFnet backbone had to be upgraded to a high-speed leased line to cope with the demand. In 1990, the name ARPANET was officially dropped and the term Internet was adopted instead – and it was now run by NSFnet.

Meanwhile computer technology had moved on apace. By the start of the 1990s, every stock market in the world had changed from dealing by paper and phone to using computer terminals. The 1991 Gulf War proved the importance of the Internet as an immediate way of broadcasting uncensored material around the world – in this case, reports from residents and journalists via IRC and newsgroups. Banks, media organisations and other commercial interests were now clamouring to be allowed to use the not-for-profit Internet to transfer data around the world.

In 1991, NSFnet dropped the 'no commerce' rule and opened the Internet to companies and the general public. Commercial Internet Service Providers (ISPs) sprang up to act as middlemen between the users and the network. The biggest ISPs grouped together to form a commercial alternative to NFSnet, a central hub called the Commercial Internet Exchange (CIX), to get their own plug in to the Internet.

Over the next few years, the number of companies joining the net began to grow at an astonishing rate. By the mid-1990s, there were more commercial organisations (who were assigned domain names ending in '.com') than the original educational establishments (whose domain names end in '.edu').

The World Wide Web is spun

The web was developed not by a military department or a company but by Tim Berners-Lee, a British scientist working at the CERN laboratory in Geneva. He developed the idea of adding links in documents to reference other documents on other nodes (computers) on the new Internet. He tried this out in 1980 with a program called 'Enquire Within Upon Everything', and by 1989, he had published a proposal for hypertext, a system of setting up instant links between documents.

A year later, Berners-Lee started to develop the method of describing the links and a program (a browser) to view and navigate them, coining the name 'World Wide Web' for the project. The basic technology and method of coding the links (called hypertext markup language or HTML) has changed very little since then; the sound, video and snappy design of today's websites are all based on add-on technology.

Software companies got to work developing their own web browser programs to display web page written in standard HTML. One company – Netscape – was way ahead of the competition with its browser. It dominated the market and helped push forward new standards to improve HTML. It even developed its own extension to HTML called JavaScript – now used to produce special effects on almost all the major websites.

Meanwhile the biggest software company in the world – Microsoft – had its head in the sand. Only in 1995, when Microsoft launched its Windows 95 operating system, did it supply its own web browser, called Internet Explorer (IE). If you bought a PC with Windows 95, you had a complete, easy-to-set-up package that was Internet-ready. The web browser market is now dominated by Microsoft – it built more than half the browsers in daily use, with Netscape trailing on a quarter share.

The future

As you've discovered from the historical background above, the Internet started off carrying text. It was never designed to carry the whole range of multimedia information that's now delivered from every trendy website.

You can now send video, sound and pictures over the Internet, but it's slowing everything down. The main connection that links the servers together is called the backbone and, although fast, it has nearly reached its capacity to carry information (this capacity is called its bandwidth).

This problem of speed can be solved by improving bits of the Internet, but it's rather a patchwork solution – like replacing short sections of country lane with dual carriageways. The future lies with Internet2, a new high-speed replacement that's being developed, with the aid of massive government grants, within the United States. Once you're online, find out how far they've got by visiting their website at **http://www.internet2.org**.

Website designers are demanding new ways of producing stunning sites. The original HTML language was not really designed with page layout in mind – it was only designed to provide hyperlinks. Over the years, we've had new versions of HTML with a bunch of design-led enhancements. But as each version of HTML is approved, the web browser developers and the site designers try and outdo each other with new tricks.

As the backbone for the Internet is being improved, so too is the functionality of all the separate elements within the Internet. Email is a good example. Future developments will make it even easier to send mail from any electronic device. New telephones have flip-out keyboards and a mini screen to provide simple email without a computer, cellphones are starting to provide email alerts and there's even a watch that tells you that you've received new email.

Email's biggest problem is that there aren't any central directories. The work of compiling has started and a standard way of using the directory, called IMAP, has been agreed. However, until everyone implements the standard, the only sure way of finding someone's address is to phone him or her.

Internet telephony Chat looks certain to grow into the most active part of the net – particularly instant messaging, which is even more convenient than email. Mailing lists and newsgroups are set to stick around with few changes. The only real change will be phone calls over the Internet. Several countries have already banned this technology because it has the potential to drain the profits of the established telephone companies. But something has to give – either phone calls will come down in price or Internet telephony will take off.

Where next?

Compared to the original users struggling on a slow, text-based network in the early 1980s, we have it good. We have unlimited access to what is effectively a free network, with access to vast tracts of information, news, music, films and software. Once you've tried the Internet, you'll soon rely on it to deliver email and news. Just like the telephone network, it's no longer a luxury – it's a right. The point is that we should be able to take it for granted. The Internet is grown up now and ready and able to earn its way. The techies who built it and still defend it will always use it, but they can no longer control it – it's just too big and powerful.

The arrival of cheap high-speed links (such as ADSL) from your home will mean that you receive more information, faster. But there's a problem. The original backbone connections that form the Internet were not designed to carry such quantities of information. There could soon be a traffic snarl-up and gridlock.

The long-term picture, however, looks very bright. The net is a fantastic resource that links the world, provides free speech, endless entertainment and has changed the business model for both new and established companies. We're in the middle of a major evolution in human history. Grab a computer, get online and be part of it.

//ADDRESS BOOK

About the Internet

Internet Society **http://www.isoc.org**
History, current status and developments of the Internet.

Internet 2 **http://www.internet2.org**
Developing the next generation of Internet.

w3 **http://www.w3.org**
Provides standards for HTML, web and Internet definitions.

NCSA **http://hoohoo.ncsa.uiuc.edu**
(National Center for Supercomputing Applications)
One of the organisations that developed the first web browser.

2//GETTING ONLINE

Before you can start to explore the Internet, you've got to get online. This can be the most difficult part of the whole process – and it normally causes people the most headaches. Once you have chosen a computer, you will also need to set up an account with a company called an Internet service provider (ISP) that supplies you with a route on to the net. Finally, you will need to install and configure special software to work with this company (although almost all new computers now come with all the software pre-installed, so you'll face just a few steps to get online).

This chapter tells you what equipment you'll need, how to choose it and how to set up your basic connection. We cover how to choose an ISP, setting up your link, web browser, email and newsgroup reader. Once you're online, you can consider using more advanced features, including online chat and making phone calls over the net – for details, see chapter 7.

//WHAT SORT OF COMPUTER DO I NEED?

In theory, any computer can be connected to the Internet – from a high-powered graphics workstation to a pocket-sized personal organiser. Using the Internet is not particularly demanding on your computer's resources. Most computers can be coaxed into going online, but if you've a computer that's over three years old, you'll find that your Internet provider is unlikely to support the special software you need. If you bought your computer new within the last year, you'll have no problems getting online. If you're still shopping for a new system, here are the basic guidelines you should follow.

When you buy a new computer, you have two basic choices: do you buy a PC-compatible or a Macintosh? The two options provide different ways of designing what's inside the computer, what sort of central processor chip is used and what sort of software can be run. In practice, PCs dominate through sheer range of software and accessories. Macintosh computers tend to look nicer but any extra software or hardware can be more expensive. Software and hardware for one type doesn't easily work on the other platform.

You don't need to invest before you surf. For just a few pounds, your local library provides very cheap access to the net, or if you want help and a coffee, try a local Internet café.

PC-compatibles Ensure that you're getting Windows 98 pre-installed. You need a reasonably fast processor: anything running at 250MHz or faster will be adequate. The latest speediest Pentium processor from Intel will speed you along but from an Internet point of view, a K6 from AMD will work just as well. You'll need at least 32Mb of main memory (RAM) – most new PCs are supplied with 64Mb. Buy the biggest hard disk you can afford: however big the disk, it'll soon fill up so ensure you've got at least 4-6Gb on board. Lastly, get a monitor and graphics adapter that can display images at a resolution of at least 800x600 (most web pages are designed to be displayed at this resolution).

Macintosh Make sure you have System 8 installed (you can make do with 7.5 but anything older is hard work). Any new Mac will be running a PowerPC processor. For those who prefer the Macintosh experience, the price of new Macs – notably the Internet-ready (and cute with it) iMac – has dropped dramatically. Aim for at least 32Mb of main memory, though 64Mb is preferred. Your hard disk should have a capacity of at least 4-6Gb and the graphics adapter/monitor combination needs to support a minimum resolution of 800x600 with 256 or more colours.

Multimedia and extras

The Internet is rapidly turning into a multimedia experience so, for either system, make sure you have a sound card and speakers. Software is almost always sold and distributed on CD, so you'll need a CD-ROM drive in your computer (get the fastest you can, with a spin speed of at least 20x). If you're buying new, make sure your CD-ROM drive is DVD-ready. It'll save an upgrade in a year or two.

//HOW DO I CONNECT?

Before you set out to explore, you need to link your computer to the net. Your shopping list has three items on it:

- a box that connects your computer to the phone line (called the modem).
- an account with a company called an Internet service provider (ISP) – that provides a doorway to the Internet.
- a normal telephone line (you can always upgrade later).

To get on to the Internet, your modem dials the telephone number of the ISP and connects your computer to the ISP's own large, powerful computer (called a server). The server is your doorway to the rest of the Internet – once connected to it, you'll be able to view web pages, read newsgroups and send email.

Modems

You need a modem (short for modulator-demodulator) in order to convert the digital data from your computer into analogue sound that can then be sent over a standard phone line. The modem also has sophisticaed features to cut out any hiss, crackle and pops you might normally hear on a line that would otherwise scramble data.

Modems are cheap, work with your existing phone line and let you connect to any Internet service provider. On the downside, they are relatively slow and can take up to

a minute to go through the tedious business of actually dialling and connecting to the Internet.

You can get modems tucked away inside your computer (an internal model) or in the form of a little box that connects to the serial port at the back of your computer (an external model). Both models do the same job – an external model is a little more expensive but it's easier to move from one machine to another if you upgrade.

Modem standards, which define the speed at which a modem can transfer information, are always on the move, constantly being developed and improved. Within a year, your new modem will be considered as slow as a ... well ... a very slow thing. To get out of this trap, check that the modem supports software upgrades (often called Flash-ROM or Flash upgrades). Whenever a new specification is developed, log on to the modem manufacturer's website and follow the instructions: new configuration data will be automatically transferred to the modem and it'll run at the new speed.

When buying a modem, refer to the following checklist:

1 Buy the fastest modem you can. Make sure it supports a transfer rate of 56Kbps (the current standard is called V90).

2 Ensure it supports upgrades to Flash-ROM so you can keep up with the latest standard.

3 Some modems include a built-in answering machine – do you really want to pay extra for this? Unlikely.

4 Almost all modems are capable of sending and receiving faxes – it's a nice extra that shouldn't cost any more.

5 Internal modems are cheaper but are more difficult to install.

6 Make sure it's BABT-approved (the box will display a sticker

with a round green spot) that legally lets you connect it to your telephone socket.

How fast is fast?

The speed of a communications channel describes the amount of information that it can carry every second – the maximum is called its 'bandwidth'. The speed is usually described with the 'Kbps' or 'Mbps' acronym. Kbps (kilobits per second) describes the number of thousand individual pieces of digital information that can be transferred every second. Mbps (megabits per second) is faster and describes the number of million individual pieces of digital information transferred per second.

The theoretical maximum speed of your modem is just one factor in deciding the real speed of the connection. You need a good, clear telephone line and an ISP that uses the same high-speed modems. In practice, you'll never hit the maximum speed of your modem; instead, you'll generally cruise at somewhere between 60-80 per cent of the maximum.

Faster, faster

Most people connect to the net using a modem, but it's hardly the fastest technology available. You could upgrade to Home Highway, but if you plan to use the Internet every day or you have your own busy website to manage, you might consider upgrading to a faster connection.

Each of the following technologies will cost you more than a standard modem connection. First, you'll need a new box to link your computer to the new communications channel and, second, the monthly rental is generally higher than a standard phone line. Lastly, every ISP supports links via a modem, but not all support these higher-speed technologies.

ISDN (integrated services digital network) is an all-digital high-speed alternative to a modem; it easily outpaces even the fastest modem and can make the call and connect you to the Internet in less than a second. In the UK there's a big push from telcos (telephone companies) to increase the number of customers (primarily businesses) that connect via ISDN; home users will find Home Highway a better solution, unless they can wait till ADSL arrives in their area.

Once you have an ISDN line (or Home Highway), you need to ask your ISP for a special ISDN dial-up account. Most providers, including the free ISPs, support ISDN.

Home Highway
Home Highway is a cut-down version of ISDN that's easier to understand, cheaper to install and is still faster than a modem.

The problem for BT is that once it announces full access to ADSL (see opposite), it will probably be forced to stop supplying the slower Home Highway system.

Your old line will be converted to two digital lines (with two numbers) and you'll get a neat box in the corner of your room. Plug in your old phone and your new ISDN terminal adapter (TA) to connect your computer and you're off. Dedicated surfers will like Home Highway but, again, there's better technology around the corner.

Cable modem If you have cable TV running into your home, you're looking at the best route to potential high-speed Internet access with little effort and cost. We say 'potential' because it depends entirely on the whim of your cable provider.

A cable modem sits between your computer and the raw cable from the cable TV company. You'll need the cable modem itself (called a head-end) and a network adapter card for your computer. Once you're set up, you have the potential to use the full capacity of the cable. You'll have to share this capacity with other users in your area but it's still a mighty fast link from home to net. In practice, you could expect to receive data at up to 10Mbps (almost 200 times faster than a standard modem) – though a more realistic figure is likely to be around 2Mbps (still a respectable 40 times faster). When sending information to the Internet, you use a slower channel over the same cable, running at a maximum of around 128Kbps.

The biggest providers in the UK, Cable and Wireless (**http://www.cwcom.co.uk**), NTL (**http://www.ntl.co.uk**) and Telewest (**http://www.telewest.co.uk**) have begun to carry out trials in some areas, but you'll have to call to ask when this might happen near you. Keep in touch with developments via the Cable Communications Association (**http://www.cable.co.uk**) and read about the first cable modems from 3Com (**http://www.3com.com**) and Motorola (**http://www.mot.com**).

DSL and ADSL ISDN's new cousin, DSL (Digital Subscriber Lines), is beginning to appear. It's another way of providing a high-speed digital link to the Internet but its great advantage is that it can work over standard telephone cabling. There are several different versions of DSL technology, with ADSL (Asymmetric Digital Subscriber Lines) just around the corner and even a reality in many countries.

Like ISDN, you'll need a special adapter that connects your computer to the line. Unlike ISDN, ADSL pumps data along the wire at an astonishingly fast rate. It can send data from the Internet to your computer at a staggering 32Mbps (that's 50 times faster than basic ISDN) and lets you transmit data on to the Internet at a variable rate of between 32Kbps and 1Mbps. This split rate works fine in practice as you'll normally receive far more information than you send.

The second main difference is that ADSL is 'always on'; this means that you effectively have a permanent connection to the Internet – for home users, this means no delays when dialling, for business users it means the chance to set up their own server. Instead of paying for calls by the minute, you pay a flat, fixed monthly rental. In some countries this is affordable for home enthusiasts, but in the UK the price is between £40-150 per month – more than you could ever run up on the phone bill.

There are few problems with ADSL. The main catch is availability. You'll have to check with your telephone company and ISP to find out when it'll be installed in your area.

If you do get set up with ADSL, it should cost no more to install than an existing ISDN line. The terminal adapter will be a little more expensive (around £150) and running costs are built into the monthly rental charge.

Leased line If you're running a large company – or your own popular website – you might consider a permanent line from your office to the ISP. This is called a leased line – it's your own dedicated, direct link. You don't dial a number as you're always online. This is not really an option for any home user and your telco would probably laugh if you asked.

Satellite Yes, you can use a direct satellite link to connect to the Internet. The main service provider is DirecPC (**http://www.direcpc.com**) who install a dish on your roof and direct it to the right spot in the sky. Oddly, the service can only send you information; you can't transmit back (you'd need something similar to Goonhilly for satellite transmissions). Instead, your computer is linked up to a standard modem that's used with your normal phone line.

Why is it so slow?

The speed of your modem determines how fast you can transfer information to and from your computer. But even with a high-speed modem you will still find the net can be unbearably slow. You are at the mercy of congestion on the backbone (the motorway that links your ISP to all the other ISPs). As more users log in at peak time, the motorway chokes up – so avoid early evening or your local time equivalent to when the United States wakes up.

Even with a clear run on the main route across the Internet, you still need the equivalent of fast local roads. Your link to your ISP needs to be fast and so does the ISP's link to the backbone. And lastly, if you're trying to view a website, your overall speed will depend upon the speed of the remote web site's computer, link and ISP.

//CHOOSING AN INTERNET SERVICE PROVIDER

Your computer's running. The modem's plugged in. Now you need to choose an Internet Service Provider (ISP). An ISP works as a necessary middleman; it provides a local telephone number for your modem to dial to connect to their big computers that form part of the Internet. Only the very biggest sites or corporations link directly to the Internet while everyone else makes use of ISPs and leaves them to manage the techie network connections.

Choosing an ISP can be a problem. Some are vast international companies that are financially and technically solid, provide great support and a good service. Others are two-bit fly-by-nights who could go bust or could ruin your surfing experience by providing crummy service. To help you choose the right provider, run through the top tips on page 25.

Check that your intended Internet provider supports local-rate calls in your area or you'll end up with a vast phone bill each month.

What's the difference between the ISPs?

There are lots of different ways of grouping and classifying ISPs but, essentially, there are now just two types of company: one charges and the other is free. Why, you're wondering, can some companies still get away with charging for Internet access when there are so many free services? Your first instinct might be to plump for the free service, but you might find that you're better served by one of the companies that charge. Here are the main differences.

Free ISPs

Some countries, notably the UK, have such aggressive marketing from telephone companies and ISPs that you can now sign up for free Internet access. A free ISP aims its services at home and personal users and provides local-rate access numbers in a particular region. You don't pay any monthly subscription, just the usual telephone charges. In return, you get web space, an email account, access to newsgroups and free software to get you started.

These companies survive by selling advertising or by splitting the profit on the cost of the phone call with the telephone company. Slim margins, but still profitable.

A couple of ISPs are even experimenting with providing free Internet access and free phone calls. Scour the newspapers for details – they are normally heavily promoted to boost the profile of the ISP and only available at certain times of the week (such as the weekend).

Pros: it's free!

Cons: can be very busy in the evenings and weekends, making it hard to get online. You might have to put up with lots of advertisements and you cannot run a business or create cutting-edge websites – though you can create simple websites for free.

Why pay?

Many ISPs still charge a monthly subscription fee to connect you to the Internet. For your money (normally between £5-10 per month) you get full access to the Internet (just like a free ISP) but there are several extra benefits: first, there's no advertising – just the plain Internet. Second, you should be able to create a more sophisticated website of your own and, third, you should also receive a handful of email addresses for you and your family.

If you're just starting out, you might need to call technical support if your computer refuses to connect. Free ISPs often charge premium rates to reach technical support – you should receive free 24-hour support from an ISP that is charging you a monthly subscription.

Many ISPs that charge are now re-aligning themselves to provide e-commerce and other business-related extras – to allow companies to register their own, unique identity on the Internet (called their domain name) or set up a shopping site.

Content providers

Some ISPs provide much more than a 'plain vanilla' connection to the Internet. In addition to the full access to the net, you can also use the company's own, internal database – a sort of private Internet for subscribers.There are plenty of ISPs that have set up to publish their own content; national companies include AOL, CompuServe, LineOne and Virgin Net. To confuse matters, some content providers charge a subscription, others are free (see the list at the end of this chapter for full details).

AOL and CompuServe

The two biggest ISPs in the world are AOL (America Online) and CompuServe (AOL owns CompuServe) – AOL alone has 16 million subscribers. These two companies take a different route to providing

Internet access to subscribers. They are both content providers – they have put a huge amount of effort into building up their own private community for subscribers that's like a mini-Internet: it's got news, sport, music, reviews, games, and lots of discussion groups and chat rooms.

In addition to this extra content, you can also use the company's international network of telephone access numbers – which is great for travellers but not relevant to anyone else. Great if you want to check your email when you're on holiday – you simply use the local access number in that country – with a standard ISP you would need to make a long-distance call.

The other main difference is that you use custom-written software that attempts to make your Internet experience as foolproof as possible. This custom software includes useful features for families: parents can define the type of content their children can view.

AOL has two different ways of charging for its services. Either pay a low monthly subscription, which includes a quota of a few hours online (you'll pay by the minute once you've used up this quota), or pay a higher subscription for unlimited time online. To add a degree of confusion, AOL has launched its own free ISP service, called Netscape Online (**http://www.netscapeonline.co.uk**), but this is not the same as the original AOL and doesn't have the custom software, discussion groups or parental control.

Choosing an ISP

We've listed the major national ISPs in the Address Book at the end of this chapter. You'll find hundreds of local ISPs near you that offer great service but might not have the technical infrastructure to give you the fastest connection to the Internet. Free ISPs are great for home use but often have a limited range of advanced features.

Pick the right ISP Who's going to get your account? Is it to be a free ISP or a global giant like AOL? To help you decide, have look at the statements below, and see which one(s) apply to you:

1 **'I'm stingy'** – go for an ISP that offers free Internet access.

2 **'I'm stingy and broke'** – go for an ISP that offers free Internet access and free phone calls.

3 **'I've a reputation to maintain'** – go for an established national or international ISP.

4 **'I want to set up a website for my business'** – you'll get better service from a standard ISP that charges.

5 **'I only plan to surf during evenings and weekends'** – you'll have a few busy signals from free ISPs during peak time.

6 **'I want my own domain name, ISDN and lots of support'** – a standard charging ISP is best for all this.

7 **'I don't want busy signals'** – make sure the ISP has no more than 10 users per modem (ask them for this ratio).

8 **'I want to connect with Home Highway or ISDN'** – most ISPs, including the free ones, support this but ask first.

9 **'I want to check my email as I travel around the world'** – your best bet is an account with AOL or CompuServe that you can access anywhere, or to sign up for a free web-based email service (see page 64).

10 **'I want to surf each night till my eyelids droop'** – avoid CompuServe and other ISPs that charge by the minute. Choose either a free or charging ISP that doesn't limit your time online.

11 **'I don't want to worry about configuring things, so just get me online quickly'** – Almost all major ISPs have easy-to-install software that loads automatically from a CD-ROM.

//GETTING ONLINE

To use the Internet you need to install and configure special software on your computer. Setting everything up is normally very easy and takes just a few minutes. Best of all, most friendly ISPs will send you a starter-pack and CD-ROM when you subscribe – this includes pre-configured versions of all the essential software that you will need. If you don't get a CD-ROM, you can still get online as almost all the software you need is pre-loaded (it's part of Windows or the Macintosh operating system bundle) – but you will need to configure it correctly.

If friends and local children cannot get your system online, try the support line. But watch out – many free ISPs will charge you by the minute for this privilege.

Get ready to connect

When you subscribe to an ISP, you'll be sent a list of configuration details that need to be typed in to set up your computer so it knows how to connect to the net. (If you've subscribed to AOL, CompuServe or an ISP that provides a complete automated installation package, you don't need to read this section – you're all set to go.)

Before you start to configure your computer, make sure that the modem is connected to the computer and telephone socket and switched on. Your ISP will have sent you a list of local phone numbers (called POPs – point of presence) that your modem uses to access the Internet. You also need your pre-assigned email address and the 'domain name' of the ISP computer. The domain name is a series of numbers that uniquely identifies every main computer on the Internet – it will look something like '198.122.22.3'. Once you've got these bits of information, you can configure your computer.

Connecting a PC to the net Before you can connect to the Internet, you need to configure Windows so that it knows how to access your ISP. Microsoft Windows controls your PC and provides all the features you need to get on to the net – it also has a helpful Wizard that takes you step-by-step through the process of entering the information you need to configure your computer. If you are running an older version of Windows, such as 95 or even 3.x, you'll need to follow some extra steps that are explained on page 30.

Steps to configure your PC:

1 Double-click on the Internet Connection Wizard icon on the left of the Desktop. If there's no icon visible, the Wizard could be in one of two possible places: Start/Programs/ Accessories/Communications or Programs/ Internet Explorer.

2 The Wizard asks what type of new connection you want to create – choose the middle of the three options to set up this computer to access your own ISP.

3 Make sure that your modem is plugged in and switched on; click on the Next button and the Wizard will automatically dial Microsoft and display a list of recognised ISPs.

4 Choose your ISP from the list and click on the Next button. The Wizard will automatically retrieve almost all the configuration information required to connect to this ISP – you'll only need to type in your user name, password and email address.

5 If your ISP is not on the list, go back to step 3 and select the last of the three options to configure Windows manually. You'll have to follow a series of steps and type in the telephone number used to access the ISP, then the configuration settings provided by the ISP, together with your user name, password and email address.

6 You'll also be asked to configure the way in which you access email and newsgroups. For these steps, you'll need the name of the mail servers used to send and receive messages (these are sometimes called the SMTP and POP3 servers): their names will look like 'smtp.virgin.net'. To access newsgroups, you'll need the address for the newsgroup server (also called the NNTP server): it will look like 'news.virgin.net'.

7 Once you have entered the information, it is stored in a profile within the Dial-up Networking folder in the My Computer icon.

Now that you have configured Windows, you can connect to the Internet and use your web browser or send and receive email messages. The Connection Wizard will have configured your computer so that when you run a web browser, it automatically dials and connects to the Internet. If, for some reason, you find that this doesn't happen automatically, double-click on the My Computer icon, open the Dial-up Networking folder and double-click on your connection profile, which you created in the previous steps. This will connect you to the net.

Connecting a Macintosh to the net Before you can connect to the Internet, you need to configure your Macintosh so that it can access your ISP. If you have a new Macintosh that's running System 8, you'll get plenty of help from the Internet Setup Assistant. It takes you step-by-step through the process of configuring your Mac ready for the net. If you have an older machine, look to the box on page 30.

Steps to configure your Mac:

1 Double-click on the Internet Setup Assistant icon (or choose the Internet Access option from the Apple menu, then select Internet Setup Assistant).

2 Click on the 'yes' option to set up a new Internet account.

3 You'll follow through a series of simple screens. Each asks you to enter one of the bits of information supplied by your ISP (email and newsgroup server, telephone number, etc.).

4 Once you've finished, your Mac is configured. You're ready to go online.

Now that you have configured your Macintosh, you can connect to the Internet and use your web browser or send and receive email messages. The Setup Assistant should have configured your computer so that when you run a web browser, it automatically dials and connects to the Internet. If you find that this doesn't happen automatically, choose the Remote Access Status option from the Apple menu to make the connection.

If you keep getting disconnected from the Internet, make sure that you've disabled the 'call waiting' feature on your phone and that someone upstairs isn't trying to dial out at the same time.

Am I connected yet? If you double-click on the web browser icon on your Desktop, this will automatically start the Windows program that dials the ISP's access number and connects your computer to their bigger computer, which provides the doorway to the Internet. First of all, you'll see the Dialer warn you it's trying to dial the ISP's access number. Once it's connected, the Dialer window disappears and the web browser window appears. You're now connected to the net – you're online.

When you're online, Windows 98 displays a tiny icon in the bottom right-hand corner of the screen (next to the time) with two tiny green squares linked. If you see this, you're online. The squares should flash bright green to show information is being transferred. The top square is the distant computer at the ISP and the bottom square represents your computer.

Your best support channel is that geeky friend that you've been patiently buttering up for years. Just make sure he really does know what he's talking about.

Trouble getting online? If you're having problems getting online, here are some of the common problems that beset new users:

1. When you start your web browser, does a window pop up (called the Dialer) to tell you the software is dialling and trying to connect to the net? If not, connect manually (see the 'Steps to configure' sections above).
2. When the Dialer pops up, does it say 'Dialing'. If not, there's a problem with your modem or modem settings. Make sure the modem is plugged in and switched on.
3. If the Dialer tells you there's 'no answer', make sure that you entered the access telephone number correctly.
4. When the Dialer connects, it displays a message that it has connected. Next, it sends your user name and password. If you see 'Authorisation error' or similar, there's a problem with your user name or password – they are case-sensitive, so enter them carefully.

Connecting an older computer to the net

If you have a computer that uses Windows 3.x or a Macintosh that uses System 6 or earlier, it's rather more difficult to get online. It's not impossible, but you'll have to use older software that rather lacks the friendly touch of the latest Wizards and Assistants.

First, ask your ISP if they have a setup CD for your type of operating system. If they do, it'll save a lot of bother. AOL and CompuServe also have versions of their custom software that runs on older computers. If your ISP can't supply a setup CD, you'll need to find the software elsewhere. The best place to look is on the front cover of Internet-related magazines in your newsagent's or visit a local Internet café or your library and spend an hour searching a site such as CNET (**http://www.cnet.com**) or TUCOWS (**http://www.tucows.com**) for suitable software.

Starting out with electronic mail

To send or receive electronic mail messages, you need an email program and an Internet connection. The easiest way to start is to use the email software that's supplied with the web browsers from Microsoft or Netscape. If you used the Windows Wizard or Macintosh Assistant to help you set up your Internet connection, you will have been given the option to configure your email program. If you didn't, see below for the manual option.

Choosing an email address When you sign up with an ISP you'll be asked to choose an email address that will be unique to you and used by your friends to send you messages.

When you choose your email address, you'll probably type in your first name and your surname. For example, if you're signing up for Freeserve, you might type in 'john@smith.freeserve.net'. Unfortunately, because of the huge number of other subscribers, you can be pretty certain that your name has already been assigned to someone else. The ISP will suggest an available address, like 'john@smith72.freeserve.net'. If you don't mind the number, fine. However, why not try a few alternatives to get a really unique address. You could try 'john@smith_family.freeserve.net' or, as you get more desperate for a unique name, even your hobby, nickname or house name.

If you're setting up different addresses for each member of the family, make sure that you pick a provider that offers multiple email addresses – for everyone in the gang. The simplest solution is to use the Windows Profiles feature to create totally separate views of Windows, email and browsing for each member of the family. Open the Start/Settings/ Control Panel window and double-click on the Users icon.

Setting up your email program If you are running the installation software from your ISP, or if you used the automatic Wizard or Assistant to configure your Internet connection (see earlier in this chapter), then you will be asked to type in the email address you've chosen and a password. Once you've done this, your email program will automatically configure the email program for you – you're now ready to send and receive messages.

To check if everything works, start the email program. It should start the Dialer automatically, connect to the Internet and contact the post office server. If you get to this stage and you see an error message, you've entered either the wrong address for the post office or the wrong name and/or password. Check all three and try again.

The manual option

If your ISP didn't supply a friendly installation program or you didn't use the Wizard or Assistant to do the hard work for you, you'll need to set up your email program yourself. You'll need to open the setup screen for your email program: in Microsoft's Outlook Express, this is under Mail/Options; in Netscape Messenger, it's under the Edit/Preferences menu. You'll see fields for your email address and password (normally the same as your standard Internet password) and fields for the names of the two email servers (supplied by your ISP). Type in the information and you're ready to go.

Setting up for newsgroups

Newsgroups are one of the most active areas of the Internet. To join in, you'll need special software called a newsgroup reader, which lets you read notices and submit your own, and a normal connection to the Internet. There are tens of thousands of individual newsgroups, each providing a discussion forum for a particular subject. They work rather like a notice board – anyone can post a message that can then be read by any other user. Once you're online, skip to Chapter 6 for details on how to use newsgroups.

Both Microsoft and Netscape include a newsgroup reader with their free web browser programs – there are alternative programs that you can download from the web, but the built-in readers are a great way to get started. If you used a special setup CD-ROM from your ISP or configured your web browser using the setup Wizard or Assistant, it's almost certain that your newsgroup reader is ready to use.

How to configure your newsgroup reader

When you first start your newsgroup reader, and if it's not already been configured, it will automatically ask you to enter the address of your ISP's news server – sometimes called the NNTP server (the special computer where your ISP stores newsgroup messages). Type in the address, for example 'news.virgin.net' and you'll see a new icon displayed with this name in the panel on the left of the screen. You're now ready to use your newsgroup reader – skip over to chapter 6 to see how.

//ADDRESS BOOK

Major ISPs

This modest range of ISPs comprises some of the larger companies that have been providing Internet access for several years. There are hundreds of other ISPs – some small, local companies, others offering national coverage. These companies will set you up with an account for a monthly payment; each provides basic dial-up access for users with modems but most can scale up to businesses with high-speed ISDN links or specialist requirements.

AOL 0800 376 5432 **http://www.aol.com**
BT Internet 0800 800 001 **http://www.btinternet.com**
CompuServe 0990 000 200 **http://www.compuserve.com**
Demon 0845 272 2666 **http://www.demon.net**
Direct Connection 0800 072 0000 **http://www.dircon.net**
Easynet 0845 333 4000 **http://www.easynet.net**
Global Internet 0870 909 8042 **http://www.global.net.uk**
Netcom 0990 668080 **http://www.netcom.net.uk**
Uunet 0845 0884455 **http://www.uunet.co.uk**

Free ISPs

Getting in touch with free ISPs by phone is hard work – they only like to give out premium rate support lines. For BTClick, ask the operator for a CD; for Freeserve, visit Dixons or PC World; X-stream and LineOne expect you to download their software from their websites; Virgin Net will send you a welcome pack and CD.

BT Click **http://www.btclick.com**
LineOne **http://www.lineone.net**
Netscape Online **http://www.netscapeonline.co.uk**
Virgin Net **http://www.virgin.net**
Freeserve **http://www.freeserve.co.uk**
X-stream **http://www.x-stream.co.uk**

3//SURFING THE WEB

The web is the part of the Internet that gets all the attention – it's easy to use, pretty to look at, full of exciting gimmicks and can be incredibly useful. You can check share prices, analyse sports results (or watch the match), listen to music, read books, shop till your credit card expires, scan the news and weather or do just about anything you choose – with a click of your mouse. It's also one of the biggest timewasters ever invented. There's something wickedly addictive about following links that lead into a series of increasingly random or irrelevant websites.

//WHAT IS THE WEB?

The World Wide Web is a collection of millions of individual websites. Each site is made up of individual web pages. The Virgin Publishing site (**http://www.virgin-books.com**) contains hundreds of web pages, stored as files that tell your computer what to display on screen, each of which might be about a particular book published by Virgin. These files contain commands that define the layout of the page, written in a language called hypertext markup language (HTML).

The clever bit about HTML is called hyperlinks: it allows the page designer to define text or pictures as hotspots; when you click on a hotspot, you jump to another page on the Internet or to another point on the page. Links are normally displayed as coloured, underlined text – when you move your mouse pointer over a hyperlink, it changes shape from an arrow to a pointing hand. Click on a hyperlink and the new page is displayed.

A page can also include graphics, sound or video clips – these are all stored in separate files and referenced using HTML commands (see Chapter 8 for more details on HTML). Each file has a name and usually ends with the file extension 'html' – like 'news.html'.

Sometimes, pages have an 'htm' extension – but it means the same thing. If you see a page ending 'asp' (for example, 'news.asp'), you're seeing a special kind of page that is filled with information only just before it is displayed.

Sites and home pages

A website is a collection of web pages that stands on its own. The Microsoft website (**http://www.microsoft.com**) has thousands of pages about the fruits of the Gates empire. Each site has a home page – it's the first page that's displayed when you visit the site. The home page is almost always stored in a file named 'index.html'. If you type in a website address without a specific web page, you'll see the home page. Visit '**http://www.bbc.co.uk**' or '**http://www.bbc.co.uk/**index.html' and you'll see the same opening page.

Often, you'll see an address like '**http://www.compuserve.com/simon/**' – this is an example of a small individual site located in an all-encompassing larger domain of an ISP. It's still a website with its own collection of web pages and it is totally different from '**http://www.compuserve.com/fred/**'.

Web addresses

Every website, page or image has its own unique address on the Internet. A website has a unique address called a 'domain name' – so the BBC's website (**http://www.bbc.co.uk**) has the domain name 'bbc.co.uk'. Each page on every website also has its own unique address, called its URL (uniform resource locator). A URL points to a particular web page, file, image or sound, whereas a domain name points to a site in general.

Save typing effort – you don't need to type in the 'http://' prefix in front of a URL. The browser will fill it in for you.

If you want to specify a particular web page on a website, you'll need to include the name of the file and the folder that contains the file. For example, if you want to see the latest news from the BBC, you could enter the URL '**http://www.bbc.co.uk/home/ today/ index.shtml**'. Thankfully, it's very unusual to have to type in such a precise link – you'll normally find a page by clicking on a link.

Guide to the parts of a web address
You'll see plenty of different types of web address, so here's a guide to the various elements:

http:// the first part of any web address is '**http://**' – it tells the browser you want to view a website.

https:// this is an indication (along with the closed padlock icon at the bottom of the window) that you're viewing a secure website.

www.bbc.co.uk the name of the computer that contains the pages for this site – called the domain name. Normally, computers that store websites start with 'www' but, on some vast sites, you might see a web address like 'reg.bbc.co.uk' that indicates you are on a secondary machine, called 'reg', but still viewing the same domain name of 'bbc.co.uk'.

194.207.0.252 the number that uniquely identifies every domain name on the web.

index.html the name of the file that contains one web page.

You can also see that '**http://www.bbc.co.uk**' is identical to '**http://194.207.0.252**'.

How do addresses work?
The key to websites – and every other element of the Internet – are IP addresses (part of the all-encompassing TCP/IP standard that

defines how everything fits together on the Internet) that uniquely identify every computer on the Internet.

Every main website on the Internet is given a unique IP address written in the form '194.207.0.252'. Since it's hard to remember an IP address, it's also given a name – such as 'bbc.co.uk' – that's called its domain name and is far easier to remember. If you want to try out this numbering, type in '194.207.0.252' in your web browser – it will take you to the BBC site in just the same way as entering 'www.bbc.co.uk'. The translation process between number and name is carried out in a huge table called the DNS (domain name system).

When you type a web address into your web browser, the browser looks in the DNS table to convert the name back into its numerical form. Once it's got the address as a number, the web browser has the equivalent of a map reference and knows exactly where to find the site.

//WEB BROWSERS

To view and surf web pages you'll need special software called a web browser. Its job is simply to decode the instructions stored in a web page file and display the formatted results on screen.

There are two main contenders in the browser market: Microsoft's Internet Explorer and Netscape's Navigator. Each company tries to introduce new technological trickery that will improve the web – and foil its rival. Both have leapfrogged each other over the years so now there's little difference between the two. And there's no price difference either – both are free (from **http://www.microsoft.com** and **http://www.netscape.com**) and both run on PCs and Macs. Both also provide a complete suite of Internet software – with email, newsgroup reader and web browser built in.

Net users who want to shun the nasty big corporations have several excellent smaller rivals to choose from including Opera (**http://www.operasoftware.com**). There are browsers for almost every type of computer and operating system; even if you have an old pre-Windows computer, you can still view web pages using the Arachne browser (**http://arachne.browser.org/**).

Using your web browser

To start surfing, run your web browser and it will automatically start the dialer program that dials the access number and connects you to the Internet. It normally takes just under a minute to connect to the net – the dialer tells you what stage you are at.

Once you are connected, the web browser automatically displays a 'home page'. This will probably be your ISP's main page, for example the Freeserve or Virgin Net page. You don't have to stick with the pre-assigned 'home page' – it's easy to change your web browser so that it displays your favourite sports page, shopping site or newspaper.

How to change your browser's home page:

1. Start your web browser, connect to the Internet and visit your favourite site.
2. With the main page of the site displayed, select the Tools/ Internet Options menu in IE or Edit/Preferences in Navigator.
3. A new dialog box is displayed: near the top there's a field with the site address of the current home page. Click on the button 'Use Current Page' to automatically insert the current site address.
4. Click on the OK button to confirm. Now, each time you start your browser, it displays your favourite page.

Navigating There are several different ways of moving (surfing) from one website or page to another:

- Move to a new site or page by typing in the address in the address window in the top left corner.
- Jump from one page to another by clicking on links in the page.
- Move back through the previous pages that you visited in this session by clicking on the back arrow in the button bar.

Visiting a site Just under the menu bar in the top left-hand corner is the Address window where you type in the URL for the website you want to visit. Click in the window and type in the address of the site you want to visit – for example 'www.bbc.co.uk' for the BBC's excellent website. You don't need to type in the initial 'http://' bit of an address – the browser fills this in for you. Once you have typed in the address, press Return and the web browser tries to find and display the page. If it cannot find the site or page, you'll see an error message. If this happens, check you have typed in the correct address and try again (see Chapter 4 for more information on finding websites).

Surfing The main part of the web browser window displays the web page. You'll see the text and layout defined according to the HTML instructions in the page. Hyperlinks normally appear on the page as underlined text. As you move your pointer over a link you'll see it change to a pointing-hand icon. Click once and you'll jump to a new page.

You can display several separate copies of the browser window by pressing Ctrl-N (or Apple-N on a Mac). Each window works independently, so you can view separate sites or pages in each – for example, viewing share prices in one window while you browse sports results in another.

One extra tip that's particularly useful when using a search engine is to press down the Shift key when you click on a link. This opens the new page in a new browser window – it's an ideal way of keeping search results in one window while you're checking out the site in another. If you don't use this time-saver, you'll have to click the Back button to flip back to the search results.

Bookmarking your favourite sites If you visit a site or page you're likely to visit again, you can bookmark it: choose the Bookmarks menu option in Netscape (or the Favourites menu option in Microsoft IE). Another way to do this is to press Ctrl-B under Windows or Option-B on your Macintosh. To go back to a bookmarked site, just click on the entry in the list.

As you start to create more bookmarks, you can create folders for different categories and neatly store your bookmarks in separate folders. To create a folder in Netscape, select the Communicator/Bookmarks/Edit Bookmarks menu option. From the new window that's displayed, select the File/New Folder option. In Microsoft IE, choose the Favourites/Organize Favourites menu option and click on the New Folder button.

Security If you're about to type in any important personal or financial information at a website – such as your credit card number when paying for shopping – make sure you are aware of security. The Internet was not designed to transfer private, personal information: if you send anything over the Internet, it is transferred in its plain, readable form. If a hacker is tapping your phone line, he or she could read whatever you send or receive. To counter this threat, sites that ask for personal information make sure that this information is sent in an encrypted, scrambled form and provide a secure channel between your browser and the website.

When your browser has established a secure channel, a tiny closed padlock icon is displayed in the status bar at the bottom of the browser window. All the new, current versions of web browsers support SSL. If you have an older version of a browser or just want to check everything is working, visit the VeriSign site (**http://www.verisign.com**) and use the online test that tells you if your browser is SSL-compatible.

Only type in your credit card details or other personal information when you see the closed padlock icon in the bottom line of your web browser.

Printing pages You can print any page that you display. If the page uses frames for layout, the print options window will ask which frame of the page you want to display. To get something that looks just like the original on screen, choose the 'As Laid Out on Screen' option.

Cookies

These are not for eating. A cookie is a scrap of information created by a website on your hard disk that lets the website store information to help it keep track of you. When you revisit the website, it reads the cookie, which tells it when you last visited or what you were interested in. For example, if you customise the Excite! (**http://www.excite.co.uk**) or MSN (**http://www.msn.co.uk**) portal pages so that they display the weather in Manchester and the latest cricket scores, these choices are stored in a cookie.

To switch off cookies, change the security settings in your web browser: for example, in Microsoft IE, choose the Tools/Internet Options menu, click on the Security page tab and click on the Custom Level button. Scroll down till you see 'Cookies' and change 'Enable' to 'Disable'.

It can be disconcerting to visit a site and be welcomed with 'back again? You were only here yesterday evening'. Most sites only use cookies to keep track of your visits and your custom options – giving them valuable marketing information that helps tailor their site. You can switch off support for cookies, but you'll lose out on lots of neat features and shopping services.

//SAVING INFORMATION FROM THE WEB

Anything that's displayed on a web page can be saved on to your computer, except for some types of video and music playback. Here's how to do it.

Copying text Select the text you want to copy from the page by clicking and holding down the button while moving the mouse. Press Ctrl-C to copy the text to the Windows Clipboard or Apple-C on a Mac. Switch to your word processor and press Ctrl-V to paste the text in Windows or Apple-V on a Mac.

Saving an image Move the pointer over the image you want to save and click once. Select the 'File/Save Image As' option from the main menu bar. Under Windows, move your pointer over the image then right-click to display the pop-up menu and choose the Save Image As option to store the image as a separate file on your hard disk.

Copying the code If you are developing your own website, you'll find it useful to see how the pros have pushed HTML to its limits to create their sites. Visit a site you particularly like and select the 'View/Source' option from the main menu bar: a new window pops up displaying the HTML source code for the page. If the page has been designed with frames (most advanced pages now use frames), move the pointer over the area of the page you want to investigate and again choose 'View/Source' to see the code for this frame.

Saving a sound or video file Move the pointer over the hyperlink that leads to the sound or video file. Right-click over the link (this only works on a PC) and choose the 'Save Target As' menu option.

Saving the location of a page Either create a new Bookmark or Favourite entry in your web browser or click anywhere on the page then drag it on to your desktop. You'll create an icon with a shortcut to the site's address.

Download a file

The Internet has millions of files that you can pull of a website and store on your hard disk. The files include updates to software applications, images, sound, or even full programs. Most large, commercial sites display details of the file together with a hyperlink – click on the link and your browser automatically starts to download the file. The browser displays a dialog box giving you the option to save the file on to your hard disk or run the file. Select the save option and the file will start to be transferred on to your computer.

Handling compressed files

Most files are compressed before they are stored on the Internet ready for you to download – this saves download time. You can double-click on a PC file that ends in 'EXE' or a Mac file that ends 'SEA' and they will automatically decompress themselves without any extra software. If the filename ends with the letters 'ZIP' (for PCs) or 'HQX' or 'SIT' (for Macs) you'll need an unzip utility to decompress the program. The most popular is WinZip **(http://www.winzip.com)** but you'll find alternatives at Filez (**http://www.filez.com**) or CNET **(http://www.cnet.com)**.

FTP servers If a computer is dedicated to storing files ready for you to download, it's called an FTP server. A good example is **http://www.shareware.com** that stores hundreds of thousands of shareware programs. If you want to publish a website or do seriously advanced stuff, you'll need specialist software. Luckily, web browsers can manage any FTP command just fine.

Some FTP servers require a password; you'll be prompted to enter a user ID and password. Most FTP servers allow guests to enter and download files by logging in as an anonymous user. Type in 'anonymous' as a user ID and your email address as the password and you should see a listing of the folders and files available to download.

The threat of a virus A virus is a nasty but very clever little program that burrows deep inside another file. When you open or run this carrier file, the virus wakes up and does two things: first, it tries to spread to other similar files – to 'infect' them – next, it might try and wreck havoc on your computer. Many viruses are benign and simply spread themselves, but the majority will try and delete files, crash your hard disk or corrupt information stored in files. Almost any file that you download from the Internet could contain a virus, but the number of incidents is very low.

It's important to remember that you cannot catch a virus simply by downloading a file. However, if the file you download is infected with a virus, you will catch it when you open or run the file. If you download a file or receive a file via an email attachment, it could contain a virus. Only a few types of file can't contain viruses: notably image files and plain web pages (however, many web pages use extra programs, called applets, to provide multimedia or special effects – and these could contain a virus).

To stop any potential problems, you should always scan newly downloaded files with a special software program that can detect and remove viruses. Two of the most popular virus detection programs are McAfee (**http://www.mcafee.com**) and Norton AnitVirus (**http://www.symantec.com**). New viruses are always appearing, so you will regularly need to download special update files to ensure your any anti-virus software can catch all the latest strains.

Music and movies
Music and video are played on the coolest sites, providing a complete multimedia experience. Visit the All-Music Guide (**http://www.allmusic.com**), for example, and you'll be able to listen to music clips and watch video segments of thousands of bands. To experience either type of clip, your web browser needs to support the special file and transfer format used by the site. There are several competing standards that are used by different sites.

The newest web browsers include support for most standard ways of transferring music, video and animation over the web, so just sit back and enjoy. If your browser doesn't support the standard, you'll see a warning message that asks if you want to download a plug-in to add support to your browser.

Speeding up your browsing
You might find it hard to believe, but your computer does not automatically provide the most efficient settings for browsing the Internet. There is plenty of scope to improve performance by tweaking some of the settings. The problem is, you'll need to adjust the TCP/IP and internal Windows settings – and they are rather complicated to tackle.

Dozens of utility programs are now available that promise to boost your Internet access performance just be adjusting these hidden settings. Some work well, others don't. It doesn't help that the goalposts keep moving as Microsoft and the developers of these utilities each try to improve performance. Before you spend your money on wild promises, take a look at the CNET (**http://www.cnet.com**) or Zdnet (**http://www.zdnet.com**) sites and read the latest reviews and benchtest figures for the current crop of these utilities.

Browsing offline
It is relatively easy to view web pages even when you're not connected to the Internet. The first method uses the temporary

files that your web browser stores on your hard disk as you browse. When you start your web browser, click on the Work Offline button from the Dialer utility to prevent it dialling out. Now type in the URL of a page you've visited recently and the browser should be able to display it. (The temporary files are only stored for a certain amount of time, so it might not be there.) If you try and view a page that's no longer in the temporary store (called the cache), the browser will attempt to dial up and connect to the Internet.

The second method is to use a specialist utility program (see address book at the end of this chapter) that downloads the whole site on to your hard disk. This was a fine idea when websites had just a few dozen pages but try this on the CNN or BBC site and you'll wait around for days as the thousands of individual pages are downloaded. Once you have downloaded the site on to your drive, you can browse it as if you were online.

//PROTECTING THE KIDS

Because of its history as a forum for uncensored free speech, there's plenty of unpleasant material out in the big bad Internet – and most parents would rather that junior didn't find out about it just yet. There are several ways to prevent access to particular sites and newsgroups.

If you subscribe to AOL, you can use the Parental Control option to control which sites and newsgroups can be viewed by the other family accounts. Non-AOL surfers can either use a commercial program that can be set up to prevent access to a vast list of X-rated sites or you can configure your browser yourself.

If you have a whole family of different users on your PC, Windows 98 includes a special feature (User Profiles) that lets each have their own individual browser, bookmarks and email settings. Switch it on from Start/Settings/Control Panel/Users icon.

Commercial programs should help catch almost every site – but you will need to update their databases regularly to cover new ones. You'll find a complete list of the programs available from **http://www.worldvillage.com/wv/school/html/control.htm**.

The alternative is to configure your web browser to use one of the web site rating schemes. The two main rating systems are PICS (Platform for Internet Content Selection) and RSACI (Recreational Software Advisory Council on the Internet). Web sites that want to be part of the scheme include rating information that is then picked up by your web browser. You can configure Microsoft's IE browser or Netscape Navigator to use either system (in IE, choose the Options/View/Security menu command, in Navigator select Help/Netwatch then select which categories you want to block with the Content Advisor settings). The problem is, if the site doesn't include rating information (and so far, few do), it won't be blocked.

//ADDRESS BOOK

Web browsers

The free software you need to view and surf web pages:

Microsoft	**http://www.microsoft.com**
Netscape	**http://www.netscape.com**
Opera	**http://www.opera.com**

Offline browsers

Save on phone bills with these handy utilities:

Insite	**http://www.engr.orst.edu/~schonfal/inst.htm**
Teleport	**http://www.tenmax.com**
UnMozify	**http://www.evolve.co.uk**
WebWhacker	**http://www.webwhacker.com**

Parental Control

Protect your children from the muck on the net with software to block access. AOL users get this built in.

CyberAngel **http://www.cyberangel.com**
How to protect your kids when they go online.

CyberPatrol **http://www.microsys.com/cyber**
Keep the kids in the safe zone by installing this rival to NetNanny – set up restricted zones to prevent kids from visiting X-rated sites.

NetNanny **http://www.netnanny.com**
Top-selling utility that prevents your kids from visiting X-rated or anti-social websites and newsgroups.

SurfMonkey **http://www.surfmonkey.com**
Creates a fun, controlled environment with its own browser that restricts what kids can do and where they can visit.

SurfWatch **http://www.surfwatch.com**
Monitor and limit the areas your children visit on the net.

WorldVillage Parental Guide **http://www.worldvillage.com/wv/school/html/control.htm**
A complete guide to the products available for parental control.

4//SEARCHING

The Internet contains everything you could ever want to know. But how do you find what you want? With nearly a billion web pages out there, you'll need plenty of help to hunt out a site that's relevant. One way is to use this book to help find useful sites, but there's no way we can cover the enormous range of information there is on the net. Fortunately, there are plenty of special sites that can help you find information anywhere on the Internet. But because of the vast size of the net, you need to take your searching seriously – here's how to do it.

Start searching

To find a web page that contains a particular keyword, you'll need to visit a special site that contains an index to the pages on the web. As usual, the Internet provides plenty of choice, but there are two different types of site that help you find information on the net:

- Search engine – this type of site tries to include every single scrap of information that's on every site in the web.
- Search directory – this type of site limits itself to just a few hundred thousand links. A real person normally checks each one before being added.

For the gentle stroll about the web, or to find every site about a subject, try a general search engine like AltaVista or Excite! These tame monsters let you search their vast databases, which list almost every web page that's published. But be careful, with so much out there, unless you ask a specific question you'll easily get swamped with hundreds of thousands of matching results.

An alternative approach to the brutish 'I've got it all' method of a search engine is to use a directory. The top directory is Yahoo! The big Y and its lesser rivals list a select few sites under specific categories, rather like the Yellow Pages telephone directory (which is also online). You can either search the directory or browse through a particular category.

Neither the directories nor the search engines can possibly index all the web sites on the Internet. To keep up with the flood of new information, they would have to try and visit and index hundreds of thousands of new web pages every day. For the millions of sites that are listed, there are many times as many undiscovered. Recent reports have suggested that out of the near billion web pages that are on the web, search engines are indexing less than 20 per cent of this total.

How a search engine works

Search engines build up their index of sites using automatic software called robots, spiders, crawlers and other silly names. These little programs hunt out new websites. When they find something, they'll record the address in the index and then try and visit every page within the site.

When a robot finds a new page that it can add to its index it looks inside the file that contains the text for the web page to get descriptive information about its contents. In some cases, the page designer will have included special information to help the robot index the site accurately (see the chapter on creating your own site for more details). All this data gets sucked into the main index and the page address is filed under the individual words (called keywords).

Although a search engine tries to index everything that's available, directories (like Yahoo!) only include select sites in their directories. These are normally all picked by real people who have to visit the site, check that it's working and useful, and then add it to the hallowed directory.

Metasearching saves time These days, probably the best way to search the web is to use a metasearch tool. Just type in your question and the metasearcher will automatically submit it to all the main search engines and directories, then filter the answers for relevance and present you with a manageable list of answers. Sites like DogPile (**http://www.dogpile.com**), All-in-One (**http://www.albany.net/allinone**) and Metacrawler (**http://www.metacrawler.com**) are a boon.

Search assistants sit somewhere between a metasearcher and a directory – the best known is AskJeeves (**http://www.askjeeves.com**). The site lets you type in a question in plain English; it then lists all the possible answers that it knows about – or the sites it thinks might help you with an answer. It will often come up with some oddball answers but, generally, it's a great first place to look if you want to know the capital of Finland or the films that starred Sinatra.

A new system called Real Names is being promoted as the alternative to all those confusing web addresses. Instead of typing in a company's address in your browser, just type in their company name. For example, to find the London Evening Standard newspaper site, either type in **http://www.thisislondon.co.uk** or just type their Real Name 'Evening Standard'. The system is part of Microsoft IE 5, or download free software from **http://www.realnames.com** for other browsers.

Searching without a search engine If you're trying to find a particular company's site, try typing in their name as a URL. For example, Virgin is at, no surprises, **http://www.virgin.com**. All the major companies will have a site under their brand name followed by '.com' or '.co.uk'. It's the same story with many subjects: if you want gardening information, try '**http://www.garden.com**', for Star Wars film news try '**http://www.starwars.com**'. Experiment – just imagine you're the website designer trying to come up with a neat name for their new site.

//HOW TO SEARCH

Once you're connected to the net (see Chapter 2), you'll only need a web browser to search and view its entire content. Start your browser and type in the address of your favourite search engine – take a tour of the search engines listed in the Address Book at the end of this chapter and choose the one you like best. (If you're in a hurry, try '**http://www.excite.co.uk**' or '**http://www.hotbot.com**'; the first has vast resources, the second is easy to use.)

Now that you're at a search site, you'll see pride of place on the page goes to the search entry field. Type in the keywords you want to search with (some sites let you type in an 'English' question) and click the button beside the field or hit Return.

Your query is sent to the remote computer that contains the search engine software – it zips through its index of millions of websites and displays a list of matching sites. All within a second or two. The search results are usually listed by relevance.

One of the problems of this type of general search is that web sites are always changing. The information in the search engine index is always a little out of date and you'll probably find many of the search result links don't work simply because the site has closed or moved. (See page 57 for more details on how to solve this problem.)

A quick, neat and free way of adding a little zing to your web searches is to use a built-in feature of the new Microsoft Internet Explorer v5. When you've found a site you like, click on the 'Show Related Sites' menu: the screen splits and you'll see a list of sites covering the same subject.

Fine-tune your search

It's a doddle to carry out a simple search – just type in your question. But this could easily result in thousands of matches – you need to fine-tune your search question so that you weed out the irrelevant sites. Progress to status of savvy-searcher by using the power tricks in the box – these are part of all search engines. The friendliest sites for power searching are HotBot and Excite Powersearch (**http://www.excite.co.uk/powersearch/**) – both letyou define a search expression by typing in words that must or must not be matched. With HotBot it's easy to define a complicated search query that finds the cheapest holiday resort in Florida, not part of Disney and near the Keys. If you're not using HotBot, you'll need to add special symbols or Boolean operators to your search query to get the same effect.

The more advanced search sites let you type in your question as a normal sentence. Take advantage of this – don't waste time searching for 'holiday France' but simply type in 'I want to go on holiday in July to Avignon'.

As you sift through your results, you'll soon realise that the engine is searching for all your words in any order. The next step to power status is to match an exact expression. To do this, enclose the expression in quote marks. For example, if you want to find a dairy that still makes original Devon cream, type in 'Devon cream'. If you don't, you'll see sites that list the cream of Devon fishing and restaurants in Leeds offering Devon plaice with cream of mushroom sauce.

Power search techniques

If you want to use a search site other than HotBot or Excite Powersearch, you'll have to use a rather techie notation for your queries. Almost all the search engines (including Yahoo!) let you refine your query using the '+' and '-' symbols. If you put a '+' sign in front of a word, it means the word must be matched. And the '-' works in just the opposite way.

The second way to power search is to use Boolean operators. These are the simple words 'AND', 'OR' and 'NOT' that you can insert between search terms. For example, if you want to find sites about the great Ella Fitzgerald and Louis Armstrong jazz duo, you would enter "'Ella Fitzgerald' AND 'Louis Armstrong' AND jazz" (note how the two names are enclosed in single quotes to search for them together).

Dead addresses

Websites get launched, change names and get redesigned all the time. This makes it rather tricky for the search engines to keep track of what's going on and, as a result, many of their suggestions are likely to be pages that no longer exist. You'll see the problem when you start to search – many of the links thrown up just won't work when you click on them. You'll get the classic warning page that tells you the address cannot be found.

With some ingenuity and lateral thinking, you can still track down the site. One of the most common problems is that the site's designer changes the names of the individual pages within the site – the site itself is probably still available but the page index at the search engine no longer matches.

Try editing the address to delete chunks from the address after each '/' symbol. Click on the address field at the top of your browser and use the arrow and delete keys to edit the address.

//SPECIALIST SEARCH SOFTWARE

Instead of using a search engine on the Internet, you could use a special software package that runs on your PC. There are several specialist search tools on the market – they all cost good money and all effectively do the same as a metasearcher. Load the software on to your computer (it normally appears as a new button on your web browser toolbar) and type in your query – as complicated as you like. The software zips around the Internet to all the search engines to find sites that'll match your answer.

Three of the better known are CyberPilot (**http://www.netcarta.com**), Poke (**http://www.webprowler.com**) and the elderly WebCompass (**http://www.symantec.com**).

Portals

When a website decides to rule the world, it calls itself a portal. These vast sites want to be your friend and to be the starting point and one-stop solution to all your browsing needs. You'll find weather, news, sport, finance and a whole load of trendy info sources that embellish the basic search engine.

Take Excite! (**http://www.excite.co.uk**) – a couple of years ago it was a simple search engine but now it greets you by name and displays your local weather and news. It will even show the latest results from your favourite team and list your share portfolio. Sure, you can still use it to search the web but you can also use the related shortcuts to order a book, choose a new car or book a holiday.

//ADDRESS BOOK

Search Engines

AltaVista **http://www.altavista.com**
Boasts just about the biggest index on the web.

Euroseek **http://www.euroseek.net**
Europhiles head for this multilingual, multicountry search engine.

Excite! **http://www.excite.co.uk**
Mammoth index that's made a big effort to be UK-specific.

G.O.D. **http://www.god.co.uk**
British and proud of it! But no comparison to the mega-index sites.

HotBot **http://www.hotbot.com**
Just about the friendliest engine on the web, but not UK-specific.

Infoseek **http://www.infoseek.co.uk**
The best all-round player.

Lycos **http://www.lycos.co.uk**
The granddaddy of search engines that is also great for MP3 files.

WebCrawler **http://www.webcrawler.com**
Rivals AltaVista in its scope, but often a little slow.

Directories

About **http://www.about.com**
A real editor manages each subject category; friendly, cozy, efficient.

LookSmart **http://www.looksmart.co.uk**
Easier to navigate than Yahoo! and sites get a mini-review.

Magellan **http://www.mckinley.com**
Each site in the index gets a review and a star rating.

Northern Light **http://www.northernlight.com**
Vast, fast and accurate.

Scoot **http://www.scoot.co.uk**
Brilliant collection of local information from around the UK.

UKPlus **http://www.ukplus.com**
Find UK-specific sites in a hurry.

Yahoo! **http://www.yahoo.co.uk**
Dominates the web and provides half a million sites clearly organised into sections. Now provides so much extra, you might never want to leave.

Yell **http://www.yell.co.uk**
Not the easiest to use but the biggest of the UK directories.

Metasearchers

All-in-One **http://www.albany.net/allinone**
Does all the digging for you – and at high speed.

DogPile **http://www.dogpile.com**
Hardly elegant sophistication, but great for specific searches.

Google! **http://www.google.com**
Particularly good at weeding out irrelevant results.

Go2Net:MetaCrawler **http://www.metacrawler.com**
Returns a manageable few of the top results from other engines.

Inference Find **http://www.infind.com**
Clinical-looking site that surgically removes duplications and dross to give you a workable, grouped shortlist.

Savvy Search **http://www.savvysearch.com**
Searches a couple of dozen of the top search engines.

Search assistants

AskJeeves **http://www.askjeeves.com**
Great service and generally comes up trumps.

AskJeevesForKids **http://www.ajkids.com**
Only supplies safe, friendly sites for children.

5//ELECTRONIC MAIL

Electronic mail (email) is still one of the best reasons to get on the Internet. It's a fast, cheap and very convenient way of sending messages and files to any other user. Don't get stuck with voice-mail or hit with transatlantic phone bills – send them an email.

The downside is that you can get swamped with mail – a few messages a day is exciting but an inbox bulging with 200 each day is not so welcome. If this happens, use the advanced tricks later in this chapter to automatically sort and organise your messages.

If you want to know how to set up your email software and choose an email address – skip back to Chapter 2 for all the details.

Sending and receiving email

There's no mystery about sending a message: display a new, empty message template by clicking on the new message icon. In the 'To' field, fill in the email address of the person to whom you're sending the message – or open the address book and choose a name. Move to the 'Subject' field and type in a short, snappy title for your email. Now you can type in the main part of the message.

When you've finished, click the Send icon and the message will be temporarily stored in your out-tray. To complete the process, connect to the Internet and click the Send/Receive icon to allow the email program to send the queued messages and receive any new messages.

Your first email

Break the ice by sending us your first email. It's a quick way to check that you understand the simple steps for sending a message – and that you have correctly configured your email software. We'll reply in a few seconds, if you've got it right. Here's what to do:

1 Start your email program (for example, Microsoft Outlook Express or Netscape Messenger).

2 Type in the email address of our testing system – 'test@virgin-pub.co.uk' – in the 'To' address field.

3 Move to the 'Subject' field and type in 'testing'.

4 Type a quick 'hello' as the main message – or even what you think of our book.

5 Click the Send button. Now click on the Send/Receive icon (in Microsoft) or the Get Message icon (in Netscape) to connect to the Internet and send the message.

6 Once the message has been sent, wait for around 20-30 seconds and click on Send/Receive button a second time. Our automatic reply will be delivered – click on it to read it. If you don't get the message, wait a little longer and then click on Send/Receive again.

Types of account

You are probably using a standard dial-up account to send and receive your email. Your email is temporarily stored on the ISP's server until you ask your email program to collect it (by choosing the Send/Receive icon).

You might have a whole range of extra email features that you didn't know existed. The most popular, provided by lots of ISPs to paying customers, gives you several different email addresses (normally advertised as '5 POP accounts'). This lets everyone in your family have his or her own separate account, each with its own password.

Keep up to date via your email. Subscribe to a mailing list or to a daily news service, such as http://www.infobeat.com, that sends you news headlines by email.

Free email You don't need to be limited to just one email address – you can sign up for as many free email accounts as you want. It's a good way of providing separate email accounts for everyone in the family or for separate business and personal email addresses. There are hundreds of companies offering free email and there's no catch – just visit their site, fill in a few details about yourself and you'll get a new email account.

This is not the same as a free Internet account (like those offered by Freeserve, X-stream and Virgin Net). You won't get dial-up access to the Internet, just a new email address. Unlike your usual email account, these free accounts are almost always web-based. You send, receive and check your email using your web browser. This is great if you're travelling and can only visit an Internet café.

If you want a normal email account (called a POP3 account) for free – so that you can send and receive mail with your usual email software – you could open a free Internet account (for example, from Freeserve or Virgin Net).

Save money by cutting down your time online to the minimum. Write your messages offline then dial up and connect to the Internet to send all the messages in one go. While you're offline, new messages are stored in an Outbox folder (Eudora marks these with a tiny 'Q' icon to tell you it's waiting in a queue). New messages are stored in the Inbox folder until you read them.

//ADDRESSING AN EMAIL

Email addresses are horribly easy to mistype. Get one full stop or underscore wrong and the message won't reach its destination. Unlike your friendly local postman who knows that Mrs Jones lives at number 14, not 41, there's no margin of error with email. However, you can normally tell if your email message has failed to get through – it will bounce back to you with a warning that it could not be delivered.

An email address is made up of two parts. In the middle is an '@' symbol (pronounced 'at') that divides the two parts. On the right is the address of the local server that handles the mail for this person. On the left is the person's user name on this server. For example, 'simon_collin@virgin-pub.co.uk' identifies a user called 'Simon Collin' in the domain 'virgin-pub.co.uk'.

Address books Don't bother typing in addresses each time you want to send mail to your friends. Instead, use the address book feature that's part of every mail program. To open the Address Book in Microsoft Outlook, use the Tools/Address Book menu option; in Netscape Messenger use Communicator/Address Book.

There's no complete, central directory of email addresses to help you find someone's address. You've got three options: phone them up and ask, visit their company's website to see if there's a contact list or search one of the (rather limited) directories of addresses that do exist (such as http://www.Four11.com).

A neat feature of many email programs – like Eudora and Outlook – is called auto-complete addressing. The program keeps track of the addresses you've used in the past and, as you start to type in an address, the program automatically completes the address for you.

If you want to be sure someone has read your message, select the 'Confirm Read' option when you create the message. When they open the message, it will automatically generate a receipt to inform you that your message has been read. This should work, unless the person or the company has switched off this feature in their software.

Multiple addresses There are plenty of times that you might want to send a message to more than one person at a time. If you organise a club or team, you can keep everyone up to date by setting up a mailing list or group of contacts – this is a feature of your email program's address book.

If you want to send your message to just a few people, use the extra sections when you create your message:

- **To:** – type in the address of the person for whom your message is intended. You can list several addresses (separated by a comma, semi-colon or space), in which case each person gets their own individual message and doesn't realise it's been sent to anyone else.
- **CC:** – works with the 'To:' field. Type in the address of another person who should see a copy of this message. The person in the 'To:' field will be told that copies have been sent.
- **BCC:** – works with the 'To:' field (and the 'CC:' field, if you want). If you type in an address here, they'll receive a copy of the message, but the person in the 'To:' field won't be told.

If you receive a message that was sent to a list of people using the CC feature, be careful when you reply to the message. You might mean to send it to the originator but it could easily go to all the members on the list.

EMAIL ETIQUETTE

Assuming that in your pre-email days you didn't go around writing rude letters to strangers, you'll find the basic rules of email etiquette easy as pie. For a start, it's always nice to reply i[...]ediately to someone – even if it's just a quick acknowled[...] you received their message and are now dealing wi[...] that you follow these basic principles:

- For some reason, people feel it's accept[...] usual rules that govern decency and d[...] to email. If you want to gossip abou[...] via email – it's too easy to forward [...]

keep a copy to hold against you. If you're writing a letter in a professional capacity, keep it professional.

- Next, don't write emails in capital letters. On the Internet, this is how people shout – and no one likes SHOUTING.
- If you need a little help with your spelling, don't forget that there's a spell-checker built into most email programs.

Signatures

Email software includes the equivalent of a rubber stamp for your signature. An email signature is a few lines with your name and perhaps your website or business contact details. Once you have entered this into your email software, it will be added to the end of every email you send.

Business folk should limit their signatures to just four or five lines: name, company, real-world contact and website address. There's no point adding your email address – it's already at the top of the email.

You'll sometimes see, and maybe want to devise, an alternative signature – cute quotes and silly pictures drawn with text (called ASCII art). But beware – few recipients will think it's as clever as you do.

Email shorthand

Part of the trouble with email is that you can't decide how it will appear or be interpreted by the person reading the message. Be careful how you put things – emails can seem very abrupt. Save time when typing your emails by using the range of standard shorthand, some of which is given below:

AFAIK – as far as I know;

FWIW – for what it's worth;

BTW – by the way;

IMO – in my opinion;

IMHO – (sarcastically) in my humble opinion;

BFN – bye for now.

Adding feeling to a message

To add emphasis to a word, surround it with '*' as in 'It made me *very* angry'. To add colour to a phrase, use '<' as in 'I thought it was a great idea <sarcastic grin>'. Lastly, you can add expressions to your mail, or newsgroup postings, using mini expressions called smileys. Don't use them too often, but they work well in small doses. Here are a few examples:

:-) happy;

;-) winking and happy;

:-(sad;

:-o amazed.

Most email programs – such as Outlook and Messenger – let you format your message just like a word processor document. You can change the fonts, colour or even add images (such as your signature). This looks great, but don't forget that the majority of net users still work with email software that can only read plain, unformatted text.

Sending files by email

You're not limited to plain text (letters) when sending email. You can attach any type of file to your email, making it a great way to send photos, databases, spreadsheets, music or video clips. It's free, quick and convenient.

To send a file, click on the paperclip icon in Microsoft Outlook (in Netscape, click on the paperclip icon, then choose the File option from the drop-down menu). You'll see a list of files on your computer: move to the folder and select the file you want to send.

Sending to fax, pager or telephone

Emails don't just go from computer to computer. You can turn your email into a fax message, redirect it to a pager or even use email to send a text message to a mobile phone.

To send an email message to a fax machine, use one of the clever email-to-fax gateways: some are free but others will charge you for the privilege. Have a look at the gaudy Zipfax site (**http://www.zipfax.com**) or the simple Oxford University site (**http://info.ox.ac.uk/fax/**).

Although each of the main mobile phone providers lets you send text messages between phones, it's a different matter when it's web-to-phone. They're all trialling systems, but check how your network is developing its email links:

Cellnet – http://www.cellnet.co.uk

One2One – http://www.one2one.co.uk

Orange – http://www.orange.co.uk

Vodafone – http://www.vodafone.co.uk

Organise your email

Don't let all your email messages collect in one vast heap – use the folders and rules to organise messages into a model of neat, well-ordered efficiency. Every email program lets you create folders within the main Inbox: you can drag and drop messages into folders to organise them or use rules to move messages automatically.

Use rules to automatically move and organise your email (Microsoft calls this feature Message Rules, other programs call it rules or a filter). Rules are part of all good email programs and work in the background to scan new messages and then organise them according to key words.

Rules look for a word or term in a message – you could devise a simple rule that moves any message with 'pay review' in the 'Subject' field into a folder called 'Priority'.

//MAILING LISTS

Mailing lists let you share messages with all the other subscribers in the list. They are a great way to keep up to date with a special interest or with peer groups or colleagues. Everything is done through your normal email program. When you want to post a message to the group, send it to the list's management email address; this then distributes your message to everyone else on the list. Simple and effective.

What are they? Mailing lists were started, in the early days of the Internet, by academics who relied heavily on email. Now, it's grown to cover every imaginable area of discussion (it's rather like a sensible, serious version of newsgroups). There are over 90,000 specialist mailing lists that let you join and discuss everything from car spares to music (such as a list to discuss the Chemical Brothers) – though the academic topics still dominate.

How do I find a suitable list? Finding a mailing list is easy. Most of the search engines let you search the database of lists or, better still, visit one of the specialist mailing list sites such as Liszt (**http://www.liszt.com**). Search for a subject and you'll get a range of lists available. Most have mini descriptions and instructions on how to subscribe.

How do I join? If the mailing list is open (most are), simply send an email message to the address of the automatic manager, called the list server (usually written 'listserv'). In the main part of the message, you'll need to type out a special instruction to tell the list server that you want to subscribe to the list. The instruction tells the server that you want it to add your email address to the list.

Set up your own list If you really cannot find a list that suits you, create your own list. This is also a neat way of distributing information between colleagues or within a club. You can set up a list for free using the tools at CoolList (**http://www.coollist.com**), OneList (**http://www.onelist.com**) or Topica (**http://www.topica.com**).

//PROBLEMS WITH EMAIL

Fed up with junk mail? It doesn't stop with email, unfortunately. Unsolicited email is called spam. A company can send out millions of advert messages to email addresses bought from a list merchant. Many Internet providers now subscribe to a central database that lists all the sources of spam and so blocks unwanted email. To check up who's on the blacklist, look at the Blacklist page at **http://math-www.uni-paderborn.de/~axel/BL/blacklist.html**.

If you feel the need to send an anonymous message, visit **http://www.anonymizer.com**. It will camouflage your tracks and make it impossible to trace.

Worse than spam are viruses spread by email (often called mail-bombs). When you open an email program with an infected file attached, it automatically spreads the virus to your computer or could even delete or damage files on your hard disk. Very nasty. A notorious recent virus sent by email was called Melissa; it accessed your Microsoft Outlook address book and automatically generated infected messages to everyone in your address book. There was no actual damage, but it caused so much extra traffic that some parts of the Internet ground to a halt.

To avoid being hit by virus attacks or mail-bombs, be very cautious before opening any attachments. Always use a virus scanner before you run the program, view the image or read the document (the current vogue is to send Word or WordPerfect documents or

Excel spreadsheets that contain a virus). Two of the best-known virus scanners are McAfee (**http://www.mcafee.com**) and Norton AntiVirus (**http://www.symantec.com**).

//ADDRESS BOOK

Email software

Your web browser already has an email program as part of the bundle and there's often little reason to change. However, if you really want to upgrade then try these dedicated email packages that have lots of new features:

Outlook **http://www.microsoft.com**
Eudora **http://www.qualcomm.com**
Pegasus **http://www.pegasus.usa.net**

Gateways

Send mail to faxes with these sites:

Jfax **http://www.jfax.com**
Subscribe and you receive a unique telephone number in a city of your choice – faxes or voice-mail messages are forwarded by email.

Oxford University fax gateway **http://info.ox.ac.uk/fax/**
Send an email to a fax machine anywhere within the UK (and patchy coverage of the world) for free.

ZipFax **http://www.zipfax.com**
Send an email and it will resend it to any fax machine – for free. But you'll have to put up with the ads.

Free email

Almost every portal and major site now offers visitors a free email address. These are a great way of separating work and personal or newsgroup messages. The drawback is that you can normally only send and read messages using a clunky slow website. All of the following provide a similar service:

Bigfoot **http://www.bigfoot.com**
Excite! **http://www.excite.com**
Hotmail **http://www.hotmail.com**
Yahoo! **http://www.yahoo.com**

Finding an address

There's no complete email directory yet, but you can try looking up a name with the following white pages:

AltaVista **http://www.altavista.com**
BigFoot **http://www.bigfoot.com**
Excite **http://www.excite.com**
Four11 **http://www.four11.com**
Who Where **http://www.whowhere.com**

6//NEWSGROUPS

In the real world, news means newspapers, breaking stories and reports, but for a net-head it means newsgroups. To get the full effect of free speech, take a tour of the Internet's newsgroups – collectively called 'Usenet'. There are over 60,000 different discussion groups that together provide the most active, exciting, obnoxious and interesting part of the whole Internet experience.

There's nothing fancy about newsgroups – it's the plain cousin of the web – just simple text messages (and the occasional image or attached file) arranged like an office bulletin board. Somehow, this makes it an even more powerful medium for people saying just whatever they want.

Sure, you'll find scraps of news here, but it's mostly comment, opinions, rants, jobs, questions, thoughts, advice, for sale ads and all the other detritus that makes up normal life.

Since newsgroups are accessible to pretty much the entire net community of 150 million users, you'll find opinions written by the good, the bad and the crazy. But best of all, it's dynamic and great fun. If you want serious discussion without interruptions from drunks and assorted bums, you'll be better off looking for a mailing list on the subject (see the previous chapter).

Newsgroup basics

Newsgroups are grounded in content and written in plain text – there's none of the design or multimedia wizardry that you'll find in websites. Very little has changed in the way you access newsgroups since the Internet was first developed. It's as simple as email and just about as powerful.

To access newsgroups you need special news reader software and a standard Internet connection. All the web browsers include news readers, so it's easy to get started. See Chapter 2 for information on how to set up and configure the software.

What are newsgroups? A newsgroup is a discussion forum in which anyone can add a message. Since it's a public forum, any other visitor can read current and older messages. If you reply to an existing message, you are creating a 'thread' that lets you view all the replies (and replies to replies) about one original message.

Where are newsgroups stored? When you add a message to a newsgroup, it's stored on a computer called the news server. Each ISP has its own news server (that's also called a news feed); however, because of the vast amount of information that's added to the Usenet every day, most news servers can only store a few days' worth of messages. If you want to find information in a newsgroup, you should use a special search engine, such as Deja (**http://www.deja.com**), that has vast storage capacity and records all the messages posted in all the groups.

There's no single computer that stores all the newsgroups; instead, the news servers at each ISP swap information to ensure that they are all up to date. If you post a message, it will appear instantly in the newsgroup stored on your ISP's news server, but it will take a few seconds (or minutes) before it is copied to all the other news servers in the area. Over the next few hours, your message will be automatically copied to all the news servers across the world.

Which newsgroups can I access? Your ISP will normally deliver your news feed. No ISP will give you full run of the 60,000 different groups (it takes up too much hard disk space on their servers) so they will restrict the list because, for instance, some are in a foreign language (English, German, Spanish) or they might come over all prudish and remove newsgroups about porn or antisocial material.

When you first connect to the newsgroup feed, your reader will download a list of all the groups supported. If you particularly want a group that's not been made available, there are other sources. For example, if you live in the UK you'll find most ISPs filter out the local French, Spanish and German language newsgroups. First, try asking your ISP to provide a particular group – most will oblige.

If you have no success asking your ISP, you can link to one of the full, free newsgroup feeds. They can be slow due to demand, but you'll get access to the full range of groups. Visit **http://www.jammed.com** for a list of the current free newsgroup feeds available. Choose carefully. Although you can read messages, many free newsgroup servers won't let you post new messages.

The third alternative is to access the newsgroups via the Deja.com website. This provides a neat way to search and view the postings in any of the 60,000 newsgroups. It's a little slow thanks to the web interface but has enough added tricks – like ratings and filters – to make it well worthwhile.

How does it work? The Usenet works by using a very simple command that lets one server copy messages to another server – it's how news servers keep up to date with new postings. This command is part of a system called NNTP (it's a part of the TCP/IP protocol suite that runs the entire Internet). Technically, a news server is called an NNTP server (in a similar way that a mail server is called an SMTP server). Because the process of sending and reading news messages is so similar to email, news readers are often integrated into email programs, for example Microsoft Outlook, Qualcomm Eudora and Netscape Messenger.

Your news reader program is called an NNTP client – it asks the NNTP servers to send it a list of the current newsgroups. If you want to look at a newsgroup, your software asks the NNTP server to send it a list of the titles of the messages in the newsgroup. If you want to read a message, your software asks the server to send the full text for this message.

Order from chaos – hierarchies

Newsgroups are divided into seven broad categories, called hierarchies. These are:

1 **comp** – computer-related newsgroups;

2 **misc** – any groups that don't fit into the other categories;

3 **news** – discussions about the Usenet itself;

4 **rec** – hobbies and sports;

5 **sci** – science-oriented discussion;

6 **soc** – social issues;

7 **talk** – discussion of (generally controversial) issues.

In addition to these seven main categories, there is an eighth rogue category called 'alt', which contains a wild range of newsgroups and is responsible for the contentious and lewd reputation of Usenet.

Each of the main hierarchies is divided into sub-categories. For example, in the 'comp' hierarchy, there are the 'comp.ibm' and 'comp.mac' categories that contain newsgroups about PCs and Macintosh computers. Each level of organisation is separated by a full stop; it makes it a little easier for you to have a good stab at guessing what a newsgroup is all about.

//GETTING STARTED

Once your newsgroup reader is configured (see page 33), you're ready to get started. The first time you connect your news reader to your ISP's news server, the software will download the names of all the newsgroups available for you to access – it can take up to ten minutes for this information to download, so be patient.

Finding a newsgroup Once you have the current list of news-groups in your news reader software, you can browse through looking for something that sounds interesting or use your reader's filter function to narrow down the list to group titles that contain a particular word. However, until you visit the group, you'll never know quite how active, friendly or useful it really is. To start out, try one of the newsgroups in the directory section of this book – at the end of each specialist chapter are relevant newsgroups.

A good way to find a newsgroup that's of interest is to use a specialist search engine, such as Deja (**http://www.deja.com**) or Tile.Net (**http://www.tile.net**) to search through archives of newsgroup messages – you'll soon see which newsgroups are relevant. Alternatively, search for a newsgroup by its founder's description at **http://alabanza.com/kabacoff/Inter-Links**.

Identifying yourself Every message posted to a newsgroup has the sender's email address. It's up to the sender to make sure that the email address is correct – or not. The oddity is that most newsgroup users really don't want to be identified, so they provide a false email address. In fact, this isn't the crime you might imagine.

Unscrupulous mailshot companies trawl through newsgroups picking up the email addresses and adding these to a mailing list that's then sold on. You can guarantee that if you post a message under your real email address, you'll soon be bombarded with junk mail and adverts.

If you think you're anonymous when you're on the net, just visit http://consumer.net/anonymizer and see how much personal information you're already showing in public.

When you configure your newsgroup reader, you need to enter an email address to identify your postings. If you have an Internet account with the option of several email addresses, use a spare address just for your newsgroup activity. Or, better still, sign up for a free email account with Bigfoot, Hotmail or Excite and use this. It's not so much a case of hiding as protecting yourself from junk mail.

//READING AND POSTING

Newsgroup readers look and work in a very similar way to an email program: on the left there's usually a list of the newsgroups (or the selection that you have chosen as interesting) and on the right you'll see the title line of the latest postings. Click on title and the full message is displayed.

If an entry starts a new topic of discussion, it's called a new thread. The first entry has a small square beside it on the left, to show it's the start of a thread. Click on the square and you'll see all the other messages listed beneath it that were sent in reply. (You can configure your reader to display postings in strict date order, but then you'll lose the structure of the threads.)

You can post a new message or reply to an existing message in exactly the same way as creating an email. If you're using Microsoft Outlook Express or Netscape Communicator, the icons for email and newsgroup are in the same place – if you've sent an email message, you'll feel right at home.

So you don't make a complete nitwit of yourself with your first posting, there are a couple of newsgroups dedicated to newcomers trying out the system: alt.test and misc.test are the main stamping grounds of newbies. You won't get flamed or subjected to silliness – and you should even receive a nice email in return for your test message.

Cancel that message If you've just realised that, by mistake, you've given away your company's secret formula or just changed your mind about something you said, you can cancel a posting. In Outlook Express, choose Message/Cancel Message and you'll remove the entry from your local server. Unfortunately, unless you do it very quickly, there's no guarantee that you'll delete it from every worldwide server before someone reads it.

A few choice newsgroups There are way too many newsgroups to try and read them all. Instead, you can use your news reader to subscribe to the few that are of interest. This ensures that you'll keep up to date with new messages posted to these newsgroups – you can still view any other group whenever you want but, for day-to-day work, try to limit yourself to just a few favourite groups. Here's how to subscribe to a newsgroup:

1 In Outlook Express, click on the Newsgroups button to see a complete list of all the groups available on your server.

2 You can narrow this list down by typing in a key word in the field at the top of the window. If you're interested in toy cars, type in 'cars' and you'll see a cut-down list of the few dozen groups covering car-related topics.

3 Select the group that's of interest and click on the Subscribe button. The group is added to the list on the left of the screen, just below the name of your news server.

4 Now, if you want to view the messages in this group, click on the group name on the left-hand side of the screen. Outlook will always keep the list of messages in this group up to date, till you unsubscribe.

You might also find it useful to filter the people as well as the newsgroups. If one particular person has been driving you up the wall with his or her inane comments, add this person to your kill list (in Outlook use the Message/Block Sender menu option). From now on, your reader will filter out any postings from the user and ensure he or she never blights your screen again.

Where's the message? The Usenet attracts millions of new postings every day (over 500Mb of data generated per day). Your ISP's newsgroup feed cannot keep all the postings, so it stores messages for just a few days. Normally, messages will be available for between one and ten days, depending on the hard disk capacity your provider's allocated to the newsgroup server. After this period, the oldest messages are deleted to make way for the new – a process called expiring.

Reading offline Reading newsgroup messages when you're connected to the Internet is ideal – but it will hike up your phone bill. The alternative is to download all the new messages from your selected newsgroups and then hang up the phone and read them offline. If you post any replies, wait till you've read all the messages and then dial up and send off your new messages.

Microsoft's Outlook newsreader is good at managing on and offline access to newsgroups. If you want offline access, subscribe to the newsgroup then select the Synchronize button to download either some of or the entire message base for this group. Netscape's Messenger, Agent, Gravity and NewsRover also support offline message browsing but it can be a little more complicated than Outlook.

If a newsgroup name ends in '.d' then it's a forum to discuss another group (that has the same name minus the '.d').

Blocking access to kids

An uncensored soapbox like Usenet can get pretty warped. A lot of the postings are crude, obscene and can include pornographic image attachments. It's not really the place for young, impressionable minds to go exploring. However, only a few of the groups are truly offensive and, as a parent, you'll probably only need to block the porn, violence and morally unwelcome groups.

If you subscribe to AOL, there's no problem – use your Parental Control page to limit which newsgroups your children can view. Alternatively, install a product like NetNanny (**http://www.netnanny.com**) or CyberSitter (**http://www.cybersitter.com**), which limit access to newsgroups containing benign stuff.

Starting your own newsgroup

If you really cannot find a newsgroup that covers your niche subject area (and don't forget to search Deja.com in case your ISP filters the list it supplies you) then you can always start your own newsgroup. However, this is hard work and you'll have to lobby for it.

If you want to start a newsgroup in the main section (not an 'alt' group), you'll need to see what people think by putting up the idea in news.announce.newgroups and then waiting till it's discussed in detail in news.groups. There's then a vote and, if the vote has 100 more 'yes' than 'no' votes, you're up and running. To start a new 'alt' newsgroup, discuss the idea in alt.config then, if there's general approval, you'll need to convince a newsgroup administrator (a god in Usenet terms) to look after your new baby.

Newsgroups: the ground rules

You can say pretty much what you like in a newsgroup, so long as it's related to the subject. But, and this is a mighty big 'but', you must observe some basic etiquette when posting to any newsgroup. Some of the rules are simply good manners, others are specified by the newsgroup, but the majority are for your own protection. Here are the basic ground rules:

1 When you post a message, never give out your home phone number or any other personal details. If you want to chat to someone in particular, use email or instant messaging (see Chapter 7).

2 It's a wise precaution to use an alternative email address for your newsgroup postings. Set up a free email account with Hotmail or Excite! – there's too much misuse of email addresses from newsgroups.

3 Don't write commercial or business messages anywhere except the 'biz' groups – that's what they are there for.

4 Don't post the same message to a whole mass of newsgroups – called spamming.

5 Make sure your postings are relevant to the group. If you're not sure, read the FAQs (frequently asked questions) for the group that's usually posted as a message or visit **http://www.faqs.org** for a list of FAQs for all newsgroups.

6 Look and read what's being posted to a group for a day or two to get the feel of the group before you leap in.

7 Don't send a 'testing' message to a busy site – use the special alt.test and misc.test sites to try out your reader.

8 If you insist on posting antisocial messages, you'll be flamed (get a mass of hate email) or even have your Internet connection stopped.

9 When you post a message, don't SHOUT in capitals – you'll get a barrage of rude messages back (called flaming).

10 Use smileys when you're trying to be funny or sarcastic. Not everyone's got your highly developed sense of humour.

11 Don't reply to a provocative or deliberately argumentative message (a flame) or you'll start a flame war (slanging match).

12 If you download any images or programs via Usenet, virus check them before you do anything else.

13 Keep your signature file short – if you add cute quotes or dumb ASCII art, you're seen as sad, not clever.

//ADDRESS BOOK

Newsgroup readers

There's not much point switching from your web browser's integrated newsgroup reader, unless you want a change of view. If you do, here are some stand-alone programs that will do the job (some are free, some not):

Agent (PC)	**http://www.forteinc.com**
Gravity (PC)	**http://www.microplanet.com**
Hogwasher (Mac)	**http://www.asar.com**
Messenger (PC, Mac)	**http://www.netscape.com**
NewsRover (PC)	**http://www.newsrover.com**
NewsWatcher (Mac)	**http://www.filez.com**
News Xpress (PC)	**http://www.download.com**
Outlook Express (PC, Mac)	**http://www.microsoft.com**

Finding and searching newsgroups

The major search engines now extend their reach to the Usenet – including AltaVista.com and Excite.com. Otherwise, use one of the specialist search engines below:

Deja.com	**http://www.deja.com**
FAQ	**http://www.faqs.org**
Newsgroup Directory	**http://Tile.net/news**
Usenet Info Center	**http://metalab.unc.edu/usenet-i/**

Access to Newsgroups

Your Internet provider should supply your main newsgroup feed – but it's probably filtered. If you want to see the full range or don't have a feed, try these sources:

Deja.com	**http://www.deja.com**
Jammed	**http://www.jammed.com**

7//CHAT

When you're using the Internet, you're unwittingly suffering from delayed reaction to anything you type in. Even when you use a newsgroup, it can take an hour or even a day before someone comments on your message. Chat changes this. It sits somewhere in between the Internet equivalent of a gossipy telephone call and the verbal barrage from contentious talk in a crowded room full of strangers.

There are several different systems that let you chat to your friends or join in a room full of strangers. Either way, it's live – as you type out a message on your keyboard, it's immediately displayed on everyone else's screen. If you want to have a quiet chinwag with a mate, use the new instant messaging systems – you both need to run the same special software and be online at the same time. Alternatively, take your chance and join in IRC (internet relay chat) – a vast collection of chat rooms (called channels), each specialising in letting you talk about a particular subject.

If you want to let off steam or save on a long-distance phone bill or just talk for the sake of it, here's how to use the different types of chat systems on the net.

//IRC (INTERNET RELAY CHAT)

Congratulations, you've now found out where the net-heads chat till dawn. Sure, there's the web-based chat rooms and instant messaging like ICQ and AIM, but, for the real action, head to your local IRC server.

Like newsgroups, IRC is divided into separate discussion groups – called channels. Unlike newsgroups, anything you type in on your computer will instantly appear on every other channel member's screen. Remember, it's all live and in front of a small audience (if you want a one-to-one chat, try instant messaging).

Get started

To use IRC, you'll need a standard Internet connection and an IRC program – you don't need a browser or email. Unusually, IRC programs (normally called clients) aren't bundled in with the main web browsers – instead, you'll probably need to download a program web. The most popular PC program is mIRC (free from **http://www.mirc.com**) and for the Mac it's IRCle (from **http://www.ircle.com**) or ChatNet (from **http://www.elsinc.com**).

First off, you'll notice that IRC clients are the rather poor relations in snappy user interface design. They're stuck in the late 80s, when the technology evolved. There's nothing wrong with this but if you've only used Windows 98 then you'll no doubt find it clunky.

The server's the key

The IRC server is a computer that runs special software to support IRC. The server simply ensures that messages are passed between all the users in a channel. There are thousands of servers on the Internet and some are very active (so there's always someone to talk to – which is good). However, others are very slow (which is bad). Start with a local server from your ISP but try others till you find somewhere that's friendly and interesting.

Setting up IRC (Internet relay chat)

Here's how to get started with IRC:

1 Install an IRC client program (or download the program, then install it).

2 You'll be prompted to type in your nickname and email address – type in a name you want to use as a nickname (it's displayed to other users in the channel), your real name and your normal email address. Some IRC servers check that your email address is correct and will refuse you entry if you enter a fake.

3 You need to enter the name of a computer that allows chatting – the software will have a list of friendly computers (called 'IRC chat servers'). Choose one from the File menu list. (Alternatively, your ISP might host an IRC chat server that will have local users or visit Liszt (**http://www.liszt.com**), which has a database of independent IRC chat servers).

4 When you choose the chat server, your software connects to the server and displays a list of the various discussion groups available at the moment (called channels).

Your first chat OK, it's rather frightening entering your first IRC session, so let's take it step by step. When you link to the chat server, you'll see a list of channels available: channel names start with a '#' symbol. Each channel is just a forum that's been created by another user to chat about some particular topic (there might be a one-line description next the channel name to give you a clue).

Find a channel that looks interesting or active (the number of other people chatting in the channel is displayed just after its name). To enter, double-click on the channel name. You're immediately in a live session, your nickname has been broadcast to the other members in the channel and you'll see their comments flying back and forth in different colours in one window of the IRC client. On the right of the comments should be a list of the other members who are in the channel.

Now it gets rather scary. You want to give the impression that you saunter around these parts all the time – and try and find out what's going on at the same time. To be honest, your first session could be bruising, but stick with it – it's worth it. Read what's going on, then start to respond. After a few minutes, you'll get into the swing of it.

Find out about scheduled chats with celebs – check **http://www.yack.com** or **http://www.liszt.com** for details.

The advanced stuff IRC originally worked using a set of commands. There are over 100 commands that let you join a channel, chat with someone, set up your own channel and leave. Thankfully, all of these commands are now hidden behind buttons and icons in the IRC client – rather like the way a web browser hides HTML. Unlike a web browser, you can still enter the original commands in your main IRC window to get full control of the situation.

You don't need to know any of the commands but, since you're in a sector generally populated by the highly net-savvy, it's worth learning a few. Rule number one: the commands need to be prefaced by a '/' – forget this and the command will be sent as a chat line. Embarrassment all round. Here's a list of the main commands:

/AWAY <message> – displays a short message when you want to nip off to make a coffee;

/JOIN <#channel_name> – to join a channel;

/HELP – to display all the commands available;

/LEAVE <#channel_name> – to leave a channel;

/LIST – to show the channels available;

/NICK <nickname> – change your nickname;

/QUIT – leave the channel and exit from the server;

/WHOIS <nickname> – to show more details on a user.

Moderation IRC channels are a splendid example of self-moderation. If you do or say something stupid or offensive, you'll be kicked off the channel (with the '/KICK' command) by one of the operators who set up the channel (their nicknames start with an '@').

Some IRC servers and channels use bots – software that monitors what's said and automatically kicks a user off the channel if they swear or use bad language. If you are kicked off, it's a warning – you can join again immediately.

Language The language used in IRC channels is rather unusual. Nothing too strange, more super-shorthand. If you're trying to type as fast as you can think and talk, you'll try and devise as many shortcuts as possible. There's a lot of 'how r u' and so on. Like classified ads, it takes a moment to switch gear. Here's a quick guide to the most commonly used acronyms:

BBIAF – be back in a flash;

BBL – be back later;

BFN – bye for now;

BRB – be right back;

BTW – by the way;

GR8 – great;

IMHO – (sarcastically) in my humble opinion;

IMO – in my opinion;

LOL – laughing out loud;

M8 – mate;

NP – no problem;

ROFL/ROTFL – rolls on (the) floor laughing;

RTFM – read the effing manual;

TTFN – ta-ta for now;

WB – welcome back;

WTF – what the f**k.

There's also a lot of smileys scattered around to give a better idea of emotions meant by a joke or comment.

Essential advice Rather like a newsgroup, there's not much that you cannot say in a chat channel – so long as you're in the right channel and not swearing your head off. Swearing is generally fine and used as part of the chat rather than an insult. So here are the basic rules that will protect you:

1. If someone suggests typing in any command, don't – unless you know what it does. Many users have hours of fun leading newbies astray.
2. Stick to the language that's being used – it makes everyone's life easier.
3. Don't hassle any other user in the channel for something – you wouldn't like it.

To find out more about the rules of IRC, how to protect yourself and the etiquette, visit the excellent IRChelp site (http://www.irchelp.org).

//INSTANT MESSAGING

IRC has its place as an open forum but if you want a quick chat with your mates – or total strangers – there's nothing to beat instant messaging. The idea's simple: special software will tell you the moment a friend has connected to the Internet and is available for a natter.

At the start of the revolution was the giant Internet provider AOL. Since its charging scheme required it to keep track of when users logged on and off, it was easy to extend this to tell people when a fellow user was online. This is great if you're on AOL but no use for the Internet. The problem is that no other Internet provider keeps track of who's logged on to its server.

Leaping into the public ring came a simple system called ICQ (say it as 'I seek you'). It's so successful that there are plenty of rivals (including a modified version of the AOL software) that all work in the same way.

Unlike IRC, you can set up ICQ so that it provides a degree of privacy: you don't have to broadcast to the world that you're waiting to chat; instead, you can limit this news to a list of friends or colleagues. When they connect, have a one-on-one or all gossip away in your private meeting room.

Get started

To start chatting with instant messaging, you'll need some special software and a connection to the Internet. Unlike IRC and newsgroups, each type of IM software uses a different system of sending messages so, generally, they are incompatible. Although there are dozens of different programs available, three dominate. ICQ, AOL and Yahoo! Pager have the largest number of users and are easy to use. If you use the latest version of the Netscape brower or you subscribe to AOL, you are already set up to use AOL Instant Messaging. If you use a different browser or ISP, you'll have to download one of the special software systems, but it's free.

The choice really lies in how you want to use the chat system. If you only want to talk to your chums or work colleagues, you can use a system like iChat that doesn't have much by way of a directory of users. If you want to find a friend with whom you can chat about shared interests, go for a package with a strong directory – and that means ICQ or Yahoo! However, systems that use a directory also ask you to enter more information to configure the software – and your entry in the directory. Here's how to set it all up:

1 If you're a non-AOL user, you need to decide if you want to try AOL, ICQ or Yahoo! Pager. Or you can try each – first download the software from AOL

(**http://www.aol.co.uk/aim**), ICQ (**http://www.icq.com**) or Yahoo! (**http://www.yahoo.com**).

2 Install the software on your computer. The program will ask you to type in your real name, nickname, email address and (optionally) a description of yourself or your interests.

3 Next, you need to set up the level of privacy you want to use – do you want to allow any other user to call you for a chat or do you want to restrict this list to known friends?

The chat software will sit quietly in the background while you surf with your web browser or check your email – until another user asks you if you want to chat. It will then pop up and tell you who's calling and give you the option to start a conversation.

You can send files via IRC and instant messaging but it slows things down for everyone – do it by email instead.

//TELEPHONE

Typing out chat is all very well, but you can't beat a real conversation. You can make phone calls over the Internet, talking and listening to another user. And with just a little extra hardware, you can even support a videophone link so you can see the person at the other end. The quality is sometimes patchy and you might suffer an echo on the line, but with the right software, you will experience a remarkably clear line.

The costs

If you stick to calls to other users on the Internet, you'll only pay your usual phone costs to your provider. However, if you plan to dial out to a friend with a regular phone, you'll need to subscribe to a service that links the Internet to the phone system. These companies tend to change their rules – and names – even more often than other web services, so the simplest way to find them is to type in 'internet phone' in your search engine. These companies are rarely free and you might need to subscribe or put down a deposit before you can run up a phone bill.

What you need To make a phone call over the net is remarkably easy. If your computer has a sound card, microphone and speakers, and a fast modem (better than 28.8Kbps) then you're all set. In addition to a standard Internet connection, you need special software that connects you to another user or acts as an exchange to a real phone. The latest web browsers have basic functions built in, but it's far easier to use a specialist program. Some you can download for free, others are sold commercially.

//ADDRESS BOOK

IRC Software	
ChatNet (Mac)	http://www.elsinc.com
ircle (Mac)	http://www.ircle.com
mIRC (PC)	http://www.mirc.com

Instant Messaging Software	
AOL Instant Messenger	http://www.netscape.com
iChat	http://www.ichat.com
ICQ	http://www.icq.com
PowWow	http://www.tribal.com
Yahoo! Pager	http://Pager.yahoo.com

Internet Telephone Software	
CuSeeMe	http://www.cuseeme.com
Internet Telephone	http://www.vocaltec.com
Net2Phone	http://www.net2phone.com
Netmeeting	http://www.microsoft.com

8//YOUR OWN WEBSITE

Why would you want to create your own website? Everyone has something to say to the world and here are just a few examples of the reasons why other users have set up their own site:

- it's easy;
- so that your distant relatives can get the latest news about you and see your latest photos;
- to advertise a product;
- to advertise yourself – publish your CV;
- to proclaim your adoration of a film star, pop star, philosopher or model – and so get to know who else shares your passion;
- to show off your collection and get more contributions.

In the old days, you would need a degree in programming, plenty to say and a subject worth writing about. Now, it's dead easy to create a site and anyone can do it. You don't need any money to set up a site (you can use a free ISP), you don't need to be a company to set up a site, you don't need to have your own domain name and nor do you need the help of a geek hacker, artist or ace writer (although these three will help when your site is famous).

You can set up a site for free and, if the idea's good enough, retire gracefully to a sun-drenched island with a fortune when you sell on the company.

Getting web space

The collection of pages that make up your website needs to be stored on an Internet server. If you keep your web pages on your computer, you're the only one who can enjoy their depth and vision. Publish them – 'upload' them to an Internet server – and the rest of the webbed world will be able to enjoy your wisdom.

Your ISP will provide you with a certain amount of free web space that you can use to store your website. Both free and charging ISPs will supply you with web space as part of your account. If you are using a free ISP (such as Freeserve or Virgin Net) then you pay nothing – but you cannot have your own domain name, nor can you drive a complex database or store vast archives of video footage.

What is acceptable?

Anything goes on the Internet – but that's not necessarily true of the company that's providing the disk space to store your website. All web space providers have their own AUP (acceptable user policy) that spells out exactly what you can and cannot do with your account. Many won't let you sell products or run commercial sites from a free account. Others don't want your porn or offensive material. If you break the AUP, your account will be closed down and you'll have to find another provider.

Law matters

If you write something that is rude or insulting about someone else, you'll feel the might of libel lawyers. Copy text or images from another site and, again, you'll get the lawyers visiting. And if you publish porn or material that's otherwise depraved or incites prejudice or violence, your web space provider will probably cancel your account and shut you down.

//HOW DO I BUILD IT?

When you create a site, you are really creating a collection of individual, linked pages. Designing the page is rather like using a sophisticated word processor: you can type in text, add headlines, change the fonts, add in images, animation and even video clips. All these different elements of a web page are described using a special set of codes called HTML (HyperText Markup Language) – so you need to use a program that can deal with HTML.

The simplest way to create a web page is to use a special web page design program. However, you can get started using an up-to-date word processing application such as Word or WordPerfect. Use the software's File/Save As or Export feature to save any document as a web page. Use all the standard word processing formatting features to produce a good-looking document, then save it as a web page. You've created a web page without touching HTML code.

Alternatively, use your web browser. Both Microsoft's IE and Netscape's Navigator include extra programs that let you create a simple web page. With IE, choose the Web Publishing Wizard; with Navigator, it's called Composer. Whichever you use, the software looks like a word processor and lets you type in and format text and graphics.

Getting to grips with HTML

Every web page is built up using the HTML language. It's rather clumsy but it lets you define how the page works. If you're using a word processor, the page editor from your browser or a special page design program then you can avoid having to deal with HTML altogether.

However, if you want to create stunning sites and understand how the web works, you'll need to tackle HTML. To complicate matters, the language is always evolving to add new multimedia effects – visit the Builder (**http://www.builder.com**) or WebMonkey (**http://www.webmonkey.com**) sites for help, advice and tutorials on all the HTML commands.

HTML commands are words or letters stored within a pair of angle brackets ('<>'). They are decoded by the web browser, which formats the text that follows according to the HTML command. The HTML language is mostly made up of pairs of commands: one switches something on, the other switches it off. For example, <B> switches on bold type, </B> switches it off. HTML commands can be written in either upper or lower case – it doesn't make any difference.

Experiment with HTML by using the different text formatting and hyperlink commands. Text can be displayed in different sizes, fonts and typefaces.

<B> this will be displayed in bold</B>

<I> this will be in italics</I>

<CENTER> this will be centred on the line</CENTER>

<H1> Use the H codes to describe the size of the text – H1 is big, H7 is small</H1>

Any text will be displayed in the browser's default font, normally a Times Roman serif font. To get full control over the font, use the <FONT> command: <FONT FACE="arial" SIZE="-1"> displays small text in an Arial font. (If the computer that's viewing this web page doesn't have the Arial font installed, it uses the nearest equivalent – in this case, a sans-serif font.)

The HTML convention ignores any blank lines or carriage returns that might be in your text. It just runs together into one block of text. You have to insert codes to create line breaks: either use a paragraph <P> command to break a line of text and add a blank line or use the <BR> command to end a line.

Including images

To include an image on your page, use the <IMG> code. You need to store the image files either as GIF or JPEG format files (almost any paint program can save graphics to these two formats). Avoid other formats such as TIF, PCX or BMP file – they won't work.

If you're using a word processor to create your page, use the Insert/Picture menu option to include an image. If you're using a web browser add-in (like FrontPage Express) to create your web page, just click on the Image icon in the toolbar and type in the name of the image file.

For small websites, it's convenient to store your image files in the same folder or directory as the files for each page. As your website gets more complex and has more images, you might find it easier to manage the image files in their own, separate folder. If you have an image file called 'flower.gif' you can display it with the command <IMG SRC="flower.gif">.

There's a balancing act when creating images for the web. You want high-quality, colourful images that are stored in a file that's as small as possible – so they are quick to download and display. Include too many images, or use files that are too big, and users will give up on your site. Most visitors don't like waiting more than 20 seconds for a page to display.

The size of an image file is determined by the number of colours used, the size of the image and the resolution. Image editing programs, like the popular shareware Paintshop Pro (**http://www.jasc.com**), let you adjust all three till you reach the perfect balance between quality and file size.

Top tips for images

1 Use the JPEG file format for photos.

2 Use GIF files for simple images that have fewer colours.

3 Reduce the resolution to a maximum of 72dpi.

4 You can usually cut down the palette of colours used to 16 or 256 colours.

5 Reduce the file size of any image to a maximum of 30-40K

6 If you want to use lots of images, keep them very simple to keep the total file size to 30-40Kb.

Adding links The web was designed to let you link one page to another, or one site to another, so that a user can follow the links and travel around the web. A link can either be a few words of text or even a picture; your mouse pointer changes to a pointing hand when it passes over a link.

If you're using a word processor to create your page, highlight the text you want to set as a hyperlink and choose the Insert/Hyperlink menu function – then type in the full address of the destination page. If you're using FrontPage Express or Netscape's web browser-based design program, highlight the text and click on the link icon (it's got a couple of segments of a chain link). Now type in the full address of the destination page.

You can also add links anywhere in your web page by using the <A HREF> HTML code, followed by the address to jump to and then the text or image that's to be the hotspot. The line

> **<A HREF="http://www.yahoo.com">** Click to visit Yahoo!</A>

will display the words 'Click to visit Yahoo!' in the usual link style – underlined and in red. Click on these words and you'll be transported directly to the Yahoo! site.

To jump to a page within your site, use the commands with the name of the file that contains the page. For example:

> **<A HREF="flowers.htm">** Click here to see the flowers</A>

Turn an image into a hotspot by including the name of the image file instead of the text. To turn our 'flower.gif' image into a hotspot that will whisk you to the 'flowers.htm' page use the code:

> **<A HREF="flowers.htm"><IMG SRC="flower.gif"></A>**

Layout Effective websites use a clear design and are easy to navigate. A lot of this is down to the overall design of each page. Many opt for a contents list running down the left-hand side while some prefer to keep navigation information at the top of each page.

Tables are the simplest way of positioning text and pictures in a particular area of the page and it works with all types of browser. The table has individual cells (like a spreadsheet) that can contain an image or text. For better control, use frames; these are now supported by just about all brands of browser. The newest system, called DHTML, makes use of CSS (cascading style sheets). Use CSS if you want to be at the cutting edge – but only visitors with the newest browsers will see anything.

Java and JavaScript

When creating a web page, you are not just limited to HTML commands. There are several different ways of extending the features of HTML – two of the better-known systems are called Java and JavaScript; both let you add extra features and effects to your web page. Java is a sophisticated programming language that's used to create small programs (called applets) that can be run by a browser. JavaScript is a kind of extension to HTML that lets you add natty effects to your web page. When a browser loads a web page, it will follow the HTML and JavaScript commands.

Java will take you a few weeks to learn – if you go on an intensive course. On the other hand, you can pick up snippets of JavaScript and add them to your web pages whenever you like. The downside of each is that users don't like Java applets – they could do something flash or they could be malicious and delete everything on your hard disk. JavaScript is relatively benign but doesn't work in the same way on all browsers.

Visit sites dedicated to JavaScript (**http://www.javascript.com** or **http://www.webmonkey.com or http://www.builder.com**) and try out the snippets of code that they offer. Half your visitors with compatible browsers will think your site sophisticated, the other half won't see the effects at all.

Different browsers

The war between Microsoft and Netscape to gain the upper ground in web browsers has been the primary force in the high-speed development of HTML and web publishing technologies. Each company tries to outdo the other by introducing a new way of helping web designers create super sites, but then the other browser is left behind. This leapfrog game is still being played out and leads to plenty of problems for web designers.

If you use some JavaScript commands, only Microsoft's IE browser will recognise them – Netscape's Navigator won't display anything. Similarly, DHTML and CSS are supported in different ways by each browser.

If you want to cater for the widest audience, don't use the newest tricks. If you do, you'll alienate half your visitors.

Advanced features

As you visit websites on your travels, you might want to have some of the same features on your site. How do you add a discussion group, search a database or ask users to fill out a form? The answer is to create a special program to carry out these features and link it to your web page using a system called CGI (common gateway interface). It's complex, but the nub is that it lets your web page send information to a program you've written that runs on the ISP's server.

Most of these programs are written in an archaic language called Perl. You'll need to learn how to write commands in Perl and you'll need an ISP that lets you run Perl scrips in your web space (some ISPs call these 'CGI scripts'). Many of the free ISPs do not let you run Perl scripts. If your ISP doesn't let you run scripts, you can use a second ISP to run them for you, but this is often slow and a lot of bother; it's generally easier just to change ISP.

The Perl language lets you build complex sites, such as shopping sites, even search engines; you can find out more by visiting **http://www.perl.com** or, to try out some of the free Perl scripts available to anyone, visit **http://www.freescripts.com** or **http://www.freecode.com**.

If this sounds too complicated for words, try Microsoft's FrontPage web design program. It includes 'bots' that let you add these advanced features to your site without any programming. The snag is that you'll need a web space provider that supports FrontPage, and you'll probably have to pay.

//HOW DO I PUBLISH?

Once you have designed and created your website, you need to copy the individual files (that make up each page and the images you have used) to your part of the hard disk on your web space provider's server computer. This is called publishing the site – but it's no more complicated than copying files from your hard disk to a floppy disk.

To copy any file from one computer to another, over the Internet, you need to use a system called FTP (file transfer protocol). This is just a simple series of commands that let your computer tell the server computer that it wants to transfer a file. You'll need a special program that's rather like the Windows Explorer – there are dozens freely available from sites such as **http://www.shareware.com** (just search for 'ftp'). You need to configure the FTP program with your user name, password and the address of the area of web space on the server (the ISP that's hosting your site will provide all three).

If you are using any of the main web page design programs (FrontPage, HotDog, PageMill, Dreamweaver and so on), you'll avoid direct contact with FTP: the page design software will do all the hard work for you.

Your own address
Sign up with any Internet provider and you will get access to the Internet and an allocation of web space, where you can store your own website. Your website will have its own unique address (normally called its URL) that lets any other user find and view your site. When you get an account with the Internet provider, it will tell you your URL, which is normally made up of the provider's name then your user name.

To get your own personal address without the provider's name in there means registering your own domain name. The simplest way to register your own domain name is to ask your Internet provider to do the work for you. Some ISPs now offer domain names for free, such as FreeNetName **http://www.freenetname.co.uk**. Most ISPs will ask you to pay an initial registration fee and then a yearly subscription just to maintain your own domain name (it's normally between £40 and £100 per year).

Publicity for your site
You've built your site and it looks great – now you have to tell everyone about it. The first announcement is the easiest: make sure that you include your website address in your email signature (see Chapter 5 for more on email).

The most important place to start is with the search engines – you must try and register your site with all the major search engines. Each search engine and directory has a special form you can fill in to submit your site. If the search engine has an editorial policy (such as Yahoo!), you can only suggest that the editors take a look at your site – if they like it, they'll include it.

To help publicise your site, send an email to the webmaster of other sites that cover the same subject and ask if they will add a link to your page. If the subject's popular enough, there might be a web ring (a collection of sites linked together to help visitors) that you could join.

If you write anything for a mailing list or newsgroup, you should make sure that your signature includes your website. Be subtle. Do not, under any circumstances, post a 'come see my site' type message. You'll almost certainly get thrown off the mailing list or be flamed by other subscribers.

Finally, you could always create a banner advertisement for your site – the little horizontal ads that appear at the top of most sites. There are several co-operative schemes that let you swap banner ads with other similar sites – you place their ad on your site and they'll do the same for you. The biggest scheme is called LinkExchange (**http://www.linkexchange.com**), and it is free.

//ADDRESS BOOK

Advice for Site Builders

Web tools and programming systems keep changing and evolving, so the best place to find out the latest are the sites dedicated to web developers.

AnyBrowser **http://www.anybrowser.com**
Check how your site looks when seen by different browsers.

Builder **http://www.builder.com**
WebMonkey **http://www.webmonkey.com**
Two vast but easily accessible guides to building your own site.

Clipart.com **http://www.net-matrix.com/graphx/**
Thousands of icons, pictures, and animations to copy and use.

Freecode **http://www.freecode.com**
A mass of Perl programs to add advanced features.

JavaScript **http://www.javascript.com**
Add cool effects using this library of JavaScript routines.

Pages that suck **http://www.pagesthatsuck.com**
Two top designers tell you what not to do.

Web Page Editors

If you're serious about your site, you will find it easier to design and manage with one of these tools:

Dreamweaver **http://www.adobe.com**
FrontPage **http://www.microsoft.com**
HotDog **http://www.sausage.com**
NetObjects **http://www.fusion.com**
PageMill **http://www.adobe.com**

Publicity

Exploit **http://www.exploit.com**
Submit It **http://www.submit-it.com**
Will automatically submit your new site to hundreds of search engines and directories.

LinkPopularity **http://www.linkpopularity.com**
See who else has linked to your site.

SearchEngineWatch **http://www.searchenginewatch.com**
Find out how different search engines work.

WebPosition **http://www.webposition.com**
Tells you how your site is ranked with the top search engines.

9//WEBSITE DIRECTORY

There are several million websites on the Internet. We've trawled through the web to find over 1000 that work, are useful and provide a great starting point to the subject.

In each section, we've also included directory sites that list other sites (for example, **http://www.funny.co.uk** is simply a directory of thousands of other side-splitting sites); these are listed as 'Starting Point' sites at the start of the section. If you want to explore, use these as a springboard.

And to keep up to date with the alternative word from fans and other web fanatics, we have also included a range of the e-zines and newsgroups that are relevant to each section. To search the complete list of 60,000 newsgroups, use Deja (**http://www.deja.com**). The only search engine that lets you hunt down the perfect e-zine is InfoJump (**http://www.infojump.com**) – persevere, it's often very busy.

Worth a quick mention is the net equivalent of the Oscars – the Webby Awards. Each year, the web designers come out from behind their keyboards to accept awards for best design, content and more. See what the pros think is best at **http://www.webbyawards.com**.

Use these sites as a starting point for your travels; if there's something really great, please let us know (send us an email at **response@virgin-pub.co.uk**).

10//ART AND CULTURE

View the best works from the greatest artists without leaving your home – that's the promise of the Internet, and it delivers with a flourish. Let your mouse lead you around the world's galleries to view priceless private collections. World galleries use the Internet as a way of displaying current shows and archive material to a wider audience. Visit the MoMA in New York, the sleek Louvre in Paris or pop into J. Paul Getty's pad on the west coast. Or stay at home and revel in the entire works of the Tate – online.

Getting a gallery to display work is an uphill struggle for new artists, but the Internet gives everyone an equal – and cheap – way to a global audience. Online galleries like ArtNet and Art-Smart house portfolios from new and established artists.

Starting Points

Art Guide **http://www.artguide.org**
What's on display in UK museums and galleries.

Art Planet **http://www.artplanet.com**
Every fine art site listed. Museums, artists, galleries, suppliers.

ArtLex – dictionary of visual art **http://www.artlex.com**
Instant understanding. Press Ctrl-N to display a second browser window to keep this dictionary handy as you visit the other sites in this chapter!

The Art Connection **http://www.art-connection.com**
For life away from the Internet, here's the real art that's on display in London and provincial art galleries.

WebMuseum **http://www.southern.net/wm/**
The world's greatest artists brought together in one virtual warehouse. Perfect for students and classroom visits.

World Wide Arts Resources **http://wwar.com**
A vast mass of links to museums, artists, galleries and exhibitions, and a great place to start exploring.

Art for Sale

Art Deadlines List **http://custwww.xensei.com/adl/**
Impoverished artists apply here – lists of moneyed prizes and exhibitions worth entering.

Art-Smart **http://www.art-smart.com**
Hundreds of artists and their portfolios posing for potential collectors.

Art.Net **http://www.art.net/**
A community for wandering artists and art-lovers. Artists' studios and galleries show art forms from sculpture to poetry.

Museums

Argos **http://argos.evansville.edu**
Use the latest technology to navigate ancient and mediaeval studies.

ArtMuseum.Net **http://www.artmuseum.net/**
Tackles a single exhibition very well – video walk-throughs and stunning pictures cover the subject in great detail. So far, van Gogh and American painters have been profiled.

Germanisches Nationalmuseum **http://www.gnm.de**
One of the most impressive museums in the world, housing art, sculpture, cultural and folk art and design from prehistoric to contemporary.

Guggenheim **http://www.guggenheim.org**
Skip between the six museums, marvel at the cool design and enjoy selected pictures.

J. Paul Getty Museum **http://www.getty.edu**
Take a tour round the billionaire's beautiful house and art collection high above the Californian coast.

Leonardo da Vinci **http://www.webgod.net/leonardo/**
Finest Renaissance man with equal skill for painting portraits and inventing helicopters.

Library of Congress **http://www.loc.gov/**
Everything that made America great. Huge site with the best historical, cultural and political material from the official US archives.

Louvre **http://mistral.culture.fr/louvre/louvrea.htm**
Paris' palace of art, beautifully rendered. Pictures come first but, Mon Dieu, the spelling ...

Metropolitan Museum of Art **http://www.metmuseum.org**
Save the airfare. Landmark New York monument displays its stunning collection of art and cultural treasures online.

MoMA **http://www.moma.org**
Avoid the queues curling round to Fifth Avenue; the NY museum that's as famous as its exhibits puts on a great web show.

Monet **http://www.claudemonet.com**
In praise of the first and leading Impressionist painter.

National Gallery **http://www.nationalgallery.org.uk**
Greatest British collection of Western European paintings ranging from glowing Early Renaissance work by Raphael and Botticelli through to late nineteenth-century impressionists. The main works are displayed online with plenty of accompanying notes.

National Portrait Gallery **http://www.npg.org.uk**
London Gallery set up to house portraits of Brits – of a fabulous quality and range; unfortunately, very little has made it on to this site.

Picasso Official Web Site **http://www.club-internet.fr/picasso/**
The great one's work on show. His son provides the intro and experts guide you round the different styles and subject matter.

Tate Gallery **http://www.tate.org.uk**
Every gallery should follow this example. View almost all the pictures in the Tate collection together with notes on the artist and subject. Brilliant.

Uffizi Gallery, Florence **http://www.uffizi.firenze.it**
Virtual reality tour of its fabulous masterpieces including Botticelli's Birth of Venus.

Van Gogh **http://www.vangoghgallery.com**
Works and thoughts on the greatest post-Impressionist artist – best known for his fixation with sunflowers. And his missing ear.

Victoria and Albert **http://www.vam.ac.uk**
The building houses the finest collection of decorative arts in the world – from ceramics to costumes – but the web site's a disappointment with little to see.

Photography

24 Hours in Cyberspace **http://www.cyber24.com**
Project describing a day in the life of the world: photo-reporting and a riveting read from leading hacks.

ArtZone **http://www.artzone.gr/**
Black and white photography, and nothing else. Mono artists, techniques, materials and competitions.

British Journal of Photography **http://www.bjphoto.co.uk**
Take better shots. Advice and news for amateurs and pros. Cameramakers Nikon (**http://www.nikon.com**) and film producers Kodak (**http://www.kodak.com**) are alternatives for advice.

LIFE magazine **http://www.pathfinder.com/Life/**
Famous on paper and now on the web – it brings the world's best photographs to the masses.

Specialist

Department for Culture, Media and Sport **http://www.culture.gov.uk/**
How the Government spends our money.

HypArt **http://www.hypart.de**
Wild and hideous web-art project that lets you contribute your painting as part of a large, public web-canvas.

Postmodern Culture **http://jefferson.village.virginia.edu/pmc/**
Deadly serious online magazine on art and culture.

The Art Bin **http://art-bin.com**
Interesting, if odd, magazine on art, philosophy and culture. As you'd expect, it's written in English and Swedish.

Try these newsgroups

alt.binaries.pictures.fine-art
Fine art image files (moderated).

alt.culture.internet
Any culture of and on the Internet.

rec.arts.dance
Dance.

rec.arts.fine
Appreciation of fine art and artists.

rec.arts.theatre
Life and times backstage.

11//BOOKS AND READING

Whatever you want to read, you can get it, or buy it, online. Original magazines (e-zines), complete novels and cut-price paperbacks jostle for attention.

A great e-zine is a brilliant read – witty, offbeat and obsessive about its subject. They are usually written by enthusiasts for enthusiasts and ensure you'll keep up to date with news, views, gossip, reviews and background detail on any subject. If you want something to read, look to InfoJump (**http://www.infojump.com**) and search for the thousands of e-zines that cover every detail. I've included some of the best zines in the following section.

Books represent a great commodity for the web. You don't need to hold inventory and you can slash prices and ship out with minimal effort. As a result, there are hundreds of bookshops online. The bigger e-shops list every book currently in print – and have even extended their range to antique books and magazines. The battle for supremacy between the bigger organisations (Amazon, BarnesAndNoble, AlphabetStreet and BOL) ensures that net prices are way below – often half – the price you'd pay in the high street.

Best of all, pay nothing and read one of the complete texts of a novel or textbook that's been published directly on to the net. And it's not just hopeful writers; most of the classics are available in various editions, as are works from well-known authors such as Wodehouse and Brontë. If you are too tired to read, choose one of the complete audio books ready for download.

Booksellers

Alphabetstreet Books UK **http://www.alphabetstreet.co.uk**
One of the nicest, cheapest UK-based online booksellers.

Amazon.com **http://www.amazon.co.uk**
Everyone knows the Amazon bookstore – with good reason: it's

still the big cheese and its customer features are great. However, the rivals are catching up quickly. There are also plenty of price differences between the US and UK versions of the shop – prices are often lower in the US site (Amazon.com) and it includes videos, music CDs and gifts for sale, whereas the UK site (Amazon.co.uk) sticks to books.

Barnesandnoble.com **http://www.barnesandnoble.com**
The widest range of books on the net – the online bookshop equivalent to the great US chain. There's even Starbucks coffee for sale (B&N bought the company) as you browse the widest range of titles available. Also sells software and out-of-print titles.

Bibliofind **http://www.bibliofind.com**
From a first edition Wodehouse to a textbook that's just out of print, this site will help you find it. The search engine indexes over 2,000 antiquarian booksellers (mostly from the US, but they can deliver). Part of Amazon.com.

BOL **http://www.uk.bol.com**
The newest of the mega online bookshops; covers the European market and provides massive range, local titles plus a few neat features such as your own bookshelf of favourite books.

Books.com **http://www.books.com**
You've read it, now chat about it. An online bookseller whose strength is its great range of interactive forums where you can discuss books.

Borders **http://www.borders.com**
Vast bookshop chain provides masses of choice, with good service.

The Book People **http://www.thebookpeople.co.uk**
Excellent site that's doing battle by discounting furiously. At the time of writing, every other shop had just discounted to 50%, these folk were on to 75%.

The Internet Bookshop **http://www.bookshop.co.uk**

WH Smith hits the web with a standard selection of 1.4m titles, plus CDs, videos, and games. Friendly cyber-clerk Jenny will keep you up-dated on new publications.

Virgin Books **http://www.virgin-books.com**

Well, you couldn't expect us not to blow our own trumpet. All the latest news from Virgin Publishing, and loads of special offers.

Libraries

Bodleian Library **http://www.bodley.ox.ac.uk/**

See the bestsellers from the thirteenth century – a modest but interesting range of images from some of the oldest manuscripts housed by this famous library in Oxford.

Internet Public Library **http://www.ipl.org**

Stroll through the aisles, pick up your favourite book and download the full text for free. An often odd selection of books that's probably down to copyright laws.

Online Medieval and Classical Library **http:// sunsite. berkeley.edu/OMACL/**

Yes, we thought you'd be interested. Small, select range of the most influential early writers such as Chaucer. Great for students, academics and anyone bored by modern fiction.

The British Library **http://portico.bl.uk/**

No, you cannot yet browse the entire collections stored in the BL (though it's in development), but at least you can search the catalogues and get background information from the site.

The On-Line Books Page **http://www.cs.cmu.edu/books.html**

From Austen, Jane to Zola, Emile, you can download the complete texts of over 9,000 books. Should keep you busy for a while.

Vatican Library **http://metalab.unc.edu/expo/vatican.exhibit/exhibit/Main_Hall.html**
What the Pope has stored in his library. Plenty of background historical information together with images of inventory notes kept from the fifteenth century onwards.

Poetry

Reflections Poetry **http://www.crocker.com/~lwm/**
Enjoyable site that provides text and, in some cases, audio files with readings of classic poems.

The International Library of Poetry **http://www.poetry.com**
Links to poetry sites plus news on poetry competitions, reviews and discussion boards where poets can exchange ideas.

Reviews

Bookideas **http://www.bookideas.com**
Book reviews by fellow surfers. A modest range of books are reviewed and rated – and if you disagree, you can add your own comments.

Bookwire **http://www.bookwire.com**
Who's publishing what, how much were they paid and when's it coming out? US-based, but provides just about the best range of bookish resources, with links to publishers, reviews by the respected Boston Book News, library and trade news and much more.

Carol Hurst's Children's Literature Site **http://www.carolhurst.com/index.html**
Is it good bedtime fodder or a scary story? Hundreds of books for children reviewed. Easy to navigate by subject, author or title, the site also provides a regular email newsletter and teacher/parent resources with ideas for theme reading.

Discovery Online – Book Talk **http://books.discovery.com/booktalk.html**
Turns the tables on choosing books: look up a topic (such as 'gorillas') and find lists of books, experts who'll answer questions and even editors who can discuss the subject. Best for kids and schools.

London Review of Books online **http://www.lrb.co.uk**
Good writing about good writing and occasionally good writing on dross pulp. A well-designed site from this respected UK magazine; the site has plenty of well-written, incisive reviews of books by the top critics, plus some selected archives.

New York Review of Books **http://www.nybooks.com/nyrev/**
Heavy-hitting reviews, short stories and essays; there's a searchable database of selected past articles that act as a taster and tempt you to subscribe.

The Book Review Corner **http://www.tronco.com/books/**
Inspired to write a review? Add your own opinions to the small and idiosyncratic selection of books.

Magazines

Alt-X **http://www.altx.com**
Fabulously hip literary e-zine with iconoclastic fiction and post-modernist musings rendered to hypertext – no, really, it's a great read.

InfoJump **http://www.infojump.com**
Original thought on the web – if not always agreeable – is usually in e-zines. Search this huge database of almost every e-zine on the web.

Newsrack **http://www.newsrack.com**
Brilliantly simple idea done very well – stationers John Menzies provide links to (almost) every online newspaper and magazine from around the world.

The Atlantic Monthly **http://www.theatlantic.com**
Slick electronic edition of this essay-based magazine that covers just about every subject worthy of comment. Usually a good read. Alternate with Nation for even coverage.

The Nation **http://www.thenation.com**
Old, established and venerated weekly opinion magazine that provides informed essays on world events, from art to books, wars to politics – with generally very good results.

ZineZone **http://www.zinezone.com**
Mass of e-zines about hundreds of different subjects created within one community site.

Others

HarperAudio! **http://town.hall.org/Archives/radio/IMS/HarperAudio/**
Listen to the stories of several dozen classic authors – from Brontë to Thurber. Download your favourite and listen to the tale as you surf.

Macmillan US Computer Reference **http://www.mcp.com**
Create your own virtual bookshelf of the text from any of the computer books from this top publisher and view the full book for free, online.

The Literary Web **http://www.people.virginia.edu/~jbh/litweb.html**
Great writing is just a link away with this comprehensive listing of hundreds of literary sites, neatly organised in a simple layout.

Winners of the Nobel Prize in Literature **http://nobelprizes.com/nobel/literature/**
Who won the top literary prize with a mass of related links about the writers and their works.

Try these newsgroups

alt.books.beatgeneration
Kerouac and co.

alt.books.isaac-asimov
Sci-fi author's fan club.

alt.books.reviews
Let rip about a story.

alt.books.stephen-king
Nasty goings on from Mr King.

alt.books.technical
Let's read something techie.

rec.arts.books
Books and publishing.

rec.arts.books.childrens
Children's literature.

rec.arts.books.reviews
Book reviews (moderated).

rec.arts.mystery
Whodunnit?

12//BUSINESS AND OFFICE

The majority of businesses are online – and with good reason. It's a vast, fast, free library that can help you research a new project, start a business, check on current business strategies or simply buy more paperclips for the office.

The level of detail available free is impressive. If you're planning a push into Central Europe or Latin America, use the Internet to do your research. You can find background profiles and detailed reports on the economy of almost any country within a few sites.

General business advice is delivered by local government resources – such as Business Link – and by online business magazines. Most of these are US-based and very up-front about money and success, but the basic business principles still apply. However, new technology means new business models, techniques and ethics. All are explained and dissected for the next generation of entrepreneurs in magazines like Fast Company.

Starting Points

Yahoo! **http://www.yahoo.co.uk/Business_and_Economy/**
The Yahoo! selection of sites about business.

Business Link **http://www.businesslink.co.uk**
Your local guide to UK business information, advice and expertise.

Inc. Online **http://www.inc.com**
American magazine for the entrepreneur provides discussion forums, advice and a vast directory of online resources.

Advice

BT Partnership **http://www.partnership.bt.com**
Dominant UK telco dishes out news and advice for global (read Internet) business methods.

Entrepreneurial Edge Online **http://www.edgeonline.com**
Practical advice on running and growing your business. Some of the sample letters are off the mark for the UK, but the financial toolbox alone is worth the visit.

Fast Company **http://www.fastcompany.com**
The first and foremost of a new breed of business magazines aimed at hi-tech companies and entrepreneurs.

New Business Kit **http://www.new-business.co.uk**
Pitfalls to avoid when setting up a new business.

Your Business – Microsoft UK **http://www.microsoft.com/uk/yourbusiness/**
Techie-advice from the Seattle HQ to help small business owners make the most of IT.

News

For financial news and indicators, see the section on finance, starting on page 154.

CommerceNet **http://www.commerce.net/**
What's new in e-commerce – read it here first. Produced by a group of Silicon Valley companies that define the new business technology. An essential visit for any company doing business on the net.

HM Treasury **http://www.hm-treasury.gov.uk/**
Official UK Treasury site. Not exactly thrilling, but the official source of all monetary wisdom.

Marketing Week Online **http://www.marketing-week.co.uk**
The leading trade weekly; register (for free) then read the news and features or search the job bank.

Mondaq Business Briefing **http://www.mondaq.com/index.htm**
Excellent coverage of the rather dull but necessary legal, regulatory and financial matters that might affect your business.

Nikkei Net Interactive http://www.nni.nikkei.co.jp/
Business news from Japan.

The Economist http://www.economist.com
A free and essential stopping point for any businessperson savvy enough to browse online and save the weekly subscription rate to this excellent magazine.

UK Business Park http://www.ukbusinesspark.co.uk
Ambitious idea to collect business, financial and niche trade news; this newly redesigned site provides almost too much useful information. Daily news summaries for your business topic can be emailed (at a cost) on a daily basis.

Office Stuff

Ashfields http://www.ashfields.com
Furnish your office or reception with a good range of desks, chairs and sofas.

Exchange and Mart http://www.exchangeandmart.co.uk
Business classifieds – the ads have everything you'll need to fill an office.

Neat Ideas http://www.neat-ideas.com
The rival to Viking puts up a great fight online.

The office shop http://www.owa.co.uk
Staplers to printers, paper pads to PCs – at low prices.

Viking Direct http://www.viking-direct.co.uk
The office bible now online; try rival Neat Ideas for a similar range and pricing

Reference

Statistical data locators **http://www.ntu.edu.sg/library/statdata.htm**
'Jones, I want a full report on the viability of opening an office in Venezuela.' Economic information about every world economy.

The Economist Intelligence Unit **http://www.eiu.com**
Current reports on world economic trends available to browse, but the real gold mine – the database of past reports – is a chargeable extra. Try the Statistical data locators site as a free alternative.

The Internationalist **http://www.internationalist.com**
Get help with your international endeavours – advice on business and business travel around the world.

Travel

For online travel agents offering cut-price hotels and tickets, look to the travel section, page 259.

Biztravel.com **http://www.biztravel.com**
The top travel site for jet-setting business types. This US service – that supports UK customers – lets you track frequent-flyer schemes, book planes, hotels and cars. It even records your preferences for seats and meals.

Travel Etiquette **http://www.traveletiquette.com**
Before you leave on a business trip, visit this site to make sure that you don't do something that will offend, be misinterpreted or amuse your business hosts.

Buying a Business

Daltons **http://www.daltons.co.uk**
Buy a pub or get a franchise from the weekly classified magazine listing business opportunities, premises, franchises and other deals.

Exchange and Mart **http://www.exchangeandmart.co.uk**
Business classifieds – from business equipment to businesses.

Moore, Wood & Cockram **http://www.mwclicproperty.demon.co.uk**
Buy the pub or restaurant of your dreams. Don't ask them how to run it though.

Advertising and Marketing

DoubleClick **http://www.doubleclick.net/**
One of the biggest web companies no one knows about. They look after the majority of the banner advertising you see on websites; they buy space, sell ads, audit and provide PR.

Wilson Internet Services **http://www.wilsonweb.com**
Yes, Ralph's a consultant, but the site is a gem. It includes his well-written newsletters on just about every aspect of Internet commerce and marketing.

Try these newsgroups

alt.business.misc
Commerce and general business.

alt.business.import-export
Buying and selling on a global scale.

biz.marketplace.international
Opportunities too good to miss, from around the world.

biz.marketplace.international.discussion
Discussion on those opportunities.

biz.stolen
Watch out, it's stolen.

misc.entrepreneurs.moderated
Run your own business (moderated).

13//CARS AND BIKES

Why not buy your next car on the web? It's easy to carry out exhaustive research, find the best price, check availability and even haggle by email.

If you don't want the devaluation and you're aiming for a used car, the classified listing papers *AutoTrader* and *Exchange and Mart* dominate. Both have searchable databases that enable you to find cars to your exact spec and within a convenient drive from home any time. Better still, set up an email alert and you'll be the first to hear when an ad for your perfect car is placed. For bikes, it's the same story. BikeTrader lists thousands of ads or, for Italian exotica, try NetBikes.

There are plenty of sites for particular marques and models, as well as classic motoring in general. Spares feature heavily – can't think why – and when you finally realise you'll never find that missing Bugatti trim, you can sell your restoration project online or find the next autojumble. But perhaps the most enjoyable part is exchanging tales of missing widget pins and self-collapsing hoods with fellow car-nuts.

Oh. You can't drive? Well, the net will provide help and dummy runs on the theory test. Sorry, no virtual driving school – yet.

Starting Points

AutoExpress **http://www.autoexpress.co.uk**

Every tiny detail about the latest thing on four wheels. Car-crazy web addicts can wallow in the vast database of road tests, check prices and browse the classifieds (though *AutoTrader* and *Exchange and Mart* are bigger). Use the Links button to get a directory of the websites for all the major car manufacturers.

MotoDirectory.com **http://www.moto-directory.com**
Lots and lots of links to bike sites – with over 6,000 (mostly in the US) this is a good place to start exploring.

RAC **http://www.rac.co.uk**
Everything a driver needs when travelling around the UK. Includes live traffic reports, a route planner and a hotel finder.

Car Magazines

BBC Top Gear **http://www.topgear.beeb.com**
Willson and crew let rip. Road tests, features, chat and all the usual opinionated silliness.

WhatCar? **http://www.whatcar.co.uk**
A little of everything car-related has been crammed into this informative site. The main features are the road tests but there's also classifieds, used car prices, insurance and finance features.

New Cars

Auto-By-Tel **http://www.autobytel.co.uk**
The vast and highly successful US way to choose and buy your next car arrives in the UK.

CAR-UK **http://www.car-uk.com**
Dig around and you'll find gems in this badly designed site. Includes a history of the UK car industry and masses of detail on individual car makes.

Carsource **http://www.carsource.co.uk**
Azure blue, tinted glass, alloys and air-con? Of course. Use the search system that matches your requirements with new and used cars available from main dealers. Once you've found the car, there are links to insurance companies, lease and finance groups.

Classic Car Club **http://www.classic-car-club.co.uk**
See the site's name? So why does it cover modern cars? Who

knows – but there's daily news, plus a calendar of events and a club index.

Mini (UK) **http://www.mini.co.uk**
Newly revamped site that'll satisfy every fan of The Italian Job, Cooper enthusiasts and past owners. You can even design your own mini online.

New Car Net **http://www.new-car-net.co.uk**
Help in choosing your new car. Enter your basic criteria, then compare the models and read in-depth reviews on each.

Old Cars

Car Prices **http://www.carprices.co.uk**
Buying a used motor? You'll want the Glass's guide – but it's not available directly, so visit this site that has licensed the price information from Glass to give you the lowdown on the top price to pay or expect to get for the wheels.

Classic Car Monthly **http://www.classicmotor.co.uk**
Find a spare bumper for your Spitfire or a gasket for the Minor. A great site for classic car owners who want to get spares, advice, talk to other owners or show off their cars. And if you're under pressure to sell your pride and joy (or box of bits) you can find the next autojumble.

Classic Cars Source **http://www.classicar.com**
Waxed, chrome-plated site for classic car enthusiasts. This US site provides a wealth of information on marques, events, spares, clubs and cars for sale.

Exchange and Mart **http://www.exchangeandmart.co.uk**
All the classified ads without spending a day hunting through the magazine. A neat and simple search function and an email update will ensure you're the first to hear about a new entry. On a par with AutoTrader (**http://www.autotrader.co.uk**); each has different ads but similar search functions.

Glass's Information Services **http://www.glass.co.uk**
The bible of the used motor trade. Trouble is, it's not available online, unless you visit **http://www.carprices.co.uk** who license the information and display it free of charge!

Haynes shop **http://www.carnet-online.co.uk/haynes/**
The engine's in pieces and you don't know what you're doing. Download an electronic version of the classic Haynes manuals to help you put it back together again.

Triumph Web **http://www.harding.co.uk/triumph/**
Wonderful site with history, classifieds and practical mechanical advice for Triumph Spitfire, Herald and GT6 owners.

Virtual Showroom **http://www.virtualshowroom.co.uk**
An index of (mostly used) cars available from dealers around the UK. Nothing fancy and you'll see a better selection with the top two classified magazines (AutoTrader and Exchange and Mart).

Bikes for Sale

BikeTrader **http://www.biketrader.co.uk**
The biggest range of bikes for sale, with a database of over 8,000 classified ads.

NetBikes **http://www.netbikes.yks.com**
Classifieds for exotica – and a soft spot for Ducati and Triumph bikes.

Bike Magazines

BikeNet **http://www.bikenet.com**
Slick UK site with the latest bike tests, biker-talk, discussion groups, race reports and classifieds.

Motorcycle Online **http://www.motorcycle.com**
Battling with rival Motorworld.com to be the biggest bike magazine on the net. Get the benefits and visit both. Road tests

and features dominate, plus a good email newsletter. It's a US magazine with few concessions to UK riders.

Motorworld Online **http://www.motorworld.com**
Bikes only on this vast magazine site. It has a more international feel than Motorcycle.com with reviews of British and American machines and coverage of US and UK events.

Street Bike Online **http://www.streetbike.com**
Powerful street bikes driven by babes in bikinis. And reviews, advice on mechanics and features on crazee bikes.

Driving

Cyberdrive **http://www.cyberdrive.co.uk**
If you're about to take your driving test, take a virtual theory test here – till you get it right! If you've got your licence, be horrified at how little you really know.

Learner Drivers UK **http://www.learners.co.uk**
All you need to know on schools, tips, the test itself and the theory.

The AA **http://www.theaa.co.uk**
Battling it out with the RAC, this site has a hotel finder and traffic watch. There's no route planner yet, and the webcam displaying the scenery outside AA headquarters doesn't really make up for it.

Motor Racing

British Motor Racing Circuits **http://www.bmrc.co.uk**
Full descriptions of all the racing circuits in the UK together with race reports and a comprehensive diary of events.

British Touring Club Championship **http://www.btcc.co.uk**
Strange people who drive family saloons at mad speeds.

McLaren **http://www.mclaren.co.uk**
A good lesson in how to produce a great-looking site. Keep up to date with the teamall around the world's F1 tracks.

The Brooklands Society **http://www.hartlana.co.uk/brooklands/**
The history of one of the best-known racetracks with photos of ancient racers and links to race sites.

Try these newsgroups

alt.autos.peugeot
Owners delighted with their French wheels.

alt.autos.peugeot.sucks
And the owners who are not quite so happy.

rec.audio.car
Turn up the volume.

rec.autos.sport.indy
Indy car racing.

rec.autos.sport.rally
Mud everywhere.

rec.toys.cars
When you can't afford the real thing.

uk.rec.cars.kit-car
Build it, drive it.

uk.rec.cars.maintenance
How to mend it.

uk.rec.cars.tvr
Big bonnet, big noise.

14//COMPUTING

It goes without saying that the Internet is a prime resource for computer buffs. You'll find product news, reviews and features to help you get the best from your hardware and software. To find your computer manufacturer's site, try entering their name or trademark followed by '.com' or '.co.uk'. You'll hit Gateway, Dell, IBM, HP, Elonex, Dan, Time and others in this way. If you're stuck, try a quick search in Yahoo! (or browse through its computer section).

Once you've found your computer's home site, check on updates for essential software drivers that control hard disk, graphics and system board. These are always free to download and could fix some potential bug.

If you spend your free time worrying about upgrades, bookmark CNET and ZDnet. Both provide features on new technologies and how to use them. For software addicts hell-bent on trying out new software, go straight to Filez – with over one million shareware programs to download, it provides the best range. But there's no guarantee the programs are any good, unless you visit RocketDownload – they've gone to the bother of rating the software available. You could also check ZDnet for reviews of software from its magazine stable that includes PC Magazine and sister titles.

US suppliers

You'll find the US home to some of the keenest prices and sharpest discounts on new hardware and software. Unfortunately, warranties and guarantees on both rarely extend outside the country. If you're willing to risk this (you'd normally have to arrange and pay for repairs through a local repair company), you'll probably have to do some sweet-talking to convince them to ship outside the US.

Starting Points

ZDNet UK **http://www.zdnet.co.uk**
Should be any surfer's first stop for computing news, reviews and features from the expert computer magazine publishers.

CNET **http://www.cnet.com**
Packed with news, a vast shareware library, advice and step-by-step instructions on everything from building a website to using your software.

Hardware

Order your custom-built computer from these manufacturers:

Apple Store **http://www.apple.com**
DELL **http://www.dell.co.uk**
Elonex **http://www.elonex.co.uk**
Evesham Micros **http://www.evesham.com**
Gateway 2000 **http://www.gateway.com/uk/**
Viglen **http://www.viglen.co.uk**

Action Computer Supplies **http://www.action.com**
Business-oriented hardware, software and accessories supplier. Great service, good prices and a site that's informative and easy to use.

CommStore **http://www.commstore.co.uk**
Upgrade your modem, move up to ISDN or buy new Internet software.

Dixons **http://www.dixons.co.uk**
Anything that's for sale in the high-street store is available online – that means TVs, hi-fi systems, PCs, fax machines and cameras.

Inmac **http://www.inmac.co.uk**
Well-stocked warehouse piled high with hardware and software at low prices and with great service.

Microwarehouse **http://www.microwarehouse.co.uk**
Provides just about the best range of computer hardware, software and accessories – and all at good prices. Better range than Action but the search and catalogue is not quite as slick.

Morgan Computers **http://www.morgancomputers.co.uk**
Cheap and cheerful end-of-line or used brand name computers, printers and other office equipment.

TechWeb **http://www.techweb.com/shopper**
Comprehensive database computer hardware and software that'll help you decide what's best for you.

Software

CD Direct **http://www.cddirect.co.uk**
Excellent range of software on CD – from games to office applica tions. Easy navigation, good budget titles and plenty of reviews.

Download.com **http://www.download.com**
Great library of commercial application software and shareware that you can buy and instantly download to your computer – part of the impressive CNET resource site.

ECHO Software **http://www.echosoftware.com**
Masses of second-user software plus over 100,000 software titles to buy and download directly to your computer.

Free Site **http://www.thefreesite.com**
Why pay when you can download free software, screensavers and web tools? Also check out **http://www.filez.com**.

Jungle.com **http://www.jungle.com**
Sharp, snappy site full of software, hardware, videos, music and games – all at discount prices.

Macintouch **http://www.macintouch.com**
Keep your Mac bug-free with the latest software fixes and updates.

Software Paradise **http://www.softwareparadise.co.uk**

Over 100,000 software titles for sale at discount prices. Covers all platforms from PC to Mac – and from developers around the world. Very easy to use.

Software Warehouse **http://www.software-warehouse.co.uk**

Extensive range of software and peripherals – providing reviews of each product, all the brand names at low prices and, in some cases, instant download.

The Educational Software Company **http://www.educational.co.uk**

Over 1,000 of the top educational software programs at reasonable prices. There are decent descriptions for most entries and recommendations help you pick the right program for your child's age and level.

Updates **http://www.updates.com**

Make sure all your applications are up to date – this free utility will scan your hard disk to see what's installed and then tell you what needs to be updated and how to do it.

Shareware

Vast libraries of programs you can download and try out before you pay.

CNET **http://www.cnet.com**

Everything you need to know about your PC and the software to make it zing. There's news, lots of reviews, advice on fixing problems and designing websites plus the vast library of shareware.

Filez **http://www.filez.com**

Claims to have the widest range of shareware files available to download, but CNET wins on general coverage.

Rocketdownload.com **http://www.rocketdownload.com**

Another good collection of shareware files to download – the big difference here is that the files have all been rated and described (saving you the annoyance of downloading junk).

Tucows Network **http://www.tucows.com**
Great collection of all the software you'll ever need – neatly arranged into categories. Rivals CNET in ease of use but without the range of Filez.

Advice

CNET **http://www.cnet.com**
Vast library of technical advice (along with its 'how to' sections, huge shareware library and industry news).

DriverZone **http://www.driverzone.com**
Drivers are tiny, but vital, bits of software that let your computer control your modem, hard disk, monitor or printer. Check here to make sure you've got the latest version or for advice on problems.

Help **http://www.free-help.com**
Get help fast – ask an expert about your computer problem.

Linux **http://www.linux.org**
Support and files about this cult operating system that rivals Windows – and has a big slice of the Internet action.

MacFixIt **http://www.macfixit.com**
Help get your Mac working properly, for a change.

Modem Help **http://www.modemhelp.com**
If you can get to this site, your modem's probably working. If it isn't, you'll wish you could.

My Desktop **http://www.mydesktop.com**
Great advice supplied, together with news and features.

PC Mechanic **http://www.pcmech.com**
Advice on how to upgrade or build your own PC.

SquareOneTech **http://www.squareonetech.com**
A useful series of Internet guides that will tell you almost as much as this book about getting online and using the net – the difference is you first have to work out how to get online to use the guides.

Tom's Hardware Guides **http://www.tomshardware.com**
Tom the PC man provides news about hardware and software plus a series of reasonable guides about various bits of your PC.

Windows Annoyances **http://www.annoyances.org**
What Microsoft didn't include in Windows and how to fix the irritating features they did include.

News

Many of the major sites, such as CNET and ZDnet include the latest computer-industry news, as do portals such as Excite! and Yahoo! Here are some of the better news-only sites:

Brill's Content **http://www.brillscontent.com**
Top features on the information and media age. Very sharp, very readable and an essential bookmark for anyone in the Internet or media industry.

Newsbytes **http://www.nbnn.com**
Everything that's happening in high technology. Extraordinarily detailed, with stringers around the world, plus decent archives.

SiliconValley **http://www.siliconvalley.com**
First stop for any high-tech VP looking for future eBay and Amazon.com-style successes. Polished site details news from the home of the US computer industry.

The Industry Standard **http://www.thestandard.com**
The best reports, features and news about the Internet itself. The metrics section is a brilliant résumé of what's up and down in this virtual world.

The Register **http://www.theregister.co.uk**
In-depth, often hard-hitting high-tech news – who's been found out, what's delayed, and what's new and fab.

Tidbits **http://www.tidbits.com**
Weekly digest of news for Mac owners.

Reference

Developer.com **http://www.developer.com**
If you're a code hound, you'll probably already know this site for its news, discussion, downloads and online journals and books.

Macmillan US Computer Reference **http://www.mcp.com**
Create your own virtual bookshelf of the text from any of the computer books from this top publisher and view the full book for free, online. A bold move that's great for computer manuals and techie texts.

The Internet Weather Report **http://www.mids.org/weather/**
Fascinating, if techie, view of the amount of traffic on the Internet – which directly relates to its speed and capacity. See also the tools at NetToolbox (**http://www.nettoolbox.com**) which will display your data's route across the globe as you use the net.

Webopedia home page **http://www.pcwebopedia.com**
Should you be worried by the blue screen of death? An online encyclopaedia with this and thousands of other PC and web terms clearly defined.

Try these newsgroups

alt.comp.shareware
What's new in shareware software.

alt.folklore.computers
Wild stories about computers.

comp.answers
Regular help and advice (moderated).

comp.binaries.ms-windows
Programs for Windows (moderated).

comp.dcom.modems
How to get connected.

comp.home.misc
Get your home wired (moderated).

comp.multimedia
Cool, interactive technology.

comp.newprod
What's new (moderated).

comp.society
The impact of technology (moderated).

15//EDUCATION

The web is rather good at showing off its academic roots, and the best place to start is probably the stunning BBC Education website. The corporation has piled in a huge budget to fund its site – and it shows. There are guides to help with homework, advice on exams and the curriculum and news for parents, students and teachers.

If you're trying to find out about local schools, use the UpMyStreet (**http://www.upmystreet.co.uk**) reference site to show you what's available. For parents after an independent education for their child, Schools Net lists almost all in the country.

UCAS have a good search site to help find the right higher education place and check the entry requirements and application procedure for British universities. And if you want to progress to complete an MBA or Ph.D., you can search for a course or research post.

For lots more about education, have a look at this book's companion volume, the **Virgin Family Internet Guide.**

Starting Points

BBC Education Homepage **http://www.bbc.co.uk/education/**
Auntie's clear and informative site that should be your first stop for anything to do with education; provides sections for every level of education and a web guide to useful sites.

Discovery Online **http://www.discovery.com**
Not tied to any syllabus, but a great place to fire the imagination and start exploring the natural world – there are features on animals, explorers and wild places, amazing facts and even web-cams of animals.

School

Anglia Campus **http://www.angliacampus.com**

A new amalgam of the old BT CampusWorld and Anglia Interactive sites that charges a subscription but has plenty of resources and lessons for home and school study.

Dundee Satellite Receiving Station **http://www.sat.dundee.ac.uk/**

View weather-satellite images for the UK and the world – you'll need to register, but it's free and it's a nice resource for geography or environment studies.

EduWeb **http://www.eduweb.co.uk**

Provides a central location for websites created by the teachers and pupils from hundreds of schools around the UK.

EdViews **http://www.edview.com**

Listings of over 25,000 teacher-approved websites. Try and get your kids to visit some of them, for a change.

Funbrain **http://www.funbrain.com**

A friendly US site that's full of online games and quizzes to help improve numeracy and literacy for kids of all ages.

funschool.com **http://www.funschool.com**

Masses of free interactive educational software with a US slant, but still useful to help teach letters, numeracy and reading.

GCSE Answers **http://www.gcse.com**

As the title suggests, plenty of past papers, sample tests and help with the revision – but currently limited to Maths and English.

History Channel **http://www.thehistorychannel.com**

Thousands of interesting articles on past world events, plus quizzes and answers for revision.

How Stuff Works **http://www.howstuffworks.com**
Great site for kids (and dads). It does just what it says: from engines to refrigerators, batteries to rockets.

Language Arts **http://www.mcdougallittell.com**
A wide range of potted study-aids to the main works of literature used in the US and the UK (for GCSE-level English). Not full guides but useful summaries with plenty of notes to help your revision.

Latin **http://latin.about.com**
Comprehensive help for anyone studying or interested in Latin and the Classics. You can browse translations or simply ask the expert about your Latin homework.

Science Library **http://www.luc.edu/libraries/science/**
Rinse out the test tubes and light up the Bunsen burners as you browse this well-stocked science library that provides loads of resources for all science disciplines (junior school and up).

MathsNet **http://www.anglia.co.uk/education/mathsnet/**
Help junior get to grips with numbers – interesting and useful interactive testing and teaching material to help improve maths.

School Zone **http://www.schoolzone.co.uk**
A vast mass of 30,000 links to education sites, lesson plans, homework help and libraries. Sure, it's American, but it's still useful.

Schools Net **http://www.isuk.org.uk**
Online directory of over 2,400 independent schools around the UK. Includes background notes for parents about the school, entrance requirements and those crippling fees.

TerraServer **http://terraserver.microsoft.com**
Impressive database of satellite images of the world – zoom in to the towns and cities covered to get a street-level view. Great for geography – or the curious.

The Internet Public Library **http://www.ipl.org**
Stroll through the aisles, pick up your favourite book and download the full text for free. Great if you're studying a writer and/or their work.

The Virtual School **http://www.virtualschool.co.uk**
Quick, swot up on any GCSE or A level subject online. For around £60 you'll get five weeks of tuition by email or chat session.

ThinkQuest **http://library.advanced.org**
Tutorials to help you in all the major subjects – very useful, but it's hard to find your way around.

University

Postgraduate and MBA Courses **http://www.merlinfalcon.co.uk**
Follow up your degree with a postgraduate course – these guides will help you choose the perfect MBA, taught postgraduate courses and postgraduate research opportunities.

Red Mole **http://www.redmole.co.uk**
Essential guide for student life – mixing beer, music, money and, yes, study.

Student UK **http://www.studentuk.com**
Your life as a student – guides to managing meagre cash reserves, studying, sport, films and life after the three-year gig.

Student World **http://www.student-world.co.uk**
So, life as a student looks good. Here's how to find a course that suits you. Everything's included from admissions to music, and job-hunting to shopping.

UCAS **http://www.ucas.ac.uk/**
Higher-ed courses and degrees on offer in universities around the UK. Enter what you want to study and your qualifications to find out what's available, then make enquiries before the results come out and the stampede starts.

Part-time

Floodlight **http://www.floodlight.co.uk**

Every evening and part-time course available in London is listed here, ready for your application form. If you want a UK-wide picture, look at the On Course site.

On Course **http://www.oncourse.co.uk**

Over 20,000 part-time and evening courses taking place across the whole of the UK – a far broader range than the London-bound Floodlight site.

Official

DfEE **http://www.dfee.gov.uk/par_cent/**

For the official word on school assessments – or how to complain to your LEA.

National Grid for Learning **http://www.ngfl.gov.uk/**

The government's very good attempt to provide online learning resources that help parents with their children's education; you'll need to register, but it's free.

Qualifications and Curriculum Authority **http://www.qca.org.uk**

Find out what your child should be studying and the key stage examinations the poor thing will have to face – from the official UK organisation responsible for managing the different stages in your child's development.

Scottish Qualifications Authority **http://www.sqa.org.uk**

Find out how education works in Scotland – all the qualifications listed and explained.

Special Educational Needs **http://www.dfee.gov.uk/sen/senhome.htm**

The government's official page for parents of children with special needs; provides information, links and online resources covering resource material, teaching methods and advice.

Languages

ALF: Interactive French Course **http://ottawa.ambafrance.org/ALF/**
'La plume de ma tante' brought up to date with this simple written and spoken French course that uses audio files and interactive prompts to teach you the basics.

DUDEN online **http://www.duden.bifab.de/**
Online versions of the respected Duden grammar and vocabulary courses – but you'll need to understand some German to navigate the site (or try the AltaVista – **http://www.altavista.com** – web page translation service).

TravelLang **http://www.travlang.com**
Online lessons teaching 50 languages are included, with phrases, words, dictionaries and revision aids.

Try these newsgroups

alt.education.alternative
Different ways to learn.

alt.education.disabled
Education for people with disabilities.

comp.edu
Teaching folk about computers.

misc.education
A little learning is a dangerous thing.

misc.education.home-school.misc
Forget school, learn at home.

misc.education.language.english
Teaching English to non-native speakers.

16//FASHION AND BEAUTY

From haute couture to street gear, the Internet covers fashion from all angles. For a full tour of all the latest designs from the catwalk, visit the wonderful and free FashionLive or the slightly more exclusive FirstView (that will charge you for the privilege).

Talking up the designs is part of the glamour and hype and perhaps the most influential online magazines for this are the trade-weekly WWW and the consumer mag, Vogue. Both supply sites oozing style and haughtiness, but for the word on the high street, try the far busier and more accessible Elle or Women.com.

Improve and update your hair, make-up and beauty regimes with advice from any one of the specialist sites, like the useful (if biased) Clinique – all of the cosmetic suppliers have sites, but not all as hype-free as this.

Gossip is at the heart of fashion and, bravely, Lumiere and Hint both dish the dirt and the latest serious fashion news.

On the more practical side, buying clothes on the net has taken off big time. Lands End, for example, has a great virtual model that can be adjusted to your shape and colouring, then dressed and fitted out online.

Starting Points

Vogue Magazine **http://www.vogue.co.uk**
The killer site for high fashion that has everything from collections to books, jobs to who's who. Good content, great photographs and design make this the first site to head for – you can even make it your opening channel for instant updates to fashion news.

Women.com **http://www.women.com/fashion/**
It really does have everything you might want to know about mainstream fashion and beauty from a vast, sprawling but consistently good site.

Silver Subject resources **http://silver.bton.ac.uk/aem/fashion.html**
Comprehensive collection of links to costume, fashion and textile sites.

News and Magazines

About-Face! **http://www.about-face.org**
San Francisco-based group that wants the fashion industry to stop parading skinny models as the ideal of beauty.

ELLE magazine **http://www.ellemag.com**
Great general fashion and beauty site. More beauty and lifestyle features and links than the sometimes-rarefied Vogue site.

Fashion Live **http://www.worldmedia.fr/fashion/**
What's new on the catwalk – a vast database of designers provides potted profiles and pictures of the latest and past collections.

Fashion UK **http://www.widemedia.com/fashionuk/**
Alternative and avant-garde fashion that leaves the high street behind.

Hint Fashion Magazine **http://www.hintmag.com**
Great e-zine covering fashion, gossip, trends and parties.

Lumiere Magazine **http://www.lumiere.com**
Daily dose of what's in and out in fashion from this fab daily e-zine.

The Museum of Costume **http://www.museumofcostume.co.uk**
Take a virtual tour of the museum dedicated to costume and its history.

WWD (womenswear daily) **http://www.wwd.com**
Influential weekly fashion journal tells you what's in, out and cool to wear.

Make-up and Beauty

Avon Cosmetics **http://www.uk.avon.com**
Don't wait for the lady to ding-dong on the doorbell, browse and buy online from this neat, clean site.

Clinique **http://www.clinique.com**
Choose the perfect lipstick. Although it concentrates on its own range of cosmetic products, there's plenty of helpful information about choosing and using make-up and skincare products.

Cosmopolitan Virtual Makeover **http://www.virtualmakeover.com**
Not the true interactive site you might hope for, but it plugs an entertaining CD-ROM that beauty addicts will love.

Easyshop **http://www.easyshop.co.uk**
Perfume – lots of perfume – plus tights, undies and bras at discount prices that include delivery. You'll find the usual major brand names. Easy to use, friendly to shop in.

fashion **http://www.dcthomson.co.uk/mags/shout/**
Beauty and fashion for girls – nothing radical, just good advice and pretty make-up.

Fragrance Counter **http://www.fragrancecounter.com**
Vast range of smells to suit him and her – and if you're clueless, there's an online advisor. You won't save much money, but they do ship around the world.

Marlene Klein Cosmetics **http://www.marleneklein.com**
You won't find this range of US cosmetics or make-up anywhere except the Internet – so nice Marlene can sell them more cheaply than the brand name equivalents.

Buying

Best of British **http://www.thebestofbritish.com**
Nothing kitsch and few Union Jacks – just a great range of top-quality brands (Molton Brown, Mulberry, Lulu Guiness) covering fashion, food and home – plenty of discounts and nice presentation.

Charles Thyrwitt **http://www.ctshirts.co.uk**
Smart shirts in every size imaginable – plus ties, cufflinks, braces and other essentials. A very clear site design makes this super-easy to use.

Cow Town Boots **http://www.cowtownboots.com**
Stride into the office with the finest cowboy boots direct from the makers in El Paso. There's rattlesnake, ostrich, python and, for the brave, a section called 'exotic shoes'. You'll need to phone Texas for the latest rates on shipping.

Designers Direct **http://www.designersdirect.com**
Kit yourself out in style for peanuts – all the top names at up to 75% off, delivered direct from the US in under a week.

Diesel UK Virtual Store **http://www.diesel.co.uk**
Not just denim from the trendy designers – shirts, jeans and scents for men and women. Cool design, and a few web-only offers.

Fashionmall.com **http://www.fashionmall.com**
A central mall to browse a wide range of clothes stores, from D&G to Liz Claiborne. A good place to start looking for clothes but it's weak on beauty products.

Fat Face Online Store **http://www.fatface.co.uk**
Surf-world hits web-world with the funky range of outdoor and sports fleeces and shirts for the family. Online shoppers earn Fat Calories that'll add up to a 10% discount.

Kiniki **http://www.kiniki.com**
Top thongs for your main man – designer boxers, undies and swimwear for men.

Kitbag **http://www.kitbag.com**
Keeping up with your football team's latest kit is now easier. But it's no cheaper.

Lands End **http://www.landsend.com**
Basic clothes but with a fabulous feature – a virtual model you can tailor to your size, shape and hair colouring before you dress it up.

L.L. Bean **http://www.llbean.com**
Famed outdoor clothing supplier – from check-shirts to hunting boots – a super-slick site that keeps winning awards.

Paul Smith **http://www.paulsmith.co.uk**
Natty fashion meets the high street in this fusion of sound and images from Smith's range of clothes.

The GAP **http://www.gap.com**
You know the gear – basic cotton chinos, T's and polo shirts – exactly like in the shopping centre but without the crowds.

The Shirt Press **http://www.shirt-press.co.uk**
Pure cotton shirts that – wait for it – never need to be ironed.

Victoria's Secret **http://www.victoriassecret.com**
The full range of world-famous undies modelled by astonishingly pretty ladies.

Try these newsgroups

---

alt.fashion
The fashion industry dissected.

alt.gothic.fashion
Lots of make-up, purple hair spray and booties.

rec.crafts.textiles.sewing
Sewing.

17//FILM AND TV

Trivia is big on the net – and it doesn't get much more trivial than film and TV gossip. Hollywood glamour, pots of money and plenty of tales make the film and TV sites as entertaining as the celluloid end product.

The studios use the net to deliver rosy-tinted news and interviews; for the independent view, look to e-zines run by obsessive movie-maniacs. InfoJump (**http://www.infojump.com**) lists almost every zine around. And if you want gossip, you've come to the right place; the most influential is Ain't It Cool News.

If you're reasonably patient, you might be able to download a tiny clip of your favourite movie, but once the novelty has worn off, you'll probably agree it's easier to pop round to your local video shop. There's plenty to interest the serious movie fan: big-movie scripts at Drew's Script-o-rama, music at MovieTunes and even a Hollywood agent to represent your work at Highlights for Screenwriters.

If you can tear yourself away from your computer to visit a cinema, use Scoot to get listings and times for your local cinema, wherever you are.

Film Studios

The big studios all have websites to promote their backlists and forthcoming titles. Most sites are slick, with video clips and short profiles of the stars. The main studios on the web are:

20th Century Fox **http://www.foxmovies.com**
Disney **http://www.disney.com**
Dreamworks **http://www.dreamworksanim.com**
Lucasfilm **http://www.lucasfilm.com**

MCA	**http://www.mca.com**
Miramax	**http://www.miramax.com**
MGM	**http://www.mgm.com**
Paramount	**http://www.paramount.com**
Polygram	**http://www.reellife.com**
Sony	**http://www.spe.sony.com**
Warner Bros	**http://www.movies.warnerbros.com**

Starting Points

The Internet Movie Database **http://www.imdb.com**
Stunning, well-organised database of over 180,000 film titles; it's easy to search films according to title, actors, producers or directors then browse reviews, synopses and background data on each and every one.

Yack! **http://www.yack.com**
Live online celebrity interviews and chats are now commonplace but finding when and where they happen is hard work. Jump to this site for a list of who's talking when.

ZineZone **http://www.zinezone.com**
Index to the thousands of independent e-zines about directors, stars and filmmakers.

Reviews and Info

6degrees **http://www.6degrees.co.uk**
No Hollywood blockbusters here but plenty of reviews, listings and features on independent British producers.

Astrophile **http://www.astrophile.com**
Was she really in that film? Hundreds of celebrities are profiled with potted biographies, interviews, pictures and news. The flip-side Dead People Server (**http://www.dpsinfo.com**) site just tells you if the stars are dead or alive.

Empire **http://www.empireonline.co.uk**
Brilliant flick-site that includes over 4,000 reviews and features plus full film listings from Scoot.

Film.com **http://www.film.com**
Review the professionals' cinematic efforts and watch the latest trailers; but the reviews and news aren't up to the standards of Empire or Ain't It Cool News.

Filmworld **http://www.filmworld.co.uk**
Best for film festivals and obscure flicks; there are heaps of reviews – plus listings from Scoot – and, if you like the review, you can buy the video. More features but not as slick or as easy to navigate as the Empire site.

MovieGuru **http://www.movieguru.com**
Give the world the benefit of your critical notes on a new film. They'll be posted beside professional reviews and a mass of background info, archives and news on the film.

MovieReview QueryEngine **http://www.cinema.pgh.pa.us/movie/reviews/**
Sparse design hides a massive database of reviews of movies – type in a movie title then follow the links.

the daily entertainment network **http://www.theden.com**
Get your daily dose of alternative features and news about the latest TV and film releases. Well worth a visit.

Gossip

Ain't It Cool News **http://www.aint-it-cool-news.com**
Probably the most influential Hollywood gossip site provided by a very well-informed amateur. Avoid it when LA wakes up – it's almost impossible to log on as film execs check if they still have a job.

Beeb **http://www.beeb.com**
Chat, discussion, news and gossip about BBC TV and radio

programmes but less impressive and informative than **http://www.bbc.co.uk**.

Cinescape Online **http://www.cinescape.com**
Keep up with the film industry news and gossip. A manageable site that's not as comprehensive as Hollywood Reporter but it's free and bags good quotes from the stars.

E! **http://www.eonline.com**
Glitzy home of news, gossip and chat; lots of 'entertainment' personality stories with good photos and fun stories.

Entertainment Drive **http://www.edrive.com**
takes a long hard look at celebrities and publishes the current gossip and news from the Hollywood rumour-mill.

Mr Showbiz **http://mrshowbiz.go.com**
Comprehensive virtual reporter passes on the gossip on film and music celebs.

People **http://www.people.com**
Doorstep the stars and celebrities from TV, film and music with the help of the online version of the US interview magazine.

The Hollywood Reporter **http://www.hollywoodreporter.com**
One of the top sites for tittle-tattle, but it's subscription only. Better to try the free Ain't It Cool News or Entertainment Drive.

Cinemas and Broadcasts

AFI OnLine Cinema **http://www.afionline.org**
Play it again, Sam. Virtual cinema that screens classic Hollywood films.

Alternative Entertainment Network **http://www.aentv.com**
A TV station and features magazine rolled into one. You can watch a range of classic films and TV programmes or read up the 'making of'-style features.

broadcast.com **http://www.broadcast.com**
Free live broadcasts of TV, radio and interviews; no special hardware is required, just connect and select the channel you want to watch.

Eurocinema **http://www.eurocinema.com**
Virtual cinema that specialises in screening European films. There's an entrance ticket price but it's lower than a video rental.

IKCTU TV **http://www.kctu.com**
There's no escape from 24-hour live TV hell. This site broadcasts news, features, old episodes of Baywatch and other essential viewing.

Movie List **http://www.movie-list.com**
Spend ten minutes downloading a 15-second preview of your favourite movie, then never bother again.

My Movies **http://www.mymovies.net/**
Cool design with zappy animation lets you see new release trailers in a real-looking cinema setting, then check local cinema listings (via Scoot) to see where it's screened near you.

Pseudo TV **http://www.pseudo.com**
A real TV channel for the net with a good range of live and recorded programs – but an expensive way to watch the gogglebox. If you're so fascinated by TV, you'll also love the KCTU TV site.

Video and DVD

Black Star **http://www.blackstar.co.uk**
Probably the best and certainly the biggest place to buy videos and DVDs in the UK. Vast range, discount prices, free delivery and nice touches, like the hyperlinked cast list – cross-referenced to help you find all the films with that star.

DVDnet **http://www.dvdnet.co.uk**
Very strong on news and reviews, with a very good selection of well-priced DVDs – the info for each title is complete and the descriptions good. You can also buy the hardware online – plenty of special offers.

DVDplus **http://www.dvdplus.co.uk**
Impressive presentation and design, with plenty of reviews and news. The titles are reasonably priced.

DVDstreet **http://www.dvdstreet.infront.co.uk**
Impressive store selling DVDs only. Very easy to navigate, great biogs and hyperlinks, lots of news and reviews – free delivery and discounts make this a fab site.

Film World **http://www.filmworld.co.uk**
Great place for film enthusiasts – stocks an excellent range of independent, world and art films on video and DVD, neatly integrating clips from film.com and listings from scoot.co.uk.

VCI **http://www.vci.co.uk**
Particularly good on TV shows on video but with a modest selection of TV films.

Specialist

Buena Vista movies **http://movies.go.com**
The nice people at Buena Vista studios have poured a great range of previews, interviews, stills and background information to their new releases into this site.

Drew's Scripts O-Rama **http://www.script-o-rama.com**
The mysterious Drew has gathered hundreds of original scripts that aspiring screenwriters can download and study – from *Alien* through to *A Clockwork Orange*.

Hollywood Glamour **http://kohary.simplenet.com/smoke.htm**
Nothing to do with the starlets of Hollywood. Oddball pro-smoking

site listing notable actresses who have been filmed holding a cigarette.

James Bond **http://www.jamesbond.com**
Not the retro archives of guns and girls you might have expected. Instead, a good-looking promo site for the new 007 film, with interviews, clips and news. True fans should try the site below.

Jerry Springer **http://www.livingtv.com**
Mad lover's husband was my daughter's son.

MovieTunes **http://www.movietunes.com**
Composers and titles and the occasional clip of the great movie themes.

Paramount Jobs **http://www.paramount.com/homecareer.shtml**
If you're trying to get into the movie business, there are always plenty of jobs available at Paramount studios listed here. Their main site, however, is rather dull.

Popcorn **http://www.popcorn.co.uk**
Light, fluffy and fun magazine covering the news and local listings for films and TV.

SceneOne **http://www.sceneone.co.uk**
Local listings for TV, theatre, music gigs and radio; find what you like then buy a ticket or video.

Star Wars **http://www.theforce.net/**
The unofficial – and better for it – site about Luke and his adventures with a light sabre. The official site is at **http://www.starwars.com**.

The Craft of Screenwriting **http://www.wga.org/craft/**
Excellent site for any hopeful screenwriter. Interviews with established writers and advice on writing, pitching and selling your script. There's also a great automatic plot generator to help free your writer's block.

The Movie Clichés Listing **http://www.like.it/vertigo/cliches.html**

How come stars in movies always get a taxi and three-digit telephone numbers? This and other silliness that's portrayed as real life in films. Patience required – it's slow.

Toaster **http://www.toaster.co.uk**

Every TV program from every UK channel, satellite and cable supplier is listed here – but you'll have to get off the sofa to read it.

Xena Warrior Princess **http://www.xenafan.com**

Worship the Princess.

Try these newsgroups

---

alt.cult-movies

Obsessive fans of cult movies.

alt.film-festivals.sundance

Independent producers get their day.

alt.movies.kubrick

The films of Stanley Kubrick.

rec.arts.movies

Talk about films.

rec.arts.movies.announce

What's happening in the industry(moderated).

rec.arts.movies.production

How movies are made.

rec.arts.movies.reviews

The latest flicks reviewed (moderated).

18//FINANCE

From advice for savers to advanced tools for day traders, you'll find every level of news and information online. Helping on the revolution is the trend of high-street banks to offer you the chance to manage your account online, via the Internet. Many of the major banks let you shuffle money between accounts and pay your bills from your PC.

To have the opportunity to invest or save you'll need some spare cash. And to get this you need to be sure you're managing your money, savings and expenses efficiently. Blay's Guides sort through the savings accounts on offer and will show you where to find the best rates. If you're spending rather than saving, Car Quote and Screen Trade will hunt through insurance and mortgage offers to cut your payments, while MoneyNet will send you the best deal from credit card companies.

If you do want to buy or sell shares, the giant US broker Schwab sits at the top of the pile with E*trade snapping at its heels. Both provide analysis, tips, pricing and historical graphs.

Most of your share dealing will be thanks to company research and price analysis – something at which Interactive Investor International excels. However, you need to keep your ear to the ground to pick up the gossip and the latest tips. The best-known, and biggest, site for advice, tips and gossipy discussion is the Motley Fool. At the other end of the scale, use the Pigeon site for a quick roundup of which company's been tipped in the weekend papers.

Banks online

Abbey National	**http://www.abbeynational.co.uk**
Alliance and Leicester	**http://www.allianceandleicester.co.uk**
Barclays	**http://www.barclays.co.uk**
Co-op	**http://www.co-operativebank.co.uk**
First Direct	**http://www.firstdirect.co.uk**
Halifax	**http://www.halifax.co.uk**
HSBC (Midland)	**http://www.banking.hsbc.co.uk**
Lloyds TSB	**http://www.lloydstsb.co.uk**
Nationwide	**http://www.nationwide.co.uk**
NatWest	**http://www.natwest.co.uk**
Royal Bank of Scotland	**http://www.royalbankscot.co.uk**

Credit Cards

MasterCard	**http://www.mastercard.com**
VISA	**http://www.visa.com**
American Express	**http://www.amex.com**

Starting Points

Yahoo! Finance **http://finance.uk.yahoo.com**
The mega portal provides straight financial facts, news and figures.

InvestorWords **http://www.investorwords.com**
Before you buy it, check you know what it means. Clear definitions to over 5,000 complex financial terms.

Stocks and Shares

B-B-Bugle **http://www.angelfire.com/al/bbbugle/**
Gently subversive, check on directors' trades, unofficial tips and share news. Less comprehensive than the Motley Fool.

Charles Schwab Worldwide http://www.schwab-worldwide.com
The biggest online broker. Excellent resources, graphing and advice – but you'll need to register and deposit money first.

E*trade **http://www.etrade.co.uk**
The young pretender to Schwab's crown. A vast, slick and info-rich site that helps you research, manage and trade shares.

Freequote **http://www.freequote.co.uk**
One of the few sites to provide real-time share prices. You'll need to register, but it's free.

Global Investor **http://www.global-investor.com**
If you dabble in world markets, here's how to keep track with reports and prices in the global arena.

Hemmington Scott **http://www.hemscott.com/infoex/exchange.htm**
Exchange tips and information about companies and shares in this unmoderated discussion group.

interactive investor international **http://www.iii.co.uk**
Share, investment, pension and mortgage prices, news and research – but you'll need to go elsewhere for online dealing.

Market-Eye **http://www.marketeye.co.uk**
Real-time share price information – at a price (although the delayed data is available free).

Pigeon **http://www.pigeon.co.uk**
Simple site that lists every share tip from the Sunday papers.

TrustNet Limited **http://www.trustnet.co.uk**
If you worry about unit and investment trusts rather than stocks and shares, here's where you'll find news and prices.

UK Shares **http://www.ukshares.com**
Aggrieved shareholders air their views and discuss rights and tactics. Useful for any shareholder.

Updata **http://www.updata.co.uk**
Track share price movements with graphs – for a fee. If you want free data and a simple graph, use the comprehensive **http://www.co.uk**.

Advice

Blay's Guides **http://www.blays.co.uk**
Tells us which savings accounts provide the best interest rates.

Financenter **http://www.financenter.com/homes.html**
Dozens of nifty calculators that help you assess financial worries and products; for example, how does interest rate change my credit card balance? US-based, but relevant to everyone.

Financial Information Net Directory **http://www.find.co.uk**
As the title says, it's full of information about anything financial – from pensions to ISAs. Tells you what's available and how to invest.

FT Quicken – Personal Finance **http://www.ftquicken.co.uk**
Good advice for the average financial consumer. Keep your money healthy and stay up to date with news on money products.

MoneyExtra **http://www.moneyextra.com**
Compare mortgages, credit cards, savings accounts, pensions, life assurance – then pick the best.

MoneyNet **http://www.moneynet.co.uk**
Choose the perfect credit card or mortgage. Fill in a form and you'll be sent details of dozens of deals.

MoneyWeb **http://www.moneyweb.co.uk**
Good, free information on how and where to invest.

Money World **http://www.moneyworld.co.uk**
An impressively complete site that tries – and generally succeeds – to cover all aspects of personal finance. Share prices, currency movements, mortgage rates, tax bands and online calculators.

The Motley Fool UK **http://www.fool.co.uk**
These are the guys that helped start the whole online share mania, now in the UK. Clear reports and information and active discussion groups to let you share your top tips.

The Treasury **http://www.hm-treasury.gov.uk/**
What's happening to tax and interest rates? Find out from the official UK government site on budgets and economic indicators.

This Is Money **http://www.thisismoney.com**
The inescapable truth about life, death and taxes. Great for money newbies with clear but realistic news and features.

Insurance

Car Quote **http://www.carquote.co.uk**
Fill in the online forms and you'll get car insurance quotes emailed or posted to you from a range of suppliers.

Eagle Star Insurance **http://www.eaglestardirect.co.uk**
Ask for a quote and then buy the insurance – online.

Home Quote UK **http://home.quote.co.uk**
Fill in your details and you'll get house insurance quotes from half a dozen companies. That was easy!

Screen Trade **http://www.screentrade.co.uk**
Reduce your insurance by comparing umpteen different suppliers – for car, house and travel.

News

CBS.MarketWatch.com **http://cbs.marketwatch.com**
Financial news, tips and reports. All the usual excess of US market information, but the European coverage beats TheStreet.com.

CNBC Europe **http://www.cnbceurope.com**
Over-designed site from the cable TV channel. Provides summaries of business, finance and company news.

Financial Times **http://www.ft.com**

The pink pages provide one of the best global views of the economic market. Once you've registered (for free) you can read the business news, check share prices and more.

Weekend City Press Review **http://www.news-review.co.uk**

Summary of business and company news compiled from the main daily papers; a great place to research companies in which you're thinking of investing.

Try these newsgroups

alt.make.money.fast

Get rich quick, then visit jail.

misc.invest

Manage your money.

misc.invest.funds

Tips and thoughts on investments.

misc.invest.futures

Discussions on financial futures markets.

misc.invest.real-estate

Make money from houses.

misc.invest.stocks

Which shares are worth buying and selling?

uk.finance

Highs and lows of the financial markets.

19//FOOD AND DRINK

Curries, French foie gras, organic lettuces, classic wines, beer by the barrel. The number of food sites is quite awesome, providing small, local producers with a global audience desperate for good, different and original food. It's great shopping for the exotic gourmet ingredients, but for everyday groceries, you'll still need your supermarket – and it too might well be online.

Get inspiration for dinner from the two biggest foodie sites on the web – Epicurious and Global Gourmet. You'll find features on ingredients, new ways to cook and thousands of recipes. Other sites, such as Classic Recipes provide exactly what the name suggests, ensuring you'll never be left wondering how to knock up gnocchi or serve up a sauce.

Wine buffs might sniff at the idea of online tasting notes, but it's a fast, easy and free way to learn about a type of wine, grape or vineyard. If you're stuck for something to drink, try the Idrink site – enter a list of what's left in your drinks cupboard and it'll scour its database of over 5,000 cocktails for the perfect mix.

Starting Points

Classic Recipes **http://www.classicrecipes.com**
The original core database of recipes is still there but it's now surrounded by so many other foodie sections, features and guides that it can be a little overwhelming.

Epicurious Food **http://food.epicurious.com**
The message is 'If you eat, visit this site' – and it's not wrong. Vast site that shows just how much can be written about food, recipes and drink. It's US-centric but, with this amount of information, who cares?

Global Gourmet **http://www.globalgourmet.com**
A good all-rounder for gourmets and gourmands – not quite up to Epicurious but easy to manage.

Kitchenlink **http://www.kitchenlink.com**
Great site with links to almost every worthwhile culinary site on the web. Hardly slick design but a great place to start.

TuBears **http://www.tubears.com**
Strange name but contains over 50,000 recipes plus foodie discussion groups.

TuDocs **http://www.tudocs.com**
Thousands of cooking and food sites rated to help you explore without time-wasting. (And 'tu' stands for 'the ultimate', in case you wondered.)

Booze

Beer from Germany **http://www.bier.de/beer.html**
Taproom heaven: detailed coverage of the history, quality, types and techniques used in brewing German beers. Visit the CAMRA site (**http://www.camra.org.uk**) if you want trad real ales.

Berry Bros & Rudd **http://www.berry-bros.co.uk**
Fine wine merchants to the gentry. A clear, informative and rather addictive site – aimed at wine enthusiasts.

Campaign for Real Ale **http://www.camra.org.uk**
Enthusiastic site packed with information about real ales and, errm, how to enjoy them.

French Government Tourist Office **http://www.fgtousa.org**
Forget about the monuments, this concentrates on wine and foodie tours of France.

French Wines & Food **http://www.frenchwinesfood.com**
Choose your (French) wine, make sure it's a good match for the meal, then pour and enjoy.

German Wine Page **http://www.winepage.de/**
Clean-tasting Riesling and impressive reds. How to decipher the label, choose and store the perfect bottle.

IDrink **http://www.idrink.com**
5,200 things to do with the booze. Blow your head off with lethal cocktails.

Stoli Central 2 **http://www.stoli.com**
Funky site that'll overwhelm you with vodka talk.

The Good Pub Guide to Britain **http://www.goodguides.com/pubs/**
Fed up with your local? Search the full text of this guide for the best pub in your area.

Wine & Dine **http://www.winedine.co.uk**
An enjoyable monthly magazine from and for wine lovers – and it's British, for a change.

Wine Spectator **http://www.winespectator.com**
Influential and informative US mag that centres on tastings. The last two years' worth of reviews are free – for the full database, you'll need to subscribe.

WineOnline **http://www.wineonline.co.uk**
The Brit view on wine tasting, buying and enjoying.

Delis

Cheese **http://www.cheese.com**
Mild cheddar, yes, but also over 500 smellier cheeses listed and arranged by name, taste and texture and country. A similarly extensive and obsessive (if not quite so polished) site is CheeseNet at **http://www.wgx.com/cheesenet/**

Dean & Deluca **http://www.deananddeluca.com**
Wonderful, stylish site from the equally cool store in New York –

but till they ship outside the US, you can only read and drool at the oils, breads and spices.

kosherinfo **http://www.kosherinfo.com**
NY-based (where else?) but with consumer guides to kosher products on the net.

Morel Bros., Cobbett & Son **http://www.morel.co.uk**
Wonderful site for the gourmet – impressive range of 350 foods, each with masses of detail.

Organics Direct **http://www.organicsdirect.com**
The paranoids who've just visited the GM world site can rest easy here. Organic food, chocolates, even socks are delivered anywhere in the UK.

Real Meat Company **http://www.realmeat.co.uk**
Caring farmers selling meat produced without chemicals – shop online for speedy delivery.

Supermarkets that deliver to your door

Sainsburys **http://www.sainsburys.co.uk**
First, visit your local store with a bar-code gun and build up your basic shopping list. Now you can order from the website. Painfully slow and often more reliable to phone.

Tesco **http://www.tesco.co.uk**
Rival to Sainsburys' delivery service. Similar delivery rates, but you choose your items from the virtual aisles. And you can even get a free Internet account.

Guides and Magazines

Curry House **http://www.curryhouse.co.uk**
Everything about curry – where to eat it, how to make it and, thanks to mail-order supplier Chilli Willie, you can get the spices online.

Dine Online Wine Online **http://dine-online.co.uk**
One person's (very) informed reviews and news about restaurants around the UK – simple design is a little jumbled but the content wins the day.

French Gastronomy **http://www.beyond.fr/food/**
Quick guide to French culinary words and their meanings.

Food and Drink **http://www.learn2.com/browse/foo_2tor.html**
Boil an egg or clean a fish; the Learn2 site provides plenty of concise culinary how-tos for timid kitchen explorers.

Genetically modified world **http://gmworld.newscientist.com**
Spot the difference between a GM tomato and a beachball. Clear and impartial scientific coverage from New Scientist on all sides in the GM battle.

RecipeXchange **http://www.recipexchange.com**
Database of recipes tried, tested and submitted by netters. Some are classic, some unusual, some revolting.

Restaurants.co.uk **http://www.restaurants.co.uk**
Trying to find some place to eat? There are over 20,000 restaurants listed by area in Britain, and by style of food. But it only delivers name and contact details – no reviews.

Star Chefs **http://www.starchefs.com**
A collection of the favourite recipes produced by celebrity US chefs. No Gary, Delia or Ainsley here – which you might consider a plus point.

Veggies Unite! **http://www.vegweb.com**
A safe haven for vegetarians. Over 3,000 recipes, features and discussion groups.

Winnie the Pooh and Pals **http://www.winniethepooh.co.uk/owlsrecipies.html**
Owl's splendid recipes for Pooh pancakes, jam tarts and brownies.

World of Recipes **http://members.tripod.com/~WorldRecipes/recipe_links.html**
An enthusiastic cook (with obviously a very hungry family) has compiled a comprehensive range of recipes. If you want to stick to tried and tested dishes, use RecipeXchange.

Try these newsgroups

---

alt.cooking-chat
General kitchen chatter.

alt.creative-cook
new tricks with ingredients.

alt.food.fat-free
Out that fat!

alt.food.wine
Wine and wine tasting.

rec.food.chocolate
Addicted to chocolate.

rec.food.drink
(Alcholic) drinks.

rec.food.recipes
New dishes to prepare (moderated).

rec.food.restaurants
How was it for you?

rec.food.veg
A meat-free zone.

alt.gourmand
Food-lovers discuss food (moderated).

20//FUNNY

Funny ha ha, not funny peculiar – although there's plenty of both on the Internet. There's no stand-up comedy on the net, but jokes are another matter. There are databases of thousands of jokes, each one rated and categorised, with some of the best gags and top lines from the classic acts like Groucho Marx and the Pythons.

More interesting than these joke sites are the web's own very oddball humourists. Try the Centre for the Easily Amused or even the ever-topical Create-a-Clinton Story. And, sometimes, the gags go overboard – AprilFools.com is a good example of the strange and often painful things people do to each other for a laugh.

Skipping on to comic strips, you can keep the wit flowing with a daily dose of Alex, Dilbert, Garfield, Snoopy or any of the major, syndicated characters. It's illegal to print them out, though – but who's going to catch you?

For a short shot of giggles, try Dave's Web of Lies and the excellent spoof tabloid The Onion is a wonder.

Starting Point

Funny **http://www.funny.co.uk**
If it isn't funny, it's not here – that's official. A directory of comedy sites on the web.

Other Amusing Sites

Absurd **http://www.absurd.com**
Select few outlandish (but true) news stories, jokes and odd tales.

AprilFools.com **http://aprilfools.infospace.com**
Help fool some poor surfer with a mock web page describing their personal life, fake-emails and so on. Hilarious for the sadistic, awful for the victims.

Cartooning Lessons **http://www.sara-jordan.com/edu-mart/cartoon/lesson1.html**
How to draw people with funny faces and impossibly big shoes.

Centre for the Easily Amused **http://www.amused.com**
Unevenly funny site with the splendid grassCam and the ever jolly Amuse-o-matic ad lib generator.

Comedy Central **http://www.comedycentral.com**
Get your TV comedy fix with video clips from mainstream shows (including South Park) plus jokes and jolly screensavers.

Comedy Zone **http://www.comedyzone.beeb.com**
Ultimato weeko! Sketcho besti you choosi choosi, non? Still with me? From the Fast Show to Blackadder as screened by the BBC. Also worth trying is the unofficial Fast Show site (**http://www.geocities.com/athens/2694/fast.html**).

Create-A-Clinton Story **http://bobsfridge.com/storytron.html**
Wind up the storytron generator to create your own lewd report from the Oval Office.

Curse Central **http://www.tower.org/insult/**
Spit 'frothy lean-witted flax wench' and your enemies shrivel. Plus love advice from Captain Jack, and Elizabethan curse generator.

Dave's Web of Lies **http://www.cs.man.ac.uk/~hancockd/dwol.htm**
Lies unmasked – it's true, women are not 12 times more radioactive than men.

Dilbert **http://www.unitedmedia.com/comics/dilbert/**
Get through another day at the office with Dilbert and chums.

Draw and Color with Uncle Fred **http://www.unclefred.com**
Draw cartoons like a master – or at least like Uncle Fred. A good set of lessons to get you started.

Eddie Izzard **http://www.izzard.com**
Dose up with the bloke in a dress at this super-slick site or try one of the dozens of unofficial fan sites (such as **http://www.izzard.freeuk.com/** that has stacks of sound bites and sketches).

Faces **http://www.corynet.com/faces/**
Silly time-waster that's cheaper than laser surgery. Combine the various parts of celebrity faces to create truly ugly results.

Garfield **http://www.garfield.com**
Eat, sleep – well, eat and sleep – with the fat ginger cat. Yikes, there's even a Garfield credit card.

Goofy Humor **http://www.goofiness.com**
Cracked humour and general silliness from the rants of fancy pants to the very odd goofy glasses (that will rewire the internals of any web page – too hard to explain, just try it).

Groucho Marx is here! **http://www.groucho-marx.com**
Rather uninspiring design but the words, oh boy – quotes plus sound files from the man with the big cigar.

Hecklers Online **http://www.hecklers.com**
Silly jokes, limericks and funny headlines. But how do you heckle a website?

Humor Database **http://www.humordatabase.com**
Take thousands of jokes, rate them to make sure they don't offend and then store them by number. Boy, that sounds wild and wacky.

Jongleurs Comedy Club **http://www.jongleurs.com**
Cracking stand-up comics, but not on this site. Instead, buy tickets for the live shows in London.

Lee and Herring **http://www.leeandherring.com**
Behind the scenes from the pair's, err, odd and live chat show: This Morning with Richard Not Judy.

M&M's Network **http://www.m-ms.com**
Cult animation from the sweet little guys who make little sweets.

Paul Merton **http://www.users.globalnet.co.uk/~hkev/**
Solitary fan site for Mister Misery's brand of fabulous dry-as-a-dishcloth wit.

Steve Coogan **http://members.xoom.com/stevecoogan/**
Alan Partridge, Tony Ferrino and Coogan's othercharacters are worshipped here and in the Coogan web-ring. Or try the wonderfully offensive Paul Calf Shrine (**http://carlton.innotts.co.uk/~wrencomp/shrine.html**) as he helps you fight students, drink too much and score with women.

Private Eye **http://www.compulink.co.uk/~private-eye/**
The Eye's official site with classifieds, lots of links and a crossword.

Python Online **http://www.pythonline.com**
Giggles galore with the spam club, splendid online polls (choose from yes, no and piss off) and a 'chit' room for discussion.

Rethink's Chris Morris guff **http://www.rethink.demon.co.uk/laugh.html**
Probably the best of several sites about this inimitable cult satirist.

Stand-up Comedy Zone **http://www.standup.co.uk**
A warm hand for the first directory of British stand-up comedy – but it's not got its act together, yet.

The Onion **http://www.theonion.com**
Brilliant send-up of tabloid news and style. A must-have bookmark.

Willie Dancing **http://www.faeridust.com/wales/dance.htm**
Utterly pointless montage of dancing Prince Williams.

Yuk Yuk **http://www.yukyuk.com**
Cartoons and capers from the digital pen of Chad Frick.

Try these newsgroups

alt.fan.goons
Assorted silliness from the chums.

alt.folklore.college
Childish jokes.

alt.humor.best-of-usenet
One man's selection of jokes (moderated).

alt.humor.best-of-usenet.d
What everyone else thinks of his taste in jokes.

alt.shenanigans
Practical jokes.

alt.tasteless.jokes
Insulting jokes.

rec.humor
Generally offensive jokes.

rec.humor.funny
Funny jokes (moderated).

21//GAMES

Computer games – some of the biggest time wasters known to man – fall into two categories. There are nice, simple traditional games like chess, bridge, Scrabble and so on – harmless enough. Then there's multi-user Internet gaming, an absurdly addictive timewaster that can end in your total withdrawal from society.

Games are pretty much everywhere on the net. Even some serious business pages and search engines sneak Scrabble or chess into a corner of their site. You can have a game against the computer or, better still, play another user in a live clash of wits and skill. Yahoo! has a great collection of multi-user trad games with thousands of users testing their nerve at any one time.

Some traditional games run as Java programs within your web browser. For example, the nifty Rubik's cube puzzle (at Fun and Games) takes a few seconds to download and still works when you're offline. Multi-user games require you to be online and tend to use various gizmos to create a real-looking model of a chess board or bridge table.

If you fancy your chances as a card-sharp, there are several casinos and betting dens that beckon you in – you'll have to enter your credit card details to buy chips. Less stressful action takes place on ad-driven sites, like Gamesville, where you can play Bingo or other puzzles and card games for prizes – with the advantage that you don't lose your shirt if it all goes wrong.

Starting Points

Virtual Arcade 1.0 **http://www.thearcade.com**

Six rooms filled with online arcade games (that link to other games sites on the web).

Yahoo! Games **http://play.yahoo.com**
The Big Y lets you play over a dozen classic games quietly with a select band of ten thousand or more other users.

Online Adventure Games

Blue's News **http://www.bluesnews.com**
FPA (first person action) gamers will revel in this great jumbled mass of a gaming e-zine. It's full of news, tips, cheats, files, reviews, profiles and gossip.

Croft Times **http://www.cubeit.com/ctimes/**
Astonishing amount of news about curvy megababe Lara Croft and her adventures with snarling wolves in dark dungeons.

Doom **http://doomgate.gamers.org**
Get the most from Doom in its stand-alone and multi-player versions. A must-see site for Doom players.

Gamepen **http://www.gamepen.com**
Hit the therapy room when you've found out enough about forthcoming games software or chatted yourself silly in the very active discussion groups.

Game Post **http://www.gamepost.com**
How much news can an online gamer read? Just about the most comprehensive coverage of news and reviews from the gaming front line.

GamePro.com **http://www.gamepro.com**
Games on all platforms – from arcade to PC.

Gamers.Com **http://www.gamers.com**
Self-styled hardcore masters of the art of gaming grudgingly provide new-user guides to the top games around.

Gaming Age **http://www.gaming-age.com**
Busy site with news on forthcoming releases and interviews with game designers.

HEAT **http://www.heat.net/**
Arcade of online games, developed by SegaSoft, with dozens of titles like Quake and Star Wars. Free membership gives you limited access, paid membership provides access to the whole range.

Multi-Player Online Gaming **http://www.mpog.com**
All the latest and favourite games for desktops and consoles, plus a big section for online multi-player games.

Official Lara Croft Fan Site **http://www.eidos.co.uk/lara99/**
Temple to the astonishingly built, streetwise cyber chick. See also Croft Times for more (unofficial) news than most can stomach.

Simutronics **http://www.play.net/**
Destroy your fellow webbers for free for 30 days, then it's pay-time. A great bunch of online, multi-player 3D arcade games – the best by far is CyberStrike.

StarCraft **http://www.blizzard.com**
Outwit the authorities with this top-rating game of deceit, cunning and military strength – set in the distant future and ready for multi-user Internet play on a PC or Mac.

The Adrenaline Vault **http://www.adrenalinevault.com**
What's new for gamers with desktops or consoles.

The Vault Network **http://www.vaultnetwork.com**
Venture in to the dark underground centre full of news, features and tips for RPG (role-playing game) enthusiasts.

Wireplay **http://www.wireplay.co.uk**
Originally a subscription-only service from BT, now a free and fantastic place to play a good collection of online games.

Buying Computer Games

101cd.com **http://www.101cd.com**
A half-million catalogue list that carries books, DVDs, videos and

games from the UK and imports. Add your own review to any entry (rather like Amazon) or pre-order forthcoming releases.

CD Direct **http://www.cddirect.co.uk**
Good range for all platforms, plenty of reviews, promotions and budget titles, plus you can pre-order forthcoming titles to make sure you're the first to get a copy.

Game **http://www.game-retail.co.uk**
Total gaming overload with reviews, news, charts, product information – and all the games and accessories you could want.

Games Paradise **http://www.gamesparadise.com**
Great range for PCs and platforms – all at low prices. Includes charts, reviews and product details – another good site from WH Smith.

Nintendo Direct **http://www.nintendodirect.co.uk**
Wallow in the vast troughs of charts, news and reviews before browsing heaving shelves stacked high with a great range of Nintendo games.

PlayStation Direct **http://www.playstationdirect.co.uk**
From the clever company that set up Nintendo Direct – another winning specialist shop.

Special Reserve **http://www.reserve.co.uk**
Just about the cheapest, widest range of computer games available. And, if you're still deciding, there are reviews and gaming news.

UK Games **http://www.ukgames.com**
Packed with demos, news, tips, cheats, charts – and, of course, the latest and greatest games at low prices.

URwired **http://www.urwired.com**
Low prices for the latest games for PC, PlayStation and Nintendo. Unusually, prices already include delivery.

Visions Online **http://www.visionsonline.co.uk**
Exchange your PlayStation, Nintendo and Sega Saturn games.

Online Traditional Games

Action Man Island Command **http://www.actionman.com**
Kit out your action hero and play adventure games.

Alan's Dungeon Master Tools **http://www.geocities.com/Area51/8306/**
Here be monsters – together with all the other bits and bobs you need for a good game of dungeons and dragons.

Blackjack Review Network **http://www.bjrnet.com**
Heaven for blackjack junkies who want to check on prize competitions or give away their secrets in the chat rooms.

Chess Connection **http://www.easynet.co.uk/worldchess/**
My knight gets your pawn, check.

Cluemaster **http://www.cluemaster.com**
Fiendishly difficult crosswords and word puzzles.

Fun and Games **http://www.blue-planet.com/fun/**
An addictive Rubik's cube and retro Pacman provide the highlights of this small range of Java games you can run from your browser.

Gamesville **http://www.bingozone.com**
World's biggest game of bingo and other online, multi-player games that you can play for prizes.

Internet Park **http://www.amo.qc.ca/indexPark.html**
Multi-player versions of Scrabble – bizarrely, 1,500 people have registered to play online.

Monopoly **http://www.monopoly.com**
No online version to play but you can catch up on the latest news – yes, there is some – check on local tournaments and gather hints to building your empire.

MSN Gaming Zone **http://www.zone.com**
There are always thousands of people here playing interactive and multi-user games – including classics like backgammon and chess.

Nick Click **http://www.coolcentral.com/nick/**
Follow private detective Nick Click in this enjoyable online adventure game as he tries to solve clues in a Bogart-inspired creation.

Plus Lotto **http://www.interloto.li/**
Liechtenstein-based lottery that promises that it might be you.

Riddler **http://www.riddler.com**
A diverting selection of online word games, puzzles and cross-words – play by yourself or enter the online prize tournaments.

Scrabble **http://www.scrabble.com**
The official home of the Scrabble word game where there are lists of tournaments, plus tips and techniques. However, for more Scrabble words than you ever thought existed, try the SOWPODS site (**http://www.ozemail.com.au/~rjackman/**).

ShockRave **http://www.shockrave.com**
Macromedia make the ShockWave browser plug-in that provides many of the multimedia effects on websites. This is their promo site, which showcases some impressive online games.

The House Of Cards **http://thehouseofcards.com**
Hear the card-sharps shuffle as they practice the card games described in this encyclopaedic site – from solitary solitaire to gambling with poker.

The London Chess Centre **http://www.chess.co.uk**
Collection of books, videos, links to clubs and news on local tournaments. Save precious playing time and subscribe to their email e-zine.

TheCase.com **http://www.thecase.com**
Step into the sleuthing shoes of an online lawyer trying to solve a weekly case.

The Station **http://www.station.sony.com**
Allow yourself plenty of free time when you visit to try out the great selection of online games including classics like chess and the multi-player online game EverQuest.

Wild Card Games **http://www.wildcards.com**
Nifty software that lets you play card games with any other Internet user. At the moment, the software is still free, but the developers might start charging at any time.

Try these newsgroups

alt.games.doom
For the millions of fans of Doom.

alt.games.video.classic
Pacman and friends.

comp.sys.ibm.pc.games.announce
What's new for the PC (moderated).

rec.games.backgammon
Backgammon tactics.

rec.games.board
Win at Monopoly and other advice.

rec.games.chess
Chess – the art and science.

rec.games.computer.puzzle
Puzzles and riddles.

22//GARDENING

Gardening is the new craze for modern times, so it's fitting that it's also an unlikely web success story. You can plan your garden, search encyclopaedias of plants and check that they suit your garden's location with the range of databases online. Then shop for shrubs, annuals or seeds and transform that muddy patch.

The best way to use the web is to potter through the advice sites. There are advice centres for new or puzzled gardeners from the US and the UK, and chat sessions to discuss ideas with other gardeners. If you're having problems with your plants, ask an expert and find the answer.

The majority of online garden centres are based in the US, but customs regulations make it almost impossible to buy anything except a few packets of seeds. British garden centres are beginning to get online, with specialist shops getting on first – it's easier to buy seed potatoes, roses or hardy shrubs than to browse through a general garden supplier.

Climate Zones

Although the majority of the gardening sites are US-specific, choose a state that has a similar climate to the UK and you can still work with the advice. The US is split into climate zones (USDA zones) – the southern UK is equivalent to USDA 8 and colder areas of the UK are equivalent to USDA 7.

Starting Point

Garden Centre **http://www.gardenworld.co.uk**

Find your local suppliers and garden centres with this neat directory of the UK, plus events and a few Q&As.

Plants

Birstall Garden Centre **http://www.birstall.co.uk**
Very impressive garden centre selling everything – from sheds to stone slabs, seeds to roses.

British Gardening Online **http://www.oxalis.co.uk**
Friendly garden centre selling seeds, equipment and plants – plus plenty of information about gardens and garden centres open around the UK.

GardeningStore **http://www.gardeningstore.com**
Official shop from the Royal Horticultural Society with a good range of books and a few (very few) plants.

Harkness Roses **http://www.roses.co.uk**
Select specimens from this specialist dealer and news from the prickly world of rose growing.

Shrubs Direct **http://www.shrubsdirect.com**
Boost your borders with a little something ordered from the 900 shrubs available from Cheshire.

Advice

Garden Solutions **http://www.gardensolutions.com**
Ignore the advice about tropical plants, use the other thousands of Q&As in this US gardening site.

Garden Town **http://www.gardentown.com**
Friendly, community feel to this US site. Plant reference material, advice and discussion groups.

Garden Web **http://www.gardenweb.com**
The closest to leaning over the virtual fence for a natter. Lively discussion groups and good background reference material.

garden.com **http://www.garden.com**
A friendly monster of a site. Helps you design your garden, gives advice and has lots relevant to the UK.

Gardening Club **http://www.gardening-club.co.uk**
UK-specific – which is rare – advice to help keep your garden blooming. But needs more in it and more for sale.

iGarden Magazine **http://www.igarden.co.uk**
Practical garden magazine with tips and good advice for all gardeners.

RHS **http://www.rhs.org.uk**
Beautiful design from the society for enthusiastic gardeners. Unfortunately, it's weak on content and you'll find more practical advice elsewhere in this chapter.

Royal Botanic Gardens, Kew **http://www.rbgkew.org.uk/index.html**
Sparse design, great content. Events, research and news from Kew and full access to its academic database of plants.

The Postcode Plants Database **http://fff.nhm.ac.uk/fff/**
Dead begonias? Find out if your plants are compatible with your area. An essential first stop for all gardeners.

Try these newsgroups

rec.garden.roses
Pruning, growing and enjoying.

rec.gardens
Top tips for garden-lovers.

rec.gardens.orchids
Orchid care and cultivation.

23//HEALTH AND FITNESS

One of the first seriously useful things that people did on the Internet was discuss and provide help with their ailments. Sufferers of obscure, unknown and difficult to treat conditions helped to give advice on suitable methods, diet, drugs and treatments over the net. Perhaps as a result of this, there are some seriously useful websites and other resources on the Internet.

If you are worried about a particular medical condition, or just want to know how to beat this year's flu, monster medical sites such as DrKoop and IntelliHealth will offer good advice in plain English. It's often far easier, not to say quicker, to ask an automated Internet doctor about a problem than to visit your local GP – but a few minutes online is no substitute for a visit to the doctor. There are even sites that help diagnose problems, but these should be used with care. Just because you have a headache doesn't mean it's a brain tumour.

Always ask to see your GP If you're seriously injured or ill! Don't rely on the advice of websites as a cure-all.

Specialist sites provide impressive support for extreme or long-term medical problems. You'll get straightforward advice, the latest details on research and reassurance for partners and family plus the all-important chance to discuss problems – and their solutions – with others in the same position.

Since universities and labs around the world are all on the net, it's relatively easy to find out what's happening in medical research (use AltaVista or another search engine for a broad sweep on any subject). Many of these sites are aimed at fellow professionals and research students, so the language is technical, but at least you can follow what's coming over the horizon. For the non-technical, start at BBC Health or ReutersHealth – both disseminate news and research into manageable sections.

If it's prevention you're after, there's lots of good advice, with diet and workout plans, to help prevent heart disease and keep that finely toned body of yours running smoothly. If you're sagging or bulging in places that shouldn't, visit CyberDiet and HealthCalc for an instant checkup and a recommended diet that's not just bran and yoghurt.

Starting Point

Healthfinder **http://www.healthfinder.com**
Thousands of links to help you explore health, medical and fitness sites.

Medicine/Medical

Allergy Info **http://www.allergy-info.com**
One of the slowest, most over-used sites around – which is a shame since it's got everything you need to know about allergies.

Ask Dr. Weil **http://www.drweil.com**
Advice from an alternative medicine expert, who will jump at the chance to provide a personalised vitamin and supplement list for your ailments.

British Diabetic Association **http://www.diabetes.org.uk**
Quickly find specialist sites dealing with diabetes.

DrKoop **http://doctorkoop.net/**
Dumb name, great site. Everything about health, medicines and wellbeing.

drugstore.com **http://www.drugstore.com**
Virtual pharmacist provides almost every medical and health product you can imagine. Medical, beauty and nutritional information – you can even buy direct from the US. Part owned by Amazon.com.

HealthGate UK **http://www.healthgate.co.uk**
Academic answers to your medical problems. Patchy, but good on topics such as diagnostic tests and allergies.

Intellihealth **http://www.intellihealth.com**
Answers almost all your medical questions but geared to US enquiries.

Internet Mental Health **http://www.mentalhealth.com**
Packed with information about mental illness, from conditions to treatment and drugs. Don't expect a light read: the content is technical and aimed at professionals.

Irish Kidney Association **http://www.ika.ie/**
You don't have to have an Irish kidney to get support from this site. But it helps.

Mayo Clinic Health Oasis **http://www.mayohealth.org**
Rich on content and in design. Especially strong on cancer, Alzheimer's and heart disease.

The Allergy and Asthma Network **http://www.aanma.org**
Get the professional's side of the story. For plain advice, try the Pfizer or Allergy-Info sites.

The On-line Allergy Center **http://www.sig.net/~allergy/welcome.html**
Enterprising Texan allergy specialist sets out his stall, with live online chat sessions so you can talk about sniffles, rashes, wheezes and sneezes.

docnet **http://www.docnet.org.uk**
Designed to let doctors exchange notes, but fascinating for nosy patients.

Good Advice

BeWELL.com **http://www.bewell.com**

Title explains all – for wide-ranging, sensible advice.

Boots **http://www.boots.co.uk**

The high street hits the net with tips on beauty, health and medicines. But if you want to buy online, you'll have to visit http://www.drugstore.com.

Center for Disease Control and Prevention **http://www.cdc.gov/**

All you never wanted to know about diseases around the world from this US-government site. A handy chart warns travellers against current problems and epidemics.

DrugNet **http://www.drugnet.co.uk**

Tells you the risks and problems of drug and alcohol abuse then dishes out sensible advice – without the usual moralising.

Family Planning Association **http://www.fpa.org.uk**

Stop that baby.

Mediconsult.com **http://www.mediconsult.com**

Discuss your ailment with other sufferers – discussion boards for hundreds of different illnesses, advice and support groups.

Meningitis Research Foundation **http://www.meningitis.org**

Clear site leads you to the right resources by posing simple questions and providing the answers and support you might need.

OncoLink **http://www.oncolink.upenn.edu**

Leading cancer research centre delivers news and research, plus gently reassuring advice to any visitor.

Pfizer Inc **http://www.pfizer.com**

The people who make Viagra also produce lots of other drugs – and deliver piles of information on allergies and heart and sexual complaints and problems.

Repetitive Strain Injury – RSI **http://home.clara.net/ruegg/**
Cures and advice for those who have typed or clicked their way to a sore wrist and tingly sensations in the hand.

Sleep Medicine Home Page **http://www.users.cloud9.net/~thorpy/**
Hardly the most exciting of page designs – but perhaps that's the point of this site that's bursting with more information than you ever thought existed about sleep-related problems.

British Heart Foundation **http://www.bhf.org.uk**
Clear, basic guide to help you care for your heart.

Royal National Institute for the Blind (RNIB) **http://www.rnib.org.uk**
As you'd expect, very simply and clearly designed – and can be used with Braille readers, speech-synthesising web browsers or any visitor with full vision.

Health and Exercise

Active for Life **http://www.active.org.uk**
Get up, get active, get fit. Stop spending so much time peering into your computer screen, for a start.

American Heart Association **http://www.justmove.org**
The motivation to heave yourself out of the armchair and into a tracksuit. Information, activities and incentives to help you exercise to prevent heart disease.

BodyIsland **http://www.bodyisland.com**
Straight talking for frazzled aerobic nuts – plus exercise and health advice for mere mortals.

Coronary Prevention Group **http://healthnet.org.uk/healthy/**
Manage existing heart problems, minimise stress and look after your heart. There's more prevention info at **http://www.justmove. org**.

Health Square http://www.healthsquare.com
Helping women and families lead a healthier life.

Healthy Ideas http://www.healthyideas.com
Mass of ideas for women trying to stay fit.

Women.com http://www.women.com
Dedicated to women who want to know more about their health, fitness, children, career plans and illnesses.

Diet and Nutrition

Cyber Diet http://www.cyberdiet.com
A sensible route to diet, exercise and nutrition advice with plenty of motivation.

Foodwatch http://www.foodwatch.com.au/
Get started on a healthier food regime – find out about the food you should or are about to eat.

HealthCalc http://www.healthcalc.net/
Go for a quick health check – calculate your body mass and find out your perfect mix of food types. If you want advice, it's a chargeable extra.

My Nutrition http://www.mynutrition.co.uk
Step into the cool, calm clinic to find out about the perfect mix of healthy foods and vitamins.

News and Research

American Psychological Society http://www.psychologicalscience.org
Lie down on the couch and read the latest research.

BBC Health http://news.bbc.co.uk/education/health/
All the news on health, medicine and medical research.

Reuters Health **http://www.reutershealth.com**
News and stories about drugs, health, diet, exercise and medical research.

Try these newsgroups

alt.society.mental-health
Issues and support for mental health.

misc.health.aids
Coping with and research into AIDS.

misc.health.alternative
Alternatives to prescription drugs.

misc.kids.health
Your children's health.

sci.med
Products, rules and regulations in medicine.

talk.politics.medicine
The medical industry and its political activities.

24//HOBBIES AND COLLECTING

For some reason, people who collect stamps, make models or sew fine gold seem to feel at home on the web. If the Internet has wrecked your chance of free time to enjoy your hobby, you can at least use the time online to find out more, chat to fellow enthusiasts or stock up on equipment or items for your collection.

One of the major hobbies on the web is genealogy – plotting your family tree – which has really taken off in America. For this, the Internet is ideal. There's unlimited access to parish records, telephone directories, encyclopaedias, census reports and family home pages. In fact, there's so much information, you'll need the help of one of the specialist genealogy sites to point out what's relevant and how to use the information.

As an information library, you'll also find the web invaluable in learning more about your pastime. It's a great place to buy new items for your collection – try the online auctions – eBay (**http://www.ebay.com**), in particular, has hundreds of thousands of collectibles for sale every day.

Newsgroups really come into their own for collectors and hobbyists. There's an entire 'rec.' structure of groups that cater to recreation outside the net. Start up your newsgroup reader and join fellow fanatics posting messages about every pastime from collecting antique watches to taking photographs.

Starting Points

About.com **http://www.About.com/hobbies/**

A friendly welcome to hundreds of different mini-sites covering different hobbies and crafts. Each one's moderated by an enthusiast and brimming with ideas, links and encouragement.

Yahoo! Hobbies **http://www.yahoo.co.uk/Recreation/Hobbies/**
Yahoo's main directory page for hobbyists – listing thousands of sites on every pastime, collection and craft.

Crafts

Calligraphy Centre **http://www.calligraphycentre.com**
Swirling handwriting: how to do it. Plus a directory of online clubs.

ClayNet **http://home.vicnet.net.au/~claynet/new.htm**
Give up the keyboard and throw a pot. Practical information for potters of all abilities.

Drawing and Sketching **http://drawsketch.about.com**
What to do with a pencil, from the nice folk at About.com – a friendly site, packed with links.

Cass Arts **http://www.cass-arts.co.uk**
Everything you need to create your masterpiece – over 10,000 art and craft products in store, plus tips, advice and step-by-step lessons to get you started.

Cross Stitch Design **http://www.maurer-stroh.com**
Design and stitch the perfect sampler.

Empress Mills **http://www.expressmills.co.uk**
Threads of every colour and type for needlework enthusiasts.

Guanghwa Company **http://www.guanghwa.co.uk**
Brushes, inks and paper to produce Chinese art and calligraphy.

Internet Craft Fair **http://www.duban.com/craft/**
Get ideas for new projects, plus chat rooms for a natter with other crafters.

KinderCrafts **http://www.enchantedlearning.com/crafts/**
Projects for pre-school kids, from a necklace to masks and paper hats.

Lawrence – Artists' Materials **http://www.lawrence.co.uk**
Old-established artist and printmaker's supplier – from ink rollers to acrylics.

Needlecrafts **http://www.needlecrafts.com**
Embroidery and stitching.

Sew & So **http://www.sewandso.co.uk**
Old-fashioned haberdasher and needlework supplier threads into the web with considerable success.

Collecting

Horology **http://www.horology.com**
Light on design and graphics but jam-packed with well-ordered lists to thousands of links to watch, clock and related sites. For background information, auctions and discussion groups try http://www.watchnet.com.

Crown Agents Stamp Bureau **http://www.casb.co.uk**
Buy the latest UK stamps from the makers – the Crown.

Philatelic Resources **http://www.execpc.com/~joeluft/resource.html**
Vast directory of sites for stamp collectors.

Portsmouth Stamp Shop **http://www.portsmouthstamps.co.uk**
Thousands of stamps and cigarette cards from around the world.

Robin Hood Stamp Company **http://www.robinhood-stamp.co.uk**
Friendly site packed with stamps from around the world.

Stanley Gibbons **http://www.stangib.com**
A rather uninspiring site from the big name in stamps.

Models

Big Little Railroad Shop **http://www.biglittle.com**
Track to train sets, locos to stations.

Hobby Lobby International **http://www.hobby-lobby.com**
Radio-controlled boats, planes and helicopters at low prices from the US.

Tower Hobbies **http://www.towerhobbies.com**
Your first place to call for anything to do with radio-controlled models – thousands of items listed and shipped around the world.

Genealogy

Ancestry.com **http://www.ancestry.com**
Search for your ancestors across 1,600 census and marriage databases in the US – tantalises you with matching entries, then demands payment.

FamilyTreeMaker **http://www.familytreemaker.com**
Awesome range of databases but geared to families that emigrated to the USA; in most cases you'll need to ask for printed report.

Hayden Genealogy **http://www.hayden.mcmail.com**
Notes on over 950 family names compiled by enthusiast genealogist Dennis Hayden. Also provides a route on to the GenRing scheme to link genealogy sites.

Society of Genealogists **http://www.sog.org.uk**
How to get started tracing your family's roots.

UK Genealogy **http://www.genuki.org.uk/big/**
Vast range of links to research and family sites to help you trace your British ancestors.

Photography

At Your Leisure **http://www.shoppinguniverse.com**
Good range of traditional and digital cameras and film – plus guides to choosing and using the kit. Part of the vast Shopping Universe mall.

Euro Foto Centre **http://www.euro-foto.com**
Huge range of video, photographic and darkroom equipment, accessories and materials.

Kodak **http://www.kodak.com**
Clear guides to help you improve your photos.

Nikon **http://www.nikon.com**
Follow the online guide to take better snaps.

Try these newsgroups

rec.boats
Enjoying boats.

rec.crafts.metalworking
Working with metal.

rec.crafts.textiles
Stitching and knitting.

rec.models.rc
Radio-controlled models.

rec.photo
Photography as a hobby.

rec.woodworking
Enjoying woodworking.

25//HOMES AND HOUSES

Homes, houses and lifestyle are covered in enthusiastic detail by thousands of specialist sites. The Internet will probably change forever the way you'll find your new house. In the US, which is a couple of steps ahead of the UK, you can carry out the entire process – from getting a loan to choosing, visiting and buying a new home from your keyboard. Visit the MSN Home Advisor for a quick tour of the future.

There are online databases of homes for sale in the UK and overseas, and you can cover a vast area with a few mouse clicks, but the information on offer can be very patchy. Some traditional estate agents publish their lists, but for the best choice stick with the specialist virtual agents that use local stringers to provide thousands of homes for sale.

The more enterprising virtual agents let you stroll through the house with video clips or virtual-reality (three-dimensional) models. No agent has yet matched a good range of properties with useful tools to produce the ultimate site for buyers – but it's not far off.

Online DIY guides and magazine-style sites help you make the most of your new home. The UK sites from the DIY superstores are hopeless. Instead, visit the mega US sites like HomeTips and NaturalHandyman where a friendly expert will explain in simple steps how to build a partition wall, lay patios or deal with plumbing. Again, the advice is US-specific, so watch out – plumbing regulations and electricity voltages, for example, are quite different across the pond.

For Sale

CyberHomes **http://www.cyberhomes.co.uk**
Lease running out? Start looking for a new rental here.

Internet French Property **http://www.french-property.com**
Dream it, view it, buy it. An extensive selection of houses for sale and rent across the Channel.

Land.Net **http://www.land.net/**
Lottery winners, step right up. Specialist sales of islands, castles and mansions. Exotic property and land that's available around the world.

Latitudes French Property **http://www.latitudes.co.uk**
C'est formidable! Over 3,000 homes for sale in France.

MSN HomeAdvisor **http://homeadvisor.msn.com**
One day, it'll all work this way. Stylish solution to finding a home and loan in the US.

Property Sight **http://www.property-sight.co.uk**
Best range of homes for sale in the UK. Local agents keep the 7,000 listings up to date.

PropertyLive **http://www.propertylive.co.uk**
Plenty of advice to reduce the stress of moving once you've bought a house from the lists of property online.

Under One Roof **http://www.underoneroof.co.uk**
Clever display and virtual walkthrough brochures of a dozen London properties for sale. Nice idea but needs more houses and flats on its list.

DIY and Building

Architects' and Building Consultants' Directory **http://www.architect-net.co.uk**
House falling down? Need an extension? Find a decent local architect.

B&Q **http://www.diy.co.uk**
How to tackle DIY and where to buy the material. Plenty of online guides but not up to the US megasites.

Federation of Master Builders **http://www.fmb.org.uk/consumers/**
Cowboys and how to avoid them.

Homebase **http://www.homebase.co.uk**
Cool multimedia effects but minimal content to tempt you back to the DIY superstore.

HomeTips **http://www.hometips.com**
How to make and fix your home. Clear illustrations and step-by-step instructions to guide any novice DIY enthusiast. Also worth trying rival site: **http://www.naturalhandyman.com**

At Home

Better Homes and Gardens **http://www.bhglive.com**
Learn how to be the very model of an American suburban housewife.

Design-A-Room **http://www.designaroom.com**
Nifty, if useless, way of planning your room.

Furniture Wizard **http://www.furniturewizard.com**
How to remove the stain little Natasha's bottle left on your Chippendale.

HomeArts **http://homearts.com**
Coffee-morning worries. Living, lifestyle and women's mags provide plenty of advice for home and garden.

Lifestyle.UK **http://www.lifestyle.co.uk**
A list of all the sites you'll need to change your lifestyle. A good place to start browsing.

Marc Newson Design **http://www.marc-newson.com**
Cool, trendy and trend-setting furniture and objects from this London-based specialist.

Section Web **http://sectionweb.com**
Loft-living personified in this stylish, minimalist site for professional designers and architects.

UpMyStreet.com **http://www.upmystreet.co.uk**
How much is your house worth? More important, how about the Joneses at number 32? Groundbreaking site that catalogues house sales by postcode and provides all your local school and government information – often very slow, but persevere.

World of Interiors Design Studio **http://www.thedesignstudio.com**
Avoid colour clashes – co-ordinate your curtains and chairs with this database of fabric and wallpaper samples and suppliers from the famous glossy mag.

Try these newsgroups

---

alt.architecture
Discuss plans for your dream house.

alt.architecture.alternative
Discuss wild plans for your dream house.

26//JOBS

Sorting out your career should be top of the list for graduates and school leavers. You can use the musty careers office at school or college, or head for the virtual centres that provide help and guidance to help decide what might suit you – the BBC Education site is a great place to start.

Once you've decided that it's a farmer's life for you or whatever else appeals, it's time to find the job. The top employment agencies all post their job vacancy ads in vast databases. Browse through the thousands of jobs on offer in the UK or across the world. Or for something local, try JobHunter's list of 21,000 vacancies advertised in local papers across the UK. If you're still in student mode, visit Top Jobs on the Net: it saves you the effort and sends you an email when something suitable is advertised.

Since you're on a computer network, it's no surprise that the IT folk get the biggest range of jobs available. But whether it's journalism (the *Guardian* media job pages online) or sales (Taps), you'll find niche sits vacs catering for specialist job markets.

Now you've found a job vacancy, polish up your CV and brush up your interview skills with the Monster Board. On the issue of salary, try the Reed Online site for a guide to pay in various sectors (you'll find similar information in trade magazines – use NewsRack (**http://www.newsrack.com**) – to find them).

If you would rather be self-employed, there are guides from Inc. and Yahoo! to choosing a franchise, setting up a business and building up your empire. (Also flip through the business chapter for more contacts.)

Starting Point

BBC Education – Skills for Work **http://www.bbc.co.uk/education/workskills/jobs/**
Piles of advice and guidance – the ideal careers centre. Clearly explains the different types of job and helps you find your ideal job match.

Jobs on Offer

Appointments Plus **http://www.appointments-plus.com**
International appointments as advertised in the *Daily Telegraph*. Plenty of non-IT jobs listed.

Au Pair UK **http://dspace.dial.pipex.com/town/estate/tad68/**
Helping hopeful au pairs find a job in homes around the world.

BestPeople **http://www.bestpeople.co.uk**
Astonishing animation gives this site a contemporary look. Behind it all there's a database of international job vacancies with a strong IT bias.

CareerMosaic UK **http://www.careermosaic-uk.co.uk**
Goes further than other job sites to get you into work. Search its database and newsgroups for vacancies.

CareerZine **http://www.careerzine.co.uk**
Over 5,000 jobs in the science, finance, admin and health fields.

e-job **http://www.e-job.net/ejob.asp**
Small, select range of jobs in advertising, marketing and sales.

Gradunet-Virtual Careers Office **http://www.gradunet.co.uk**
Matches graduates to their perfect job.

International Language Job Centre **http://www.atlas.co.uk/efl/jobs/**
The chance of a change of scene for language teachers.

Taps **http://www.taps.com**
Thousands of IT, marketing, sales and finance jobs in Europe. The site's used to advertise jobs from hundreds of major UK and international companies, so it is always busy.

JobHunter **http://www.jobhunter.co.uk**
Gathers together jobs advertised in local newspapers – the searchable database has over 21,000 job entries.

Jobs Unlimited **http://www.jobsunlimited.co.uk**
Jobs in media, education and social areas that have been advertised in the *Guardian* newspaper.

JobSearch **http://www.jobsearch.co.uk**
Smart searches for your next job – submit your CV and your perfect job description.

JobSite UK **http://www.jobsite.co.uk**
Get a job in Paris or Petersham – scour the collection of over 7,000 jobs advertised by UK and European recruitment agencies.

Jobworld **http://www.jobworld.co.uk**
The best choice of jobs for IT professionals – over 15,000 job vacancies on offer.

Opportunities Online **http://www.opps.co.uk**
Job bank for specialists, surgeons and medical-theatre staff – you'll need to register first, but it's free.

PhD Jobs **http://www.phdjobs.com**
Top jobs for academics – a UK site exclusively for postgraduates searching for a post in academia or industry.

Reed Online **http://www.reed.co.uk**
Search for a job, calculate your potential salary and get careers advice from the high-street recruitment agency.

Response Centre **http://www.responsecentre.co.uk**
Range rather than quantity with vacancies in government, charities and the public sector.

The Monster Board **http://www.monsterboard.co.uk**
Search for a job by county or country – there are bigger lists but the range here is impressive and there's help on CVs and interviews.

Times Higher Educational Supplement – Job section **http://www.jobs.thes.co.uk**
International posts in colleges and universities.

Top Jobs on the Net **http://www.topjobs.co.uk**
The easy way to hunt for jobs – enter your perfect job description and this site will send you an email when, or if, it's advertised.

Self-employed

Inc. Online **http://www.inc.com**
Build your own international empire – advice for entrepreneurs.

The Franchise Business **http://www.lds.co.uk/franchise/**
How to choose and set up a franchised business.

Yahoo! Small Business **http://smallbusiness.yahoo.com**
Starting, running and growing your own business.

Try these newsgroups

biz.jobs.offered
Vacancies that need filling.

misc.jobs.misc
Discuss work and careers.

misc.jobs.offered.entry
The first step on the job ladder.

misc.jobs.resumes
I want a job.

27//KIDS

The web is a fantastic combination of playground and library. Since the Internet is the technology of the future, it's also essential that children are able to use and understand how to use it to best advantage. To get children interested, the web's brilliant for homework assignments (though look at Education for more sites) and a lot of fun for kids who want to make new friends or let off steam about the adults in their life. However, there's plenty of weirdness out there. See page 47 for details on how best to protect your kids without spoiling their fun.

The net gives kids freedom – a place to explore away from horrible old teachers and nagging parents. Before you recoil at the thought of little Freddie surfing the web, it's relatively easy to protect them from the unwelcome sites on the web. And instead of the worry, think of the help it can provide for homework, sport and hobbies.

On long, rainy days when the toy chest's been emptied several times and it's still not time for tea, try the web for bumper packs of activities. CyberMom and Summer Fun both have stacks of activities, recipes and things to make and do.

If you're reading this and wondering what it's got to do with your little flower who's only just learned to crawl, think again. New and expectant parents get bumper bags of advice and support from ParentSoup, Moms Online and UK Parents Online. They'll even show you how to change a nappy – but won't do it for you.

As a teenager, you'll want the parents out of your hair – then settle down for some serious surf wisdom. For a start, there are the big portal sites that are the organised discos of the net. There's plenty of chat, girl-talk, boy-talk and more advice than you could ever want. For lots more about this, see our companion book, **The Virgin Family Guide to the Internet.**

Starting Points

Berit's Best Sites for Children **http://db.cochran.com/li_toc:theoPage.db**
Safe and fun sites for kids, rated to help parents. Don't forget monitor programs that block access to unwelcome sites (visit **http://www.netnanny.com**).

Kids Online **http://www.aaa.com.au/Kids_Radio.shtml**
More sites than you can shake a rattle at.

Yahooligans! **http://www.yahooligans.com**
Friendly search engine and guide to the web. Great niche marketing by Yahoo!

Babies and Pre-school

Baby World **http://www.babyworld.co.uk**
Mega site for everyone that wants kids or has just received their first dribbling, screaming bundle of joy.

Babyhood **http://www.babyhood.com**
Get a free home page for your tiny tot; the rest of the site – dedicated to the under-2s – has some advice, but it's not up to Baby World standards.

Big Brainy Babies **http://www.brainybabies.com**
Taxing puzzles for talented toddlers.

Crayola **http://www.crayola.com**
Select a picture, print it out and colour it in. Perfect rainy-day fun, stories and games. You might find a box of crayons is handy.

KinderCrafts **http://www.enchantedlearning.com/crafts/**
Projects for pre-school tinies, from a necklace to masks and hats.

Time for Teletubbies! **http://www.bbc.co.uk/teletubbies/**
Ehh-ohh.

Winnie the Pooh and Pals **http://www.winniethepooh.co.uk**
Wonderful site with games, puzzles, recipes, stories and poems about ... Pooh. Also worth visiting the similar, charming Pooh Corner (**http://www.gironet.nl/home/awouters/**).

Zini's Activity Page **http://www.incwell.com/Zini/**
Find the Crayons, it's colour-in time – dozens of nicely drawn pages, puzzles and mazes to print and use.

Kids

Bonus.com **http://www.bonus.com**
Takes an unusual route to controlling what your kids can view: once you're here, special software traps them in the site. Luckily, the content's great fun.

Bookworm books for kids **http://www.kidsreads.com**
Recommended reads for kids aged 6-12.

Bugbios.com **http://insects.org**
Perfect for nasty little boys who like putting insects in bottles.

CyberMom **http://www.cybermom.com**
Mummy meets the Jetsons – tricks and advice to make mummy's job easier – very American, but very useful. Also worth trying Moms Online (**http://www.momsonline.com**).

Disney **http://www.disney.co.uk**
Mickey's official home in the UK – neat animations, games, and stories.

Junior Parliament **http://www.3t.co.uk/parliament/junior/**
Making politics interesting for kids is a tough job; tries hard with a range of quizzes and information for teachers and children.

Just For Kids Who Love Books **http://www.geocities.com/~abrown/kids.htm**
An extensive collection of links to sites about children's authors and the characters.

Kid's Channel **http://www.kids-channel.co.uk**
Keeping the kids amused with games, puzzles, activities, stories and colouring projects – but Kids' Space (**http://www.kids-space.org**) provides more.

Kids' Space **http://www.kids-space.org**
Gallery of pictures, music and stories submitted by children.

Looney Tunes Karaoke **http://www.kids.warnerbros.com/karaoke/**
Sing-a-long with your fave cartoon characters; rather like the uncle who gives your son a drum, this site will change your home's noise levels.

The Yuckiest Site on the Internet **http://www.yucky.com**
Gross goings on in this brilliantly conceived site. Love the pop-up instant polls: 'How often do you pick your nose?'

Teens

A Girl's World Online Clubhouse **http://www.agirlsworld.com**
Where girl power starts – typical features tell you how to turn babysitting into a moneymaking operation. Terrifying.

Cyberkids **http://www.cyberkids.com**
A controlled environment for little people: e-zines, stories, music, reviews, chat sessions, interviews and cartoons.

FreeZone **http://freezone.com**
Let your 10-14-year-olds romp around this safe environment with chat pages, discussion groups, advice and games.

Girl Tech! **http://www.girltech.com**
Chat rooms, advice, stories and interviews for girls.

Headbone Zone **http://www.headbone.com**
Self-consciously wacky coverage of all the usual kids' topics – but too many commercial sponsors. Just like children's TV, really.

KidsCom **http://www.kidscom.com**
A friendly place for kids to start exploring the Internet and themselves, exchange messages, play games and send e-postcards.

Teen Hoopla **http://www.ala.org/teenhoopla/**
Help for teenagers stuck with homework but plenty of distraction from teen-zines on sports, arts and comics.

Parents and Family

myFamily **http://www.myfamily.com**
Salvation for disjointed families. Create a family meeting point and mantelpiece for photos, memos and calendar.

Parent Soup **http://www.parentsoup.com**
Relief for parents worried about their kids – or just plain worried. There's advice on education, health and even baby names.

Summer Fun **http://db.ok.bc.ca/summer/**
Ideas for exhausted parents to entertain small bouncy people over the long break. Includes recipes (for indoor and outdoor cooking) from other exhausted parents.

UK Parents Online **http://www.ukmums.co.uk**
For new mums and dads with the energy to surf. Advice on health, managing – and how to change nappies.

Pets

AcmePet **http://www.acmepet.com**
Looking after your furry, fishy or feathered friends – advice, news, stories, polls, chat and games for young pet owners.

Equiworld **http://www.equiworld.net**
Masses of information about horses, ponies and how to look after and ride them.

geegees **http://www.geegees.co.uk**
Awful design but saddled-up with enthusiasm for horse lovers in the UK.

Haynet **http://www.haynet.com**
Slick American site for horse-mad surfers.

Pet Cat **http://www.petcat.com**
Tales from the litter tray. Kitty talk, how to look after your cat, diary of a cat and advice for young owners.

Pets Pyjamas **http://www.petspyjamas.co.uk**
A fun site aimed at kids who want to learn how to look after their cat or dog.

RSPCA **http://www.rspca.org.uk**
Packed with good advice on looking after pets – and a cute little animated fox.

Try these newsgroups

alt.kids-talk
Kids discuss life.

misc.kids.computer
How kids use computers.

misc.kids.consumers
What kids want and buy.

rec.arts.books.childrens
Children's literature under the spotlight.

28//LOVE AND DATING

Perhaps it's a verdict on our times. We find it so hard to get the right partner in our own circle that we have to reach out further and further. Searching for love on the net is a pastime of millions. From advice on chat-up lines via wedding plans to divorce settlements, there's a site for your emotional needs.

The most active sites on the net are trying to help establish LDRs (long distance romance): an email version of pen pals but rather more explicit. You can try to find a friend with chat (see Chapter 7 for details on IRC or ICQ), but specialist LDR sites provide more like-minded visitors. And it's not just about sex and surfing. There's plenty of real romance out there, lodged between the desperate offers to be your wife and the tales of a first kiss.

Rather than diving in headlong, take a moment to read the advice. It's a minefield – emotional and financial – and you'll get good instruction on what to do and expect from the Rainbow Connection, Dating Advice and Dateable.com. Some sites are great for simple online romance, others get straight down to sex. Get the two confused and you'll be flamed or barred.

If you want to find a partner for life, you can trawl the personal ads (**http://www.webpersonals.com**) or try the dating agencies. The biggest US agency has matched over 1.6 million singles but for British residents, Dateline provides a professional service without the transatlantic flights. And if you're too shy to approach the object of your desires, try joining the crush of lovesick teenagers at eCrush.

Starting Points

Dating Advice **http://dating.miningco.com**

Handholding for anyone new to love on the net. A great place to start.

Internet Dating **http://www.wildxangel.com**
A useful counterweight to the puff of many of the other love sites – this covers the dangers and problems you might encounter.

Finding Love

Cyber Wives **http://www.cyberwives.freeserve.co.uk**
Guys and gals with names like 'Ferret' ready to enter into long-lasting LDRs (long distance relationships) or even marriage. Testimonials say this, so it must be true.

Dateline **http://www.dateline.uk.com**
Probably the best way to find a British partner. But it'll cost you to gain access to their huge database of very detailed profiles.

Love Resources **http://www.loveresources.com**
Sell yourself, sweetie. Create your own web page to promote your best features and if this doesn't work, ask the love expert what's wrong.

Match.com **http://www.match.com**
Pay up and you get dates, chat and maybe even romance from the biggest US dating service online.

SinglesOnline **http://www.singlesonline.com**
Gallery of a dozen men and women ready to chat till your ears burn. But with occupations like 'sex education', I just wonder if they're real.

Swoon **http://www.swoon.com**
Nice mix of dating, mating and relating. Plenty of horoscopes, personal ads, advice and quizzes to get you started on the road to love.

Webpersonals **http://www.webpersonals.com**
Amazingly busy personal-ad site (over 80,000 entries a day); everyone's after friendship and company – oh, all right then, sex.

Advice

1001 Ways to be Romantic **http://www.1001waystoberomantic.com**
Snappy ideas to improve your hit rate. And the Romantic Tools section (guffaw) is a scorecard system to measure how romantic you are. Well, what did you think it was?

A Singles Newsletter **http://www.thesinglelife.com**
Advice for singles who'd rather not be alone. Trite advice on nightclub etiquette, recipes for lurve and the top tips for romantic dinners.

Cyber-Loving **http://www.cyber-loving.com**
Astrology charts, gifts, e-cards and chat, all aimed to help online relationships flourish.

Dateable.com **http://dateable.com**
Looking for love? Here's a good place to start with general advice, classifieds and lots of features.

Divorce Support Page **http://www.divorcesupport.com**
Let off steam, ask questions or just chat as you cry on to your keyboard. US-based but it's a friendly shoulder to lean on, with good advice.

eCrush **http://www.secretcrush.com**
Does that gorgeous hunk/babe know you love him/her? Embarrassing, very un-British, up-front stories of crushes. For the brazen, you can even place an ad announcing your crush.

How far is it? **http://www.indo.com/distance/**
You've met online – now exactly how far apart do you live?

How to Juggle Women **http://www.jugglewomen.com**
A tip a week on multi-dating without getting killed, going broke or getting completely exhausted.

Romance101 **http://www.rom101.com**
What's your best chat-up line and who's your ideal partner? Find out with the highly scientific astro-compatibility tests.

The Rainbow Connection **http://www.rainbow-connection.org**
Plenty of advice for anyone planning to use chat or mailing lists to get an LDR.

Tips for Dating Emotional Cripples **http://www.grrl.com/bipolar.html**
Girls: how to chuck that redneck/punk/president/artist that you're stuck with. Also try the main site (**http://www.grrl.com/main.html**) for pages on dating advice.

Try these newsgroups

---

alt.personals
Improbably endowed people who want to get (very) friendly.

alt.romance
Smoochy thoughts of love.

alt.romance.online
Electronic smoochy thoughts of love.

alt.romance.unhappy
Heartbreak Hotel.

alt.visa.us.marriage-based
Newsgroup for the desperate and unsubtle.

soc.men
Men and their problems.

soc.women
Women and their problems.

29//MIND, BODY AND SPIRIT

You won't be surprised to learn that almost all these New Age, touchy-feely sites have their own message – and often their own agenda (lots of the sites are simply promos for products or authors). However, dig deeper and you'll find truly helpful advice and teachings from friendly, expert and generous people (mostly Californian).

Where standard prescription medicine (see the chapter on health) and medical procedures have vast, open and very useful sites, alternative medicine has not embraced the web so warmly. There are sites that offer articles and information about herbs, aromatherapy and other techniques, but many are simply commercial sites with a service to sell.

Perhaps the main problem with this subject area is that the majority of the thousands of sites online are published by individuals. Nothing wrong with using your free web space allocation, but it does mean that the web addresses change on a daily basis. We found this to be one of the most transient parts of the web. The best advice is to try a search in Yahoo! (**http://www.yahoo.co.uk**) or AltaVista (**http://www.altavista.com**) and find the subject you're interested in – but be prepared for plenty of dead links to sites that no longer exist.

Starting Points

Holistic Medicine Web Page **http://www.tiac.net/users/mgold/health.html**
Vast resource on all things natural – including holistic healing, alternative medicine, nutrition and yoga.

Self Improvement Online **http://www.selfgrowth.com**
Your quest starts here – over 4,000 sites offering ways to improve yourself.

Natural Healing http://www.natural-healing.co.uk
Directory of real-world organisations and companies specialising in holistic healing.

Inspiration and Self-improvement

Children of Light http://www.childrenoflight.com
Awaken the consciousness of your soul with help from Ron and Robert. Lectures, advice and information – plus online guidance (for a fee) and teaching via chat rooms.

Heartwarmers4u http://www.heartwarmers4u.com
Receive inspiring emails every day of the week. Also browse its list of sites that provide inspiration and advice.

IACHT http://www.iacht.co.uk
Crystals to heal and inspire – information and sales.

Inspiration Network http://www.inspire.org
Your body, your vehicle – exercises and instruction for those seeking inspiration or attempting to instill it in others.

LifeMentoring http://www.lifementoring.com
Great thoughts, spiritual wisdom and personal development in a friendly community.

MetaTalk http://www.metatalk.com
Rebirth, growth and free personal counselling.

Thought A Day http://www.thoughtaday.com
Improve your daily meditation with a thought a day emailed direct to your desk.

Psychic and Spirit

Feng Shui http://ehost.menet.net/fengshui/
Find harmony in your life and website. The five elements analysed and described, plus a celebrity guest to up the ratings.

Mind Body Spirit **http://www.mindbodyspirit.net/**
General store for your crystals, books, tarot, aromatherapy and divining materials. Shipping available from the US back to the UK.

SpiritNetwork **http://spiritnetwork.com**
A little of everything with biorhythms, paranormal, spirituality and general wellness – and even web authoring for spiritual sites.

Stonehenge **http://www.activemind.com/Mysterious/Topics/Stonehenge/**
One take on the druid fortress/altar/temple.

The Ascension Network **http://www.ascension.net/**
Library of features on spiritual techniques and healers.

The Mystic **http://www.themystic.org**
Start at mystical awakening and progress to ascents of the mind in a year's free online guide to Eastern Mysticism.

Uri Geller **http://www.urigeller.com**
Are you a psychic force? Find out with Uri.

Viking Remote Viewing **http://www.viking-z.org**
Brush up on your psychic self-defence or read about UFOs and crop circles.

World Transformation **http://www.worldtrans.org**
Tune into the positive vibrations and find good things and peace. Synchronicity rules.

Health and Healing

Alexander Technique **http://www.alexander-technique.com**
Stand up straight with the good guide to well-being through posture and movement.

Health and Healing News **http://www.hhnews.com**
Aromatherapy and herbal remedies for you and your pets explained and discussed.

Healing Humor **http://www.learnwell.org~edu/laugh.shtml**
Laugh. It cures.

Healing Network **http://www.nucleus.com/~gateway/healing.html**
Ask the Reiki master for distance-healing advice.

Health Clinic – HealthWorld Online **http://www.healthy.net/clinic/index.html**
How to treat your chronic disease with complementary medicine.

Holistic America **http://www.holisticamerica.com**
A good place to start by exploring the directory of holistic health sites and articles from leading practitioners, such as Dr Chopra.

Holistic Healing Fundamentals **http://www.holisticmed.com/fund.html**
Newcomer's guide to what this holistic stuff is all about.

Mayo Clinic **http://www.mayohealth.org/mayo/library/htm/natural.htm**
A good gauge to traditional medicine's view of natural therapies, from the archives of the vast Mayo medical site.

Mind, Body & Soul Network **http://www.mindbodysoul.com**
Get to grips with astrology, dreams, fitness, nutrition, sex and your psychic self.

Mind-Body-Spirit **http://www.all-natural.com/art-indx.html**
A good introduction to natural healing.

Natural Health and Healing **http://home.rica.net/webassist/health.htm**
How to achieve natural health and healing with t'ai chi, meditation and a special diet.

Pranic Healing **http://www.pranichealing.com**
Overtly commercial site lauding Pranic healing centres and classes.

Reference Guide for Herbs **http://www.realtime.net/anr/herbs.html**
Herbs and how to use them for healing.

T'Ai Chi **http://www.taichi.com**
Master the slow, controlled movements for well-being and focus. Baggy white pyjamas optional.

Horoscopes

Horoscopes4u **http://www.horoscopes4u.com**
Type in your birth date and get a personal horoscope.

Russell Grant **http://www.russellgrant.com**
Horoscopes from the chirpy, chubby personality astrologer who'll tell you what'll happen next.

Tarot **http://www.talisman.net/tarot/**
Your future's in the cards.

Try these newsgroups

alt.meditation
Meditation for an improved life.

alt.meditation.transcendental
Your second-level meditation.

alt.out-of-body
I jumped out of my skin.

alt.yoga
Yoga and its philosophy.

alt.zen
Adopt a Zen-like position.

30//MUSIC

Not only is the Internet full of people who want to share their enthusiasm for their favourite bands, but there are record company sites, magazines and official band websites galore. What's more, new technology that enables you to listen to and download music has improved by leaps and bounds – you can now download remixes from top DJs almost as soon as they're done.

There are probably more sites writing about music than playing it, and providing background discographies seems something of an obsession to the bigger sites on the web. The leader by a mile is the brilliant All-Music Guide. It lists reviews, discographies, interviews, sample tracks and fanzines for hundreds of thousands of groups.

MP3 The biggest challenge to the traditional music industry is the development of the MP3 (MPEG-3) standard. This allows anyone to store CD-quality stereo sound in a relatively small file (one minute of music takes up around 1Mb of disk space). MP3 files can be played on your computer or transferred to a tiny, portable machine to replace the traditional Walkman.

Many people are copying normal CDs into MP3 format and making these copies available on the Internet. It's this illegal copying and free distribution that the music industry rightly sees as a threat, although there is some evidence that most people who download a pirated file will then go and buy the CD.

The alternative to MP3 is called Real and provides a method of transferring music over the Internet live – you never download the entire file, instead you are effectively controlling a CD-player at the other end. This instant playback is called 'streaming audio' and needs a good, fast connection to the Internet in order to work. The music industry likes it because the complete file is never transferred – so it can't easily be copied.

Music Company Sites

A&M	http://www.amrecords.com
Atlantic	http://www.atlantic-records.com
Columbia	http://www.columbiarecords.com
EMI	http://www.emi.co.uk
Geffen	http://www.geffen.com
Island	http://www.island.co.uk
MCA	http://www.mcarecords.com
Polydor	http://www.polydor.co.uk
Polygram	http://www.polygram.com
Sony	http://www.sonymusic.com
Virgin	http://www.vmg.com
Warner Bros.	http://www.wbr.com

Top Bands

To find out more about any artist or band, search the Ultimate Band List (http://www.ubl.com).

Abba	http://www.abbasite.com
Ash	http://www.ash-official.com
Beatles	http://www.hollywoodanddivine.com/anthology/index.html
Blondie	http://www.blondie.net
Blur	http://www.blur.co.uk
Bowie	http://www.david-bowie.com
Boyzone	http://www.boyzone.co.uk
Catatonia	http://www.catatonia.com
Chemical Brothers	http://www.vmg.co.uk/chemicalbros/
Corrs	http://www.atlantic-records.com/the_corrs/
Madonna	http://www.wbr.com/madonna/
Ricky Martin	http://www.rickymartin.com
Rolling Stones	http://www.the-rolling-stones.com
Spice Girls	http://www.virginrecords.com/spice_girls/spice.html
Steps	http://www.welcome.to/steps_the_web_site/

Starting Points

All-Music Guide **http://www.allmusic.com**
Everything you could ever want to know about music. A super-sized encyclopaedia of pop, rock and classical reviews, biographies and discographies rolled into one. If you can tear yourself away, also try Worldwide Internet Music Resources (**http://www.music.indiana.edu/music_resources/**).

Clickmusic **http://www.clickmusic.co.uk**
Comprehensive UK pop music site, with news, reviews,downloads, gig listings and more.

Harmony Central **http://www.harmony-central.com**
Great site for band members – masses of articles about playing and life in a band, plus a good directory of useful sites.

The People of Jazz Index **http://www.acns.nwu.edu/jazz/artists/**
Links to the top jazz resources.

Ultimate Band List **http://www.ubl.com**
Obsessed with a band? Join its fan site. Everything to help the pop-crazed bopper get a fix.

Classical

Classical **http://www.musdoc.com/classical/**
Fine collection of articles, reviews and biographies of classical composers and their works.

Classical Net **http://www.classical.net/**
Biographies and recommended play lists put together by amateur enthusiasts for enthusiasts.

Classic FM **http://www.classicfm.co.uk**
Online version of the hugely successful radio station. Brings classical music to the masses. Do we deserve this?

MDC Classic Music **http://www.mdcmusic.co.uk**
Excellent selection of classical music CDs for sale.

Sheet Music Direct **http://www.sheetmusicdirect.com**
Stuck for something to play? Buy and download sheet music for instant inspiration.

Buying CDs

*The market place is dominated by vast warehouse-style shops selling hundreds of thousands of titles at low prices. Don't forget to use MyTaxi (**http://www.mytaxi.co.uk**) or ShopGuide (**http://www.shopguide.co.uk**) to compare prices. The following megasites provide a similarly huge range.*

101cd.com **http://www.101cd.com**
Amazon.com **http://www.amazon.com**
Audiostreet **http://www.audiostreet.com**
Borders **http://www.borders.com**
CDNow **http://www.cdnow.com**
CD Universe **http://www.cduniverse.com**
Music Boulevard **http://www.musicblvd.com**
IMVS **http://www.imvs.com**

Action Records **http://www.action-records.co.uk**
Three unique points: one, they still sell vinyl; two, they also have a real shop; three, they also have their own music label. Sum – a great place to shop for indie and mainstream.

cdparadise **http://www.cdparadise.com**
Cut-price CDs, videos, computer games and books. Features 'Brad', the virtual assistant who'll keep you informed of new CD releases. Part of the WH Smith empire.

GEMM **http://www.gemm.com**
Track down hard-to-find CDs with a neat search tool that looks in all the new and secondhand online stores.

HMV **http://www.hmv.co.uk**

High-street music store for mainstream soul, jazz, pop and classic CDs, DVDs and videos.

Razorcuts **http://www.razorcuts.com**

Browse the site for tracks you want – from jazz to lounge, classic to disco – and create your own custom CD. Cool.

Tunes.com **http://www.tunes.com**

Vast CD shop that gathers reviews from AMG, over a million sound clips, news from Rolling Stone, thousands of video clips and several hundred thousand titles with reviews. Phew!

MP3

Dimension Music MP3 Information **http://www.dimensionmusic.com**

News, music and the software to play it.

Lycos **http://mp3.lycos.com**

Yes, the search engine gets an honourable mention because it's the best place to search for bootleg MP3 files to download and play.

MP3.com **http://www.mp3.com**

Plenty of news on copyright laws, the software you need to playback the files and a good range of new indie bands using MP3 to preview their sample tracks. Thousands of funky unknowns and a smattering of classical – but no major artists.

Mp3.dk **http://www.mp3.dk**

The MP3 craze – what it is, what it means, how to join in.

MP3 World **http://www.worldkey.com/mp3world/**

Read the 'is this illegal?' box as you search the archive of MP3 music to download.

MP3 Master List **http://www.iocon.com/masterlist/content.html**

Vast directory of MP3 files, but plagued by links that don't work.

mIRC-X: MP3 Search Resource **http://www.mircx.com**
Search engine focussed on MP3 format files.

RioPort **http://www.rioport.com**
Advertising its eponymous neat, tiny portable MP3 player, plus a whole mass of links where you'll find MP3 files.

Reviews and Magazines

Addicted To Noise **http://www.addict.com**
Sonic sonnets from some of the coolest tune-hacks in the US – monthly articles make this a great read.

All Star **http://www.allstarmag.com**
Music news and reviews from around the world; part of CDnow, so you can buy once you've read.

Billboard **http://www.billboard-online.com**
The famous magazine keeps you up to date with news stories and a few charts. For the full archives and all the charts, you'll have to pay – unless you visit **http://rock.yahoo.com/** where you'll see the same listings, in full, for free.

Dotmusic **http://www.dotmusic.com**
Pretty much the perfect mix of gossip, official news, previews, biogs and – to fund it all – sales of CDs.

MTV Online **http://www.mtv.com**
Hundreds of bands, mini video clips and preview tracks in a sharp new site – just like the TV show.

music365 **http://www.music365.co.uk**
Mostly mainstream pop and chart news, previews and features. Great if you love Cher or Michael Bolton.

NME **http://www.nme.com**
Serious rock 'n' roll reviews and news from the New Musical Express.

Rolling Stone **http://www.rollingstone.com**
Just a sample of the classic interviews and photos. Shame – it would be great to have the lot.

SonicNet **http://www.sonicnet.com**
Straight-talking, award-winning guide to what's up in the music scene.

Top 3 **http://www.top3.net/**
Mad about pop music? Lyrics for 200 top pop songs, MP3 samples and reviews. There's a strong bias to US bands but it's a well-stocked site.

Top of the Pops **http://www.totp.beeb.com**
Charts, news, gossip – but no strobe lights on the site of the TV show.

Broadcasts

Blues Experience **http://www.bestblues.com**
Strike a cool note, swing back and enjoy the reviews and broadcasts of blues music.

Live Concerts **http://www.liveconcerts.com**
Enjoy a gig from home.

NetRadio Network **http://www.netradio.net/**
Over 120 free radio stations playing everything from 80s pop and rock to classical. Dreadful quality, but it's fine for background music while you type. A similar alternative is Spinner (**http://www.spinner.com**).

Pirate Radio **http://www.pirate-radio.co.uk**
Pirate radio stations don't bother any more lugging broadcast gear to the top of tower blocks in the middle of the night. No, now they just play live at this website.

SHOUTcast! **http://www.shoutcast.com**
The true spirit of the Internet lives on – download a plug-in

(winAmp) for your browser, pay whatever you want for it, then either set up your own radio station or listen to a mass of others.

Timecast **http://www.timecast.com**
Tells you what's new and broadcasting on the net.

vTuner **http://www.vtuner.com**
Scan all the radio stations broadcasting live on the net. Search by style or country (the UK has 22 stations) then click and listen; each station is rated by quality of sound and speed of delivery. An alternative is **http://www.radiotower.com/** that's harder to use and with a limited range.

Music

Burbs **http://www.burbs.org.uk**
Everyone has to start somewhere. Profiles and samples of thousands of hopeful bands waiting to be discovered.

Disgraceland **http://www.nwlink.com/~timelvis/**
Meet Friz, the world's only Elvis-impersonating bird. A crazy but loving tribute site to the King.

Past Perfect **http://www.pastperfect.com**
Sounds of the 20s (and 30s and 40s) lovingly remastered to remove the crackles and scratches.

Pollstar **http://www.pollstar.com**
Check out just about every gig around the world.

SoundMarket **http://soundmarket.net/**
Country music twangs and ballads.

T-DOT Live **http://www.virtualnoise.com/tdotlive/**
If it's blowin' up and needs someone to represent, here's cool hip-hop from the beat masters.

Virgin Records **http://www.vmg.co.uk**
A lesson in cool site design, helped by the great artist line-up. But for a wider view, try the portals like AMG.

Yahoo! Music **http://rock.yahoo.com**
Neat summary of what's happening in the rock and pop scene – with live broadcast schedules, US charts and reviews.

Try these newsgroups

---

alt.fan.shostakovich
For those crazy fans of Shostakovich.

alt.music.abba
Mamma mia!

alt.music.independent
Cool tunes from the independent labels.

alt.music.world
General thoughts on world music.

alt.rap
Rappers' delight.

rec.music.a-cappella
Just voices.

rec.music.bluenote
Smooth jazz and blues.

rec.music.classical
Classical music in depth.

rec.music.marketplace
I want to trade my Beatles picture disc.

31//NEWS

Serious, daily world news is delivered from newspapers and TV channels on the web. Each of the UK newspapers has impressive sites with all the articles from the day's paper plus – the real gem – searchable archives of past news coverage. And it's free.

The Internet has proved its worth in delivering breaking news, and not just via the web – Usenet newsgroups were the only way to relay reports from civilians stuck inside recent war zones (such as the conflict in Kosovo). And some of the biggest scandals have broken on the net – the world read about the Monica Lewinsky affair first on the Drudge Report website.

The top two UK broadsheet sites are generated by *The Times* and the *Telegraph*; both vying for a similar audience, both providing excellent coverage. If you have a favourite paper, visit its website. You'll already know the format and what to expect from the *Daily Star*, the *Independent* and the *Mirror*.

Part of the joy of the web is its global outlook. If there's a story breaking in the United States, don't put up with a short report in a UK paper, visit the US sites and get all the details. The few national papers (*New York Times*, *Washington Post* and *USA Today*) all provide fine coverage of the US news with smatterings of world events, but the smaller local online papers give the true flavour of the state. To find a local paper for any country, visit Newsrack or The Paperboy.

Naturally, Internet users have created plenty of commentary on current events. Commentary sites have sprung up and offer analysis of every world event. And as a much-needed counter to the tide of facts, try the witty anti-news sites such as the brilliant tabloid spoof, The Onion.

UK newspapers

The Daily Telegraph	http://www.telegraph.co.uk
The Evening Standard	http://www.thisislondon.co.uk
The Express	http://www.expressnewspapers.co.uk
The Financial Times	http://www.ft.com
The Guardian	http://www.guardian.co.uk
The Independent	http://www.independent.co.uk
The Mirror	http://www.mirror.co.uk
The Observer	http://www.observer.co.uk
The Scotsman	http://www.scotsman.com
The Star	http://www.megastar.co.uk
The Sun	http://www.currantbun.com
The Sunday People	http://www.people.co.uk
The Sunday Times	http://www.sunday-times.co.uk
The Times	http://www.the-times.co.uk
The Yorkshire Post	http://www.ypn.co.uk

Starting Points

BBC news **http://news.bbc.co.uk**
This is where much of the BBC's massive investment in online services has gone. Not as trendy as CNN but the coverage is better. Includes features, in-depth analysis and even offers live video or audio news segments.

CNN **http://www.cnn.com**
Brimming with news, features and listings from around the world – a little US bias but not so much as the TV station. It cost millions to develop this highly original site – and it was worth every cent. The BBC has sharper European and UK coverage.

NewsPage **http://www.newspage.com**
World and business news on a grand scale – reports gathered from over 600 magazines and newspapers, then sorted into 2,500 topics. If it's out there, it's in here – but it can be rather overwhelming.

Newsrack **http://www.newsrack.com**
Brilliant, simple idea done well – links to (almost) every online newspaper and magazine site from around the world. If it's not here, try The Paperboy at **http://www.thepaperboy.com/** or Worldwide News at **http://www.worldwidenews.com/**.

Weather

BBC Weather **http://www.bbc.co.uk/weather/**
What's happening with high and low pressure systems. Local and world weather by region plus shipping and pollen forecasts. And for the groupies, check out behind the scenes at the weather centre for news about your favourite weathercaster.

European Centre for Medium Range Weather Forecasts **http://www.ecmwf.int/**
When's the Indian monsoon due? Complicated charts tell us.

The Met Office **http://www.met-office.gov.uk/**
The weather today and over the next few days. For a glossier view of the same information, visit the BBC weather site at **http://www.bbc.co.uk/weather/**.

The Weather Channel **http://www.weather.com**
The weather from around the world with 3-day forecasts and mini sat-pix. Factual but not as friendly as the BBC Weather site.

Yahoo! Weather **http://weather.yahoo.co.uk**
With its 5-day forecasts, Yahoo! predicts two days further than the Weather Channel and the BBC and three days better than rival Excite!

World Coverage

Agence France Presse **http://www.afp.com**
Full coverage of world news in six languages (French, English, German, Spanish, Portuguese and Arabic) from a leading international press agency.

Anorak http://www.anorak.co.uk

Originally sent to busy share-traders' screens to scan in their quiet moments, this site provides the quickest possible news fix. It condenses all the tabloid and broadsheet news and views into a mini commentary. Includes cartoons, showbiz, sport and great photos.

Crayon http://www.crayon.net/

Create your own newspaper from the subject sections, features and cartoons available. If you want email delivery, try InfoBeat.

InfoBeat http://www.infobeat.com

Get a custom-made daily paper delivered free via email. Not a unique service but this is the best for world coverage.

International Herald Tribune http://www.iht.com

World news but without the glamour of CNN.

NewsNow http://www.newsnow.co.uk

Gets you the news first. An impressive UK news service that provides world news updated every five minutes.

Press Association http://www.pa.press.net/

Excellent coverage of news from around the world. Less US bias than CNN and without the deluge provided by Reuters.

Reuters http://www.reuters.com

The biggest name in newsgathering includes a terrifying news ticker that rolls on relentlessly. Step off the home page and be overwhelmed by the quantity and quality of the subject-specific news.

The Christian Science Monitor http://www.csmonitor.com

Not the religious rag you might expect but a cool, balanced view on world news.

The Nando Times http://www.nando.net/

World news, regional US reports – and Dilbert – make up part of this nicely manageable rival to the big US news-busters.

The New York Times **http://www.nytimes.com**
The world view from Manhattan makes an impressive read. Everything from the paper plus the NY Review of Books and local guides to NY.

Specialist

Africa News **http://www.africanews.org**
Gathers together news and features from over 60 sources covering all of the African states.

Arab World Online **http://www.awo.net/**
Absolutely everything you need to know about the Arab world.

ASIA INC Online **http://www.asia-inc.com**
From Asia, the people, business and finance deals behind the news. For the news itself, use AsiaOne.

AsiaOne **http://www.asia1.com.sg/**
Local, national and international news from Asia.

Brill's Content **http://www.brillscontent.com**
Top features on the information and media age. Very sharp, very readable and an essential bookmark for anyone in the media industry.

China News Digest **http://www.cnd.org**
General and business news from China together with the unique Chinese perspective on world news.

Drudge Report **http://www.drudgereport.com**
Millions of visitors stop for world news headlines, gossip and scandal – often exclusive – with features by Matt Drudge and top columnists from around the world.

Globe and Mail **http://www.globeandmail.ca/**
Best-known Canadian newspaper from Toronto tells you what's happening in the vast landmass just north of the US.

InfoJump http://www.infojump.com
Find an e-zine that covers your interests and keep up to date.

Megastories http://www.megastories.com
Analysis and comment on the news and breaking stories.

Newsbytes http://www.nbnn.com
Everything that's happening in high technology. Extraordinarily detailed, with stringers around the world, and decent archives.

Russia Today http://www.russiatoday.com
The news – in English – with plenty on Moscow politics. Surprisingly Western in look and content.

SiliconValley http://www.siliconvalley.com
First stop for any high-tech VP looking for future eBay and Amazon.com-style successes. Polished site details news from the home of the US computer industry.

Slate Magazine http://www.slate.com
Enjoyable read with news and features – but hardly the wild child it once was.

Sporting Life http://www.sporting-life.com
Sports news. All of it.

SportLive http://www.sportlive.net/
News and results from the major sports – nicer to look at and easier to read than the Sporting Life but without the breadth and depth.

Tass http://www.tass.ru/english/
The Russian view on a particular story – described as a time-line through the day.

The Hindu http://www.the-hindu.com
India's national newspaper. Full text (in English) with all the news, business, sport, entertainment and classified ads.

The Hollywood Reporter http://www.hollywoodreporter.com
Tells you who's doing what with whom – and for how much.

The Industry Standard **http://www.thestandard.com**
The best reports, features and news about the Internet itself. The metrics section is a brilliant résumé of what's up and down in this virtual world.

The Jerusalem Post **http://www.jpost.co.il/**
News from Israel.

The Onion **http://www.theonion.com**
Brilliant send-up of tabloid news and style. A must-have bookmark.

The Smoking Gun **http://www.thesmokinggun.com**
Why the Senator was really found tied naked to the railings. Generally interesting, shaky facts behind the gossip.

Time **http://www.time.com**
Commentary on the news from top writers and politicians. For more up-to-the-minute commentary, try MegaStories.

Wall Street Journal **http://www.wsj.com**
Business news with a North American accent. The full edition costs, so try the Financial Times site for similar coverage for free. (Also look in the chapter on finance for alternative news sources.)

Try these newsgroups

alt.gossip.celebrities
Stars fall from grace.

alt.gossip.royalty
Palace whispers.

alt.journalism.print
Hacks congregate to chew over issues.

alt.politics.gossip
Naughty ministers uncovered.

bit.listserv.muslims
Islamic news (moderated).

bit.listserv.pakistan
News from Pakistan (moderated).

misc.news.bosnia
Reporting from Bosnia (moderated).

misc.news.southasia
News from India (moderated).

sci.space.news
New discoveries in space (moderated).

32//REFERENCE

That much-used cliché 'information overload' hardly does justice to the amount of reference material on the Internet. There are dictionaries and encyclopaedias that can be searched online, worldwide maps provide street-level detail of any local area and automatic software tries to answer even the toughest questions. This chapter covers a selection of reference sites that will solve your everyday questions. For specific information about business or science, travel or sport, look at their specific chapters.

Online encyclopaedias provide invaluable help with homework or research. The two big rivals, Microsoft's Encarta and Encyclopaedia Britannica are both online. You'll have to pay to access the full versions, but there's a cut-down version of Encarta available free that should answer most questions.

The web's a global service so it's appropriate it provides its own translation service to help translate a letter or a website to and from English using, for example, AltaVista's neat features.

You can avoid getting lost with worldwide street-level maps that can be instantly searched, displayed and printed out. If you're in the UK, you can type in a phone number and you'll get a map of its local area. Otherwise, find your way from A to B with the route-planning features of MapQuest (or visit the travel section).

Local information can be surprisingly difficult to find. What's on at the local cinema, at what time does the library open and exactly who is your local councillor? Answer them all with either the brilliant Scoot (based on the Yellow Pages directory and listings) or UpMyStreet that also has the audacity to tell you the price of the houses in your street.

Why so much reference material? It's a throwback to the days when the Internet was an educational service. Now, it's a great resource to help solve your nagging questions. You can look up the material yourself using any of the reference sites listed here, or visit one of the online gurus – type in your question and AskJeeves, Ask an Expert and Information Please will provide the answer.

Starting Points

About.com **http://www.about.com**
A neat, wonderful place to start looking – a friendly community of experts, advice and features. Every topic has its own human editor.

Argus Clearinghouse **http://www.clearinghouse.net/**
Reference sites on the web, rated and categorised. Dull but useful.

Yahoo! Reference **http://dir.yahoo.com/reference/**
The best reference sites from Yahoo!'s main catalogue.

Dictionaries and Encyclopaedias

A Web of On-line Dictionaries **http://www.facstaff.bucknell.edu/rbeard/diction.html**
Look up anything in any language; hundreds of bilingual and specialist English dictionaries – from Agriculture to Art, Hebrew to Hmong. Each comes from a different source, so the quality and bias can not always be assured.

AltaVista: Translations **http://babelfish.altavista.com**
Online translator to and from English and five other foreign languages – type in your text or point it to a web page URL and choose the language combination. It's fast and it works (kind of).

Encarta **http://www.encarta.com**
Browse Microsoft's excellent Encarta encyclopaedia. Either search the free concise version (that's good enough for most searches) or subscribe to the deluxe edition – with a 7-day free trial.

Encyclopedia.com **http://www.encyclopedia.com**
Free, concise encyclopaedia.

Encyclopaedia Britannica **http://www.eb.com**
No longer in print but constantly updated material on line. A free trial lasts 30 days, then you pay a monthly $5 subscription.

Merriam Webster **http://www.m-w.com**
Fine general US-English dictionary and thesaurus. Use A Web of Online Dictionaries for bilingual and specialist English words.

Questions Answered

Ask an expert **http://www.askanexpert.com**
Got a problem that's bugging you? These very clever people are waiting eagerly to answer your questions.

Ask Jeeves! **http://www.askjeeves.com**
Okay, it's really a search engine, but type in a question and it'll help you find the answer quickly.

Information Please **http://www.infoplease.com**
Easy reference to a vast combined resource of dictionaries, encyclopaedias, news archives and biographies.

The Why Files **http://whyfiles.news.wisc.edu**
Why oh why oh why oh ... hang on, here's the answer. Especially good on scientific and sports questions.

Xplore **http://www.xplore.com**
Answers to nagging questions – great for anyone struggling with their homework or pub-quiz bores.

Maps and Gazetteers

Active UK Map **http://www.ukguide.org/ukmap.html**
Patchy coverage of tourist and community information – but better than nothing.

CIA **http://www.odci.gov/cia/publications/factbook/**
Slightly scary site (with a CIA page for kids and your tacit agree-

ment to be monitored) gives way to the impressively accurate Factbook with world statistics, maps and socio-economic info.

City Net **http://www.city.net/**
What's going on in cities around the world – aimed at travellers but great for research or homework. Includes local transport, restaurants, guidebooks, accommodation, sights and customs.

MapQuest **http://www.mapquest.com**
Search for a place, then plot a map – in extraordinary street-level detail – for the world.

MultiMap **http://www.multimap.com**
Got a UK phone number? Type it in and get a map of the local area. A neat add-on to the site's core business of providing street-level maps of the UK.

UK Street Map **http://www.streetmap.co.uk**
Lost in Lewisham? Whip out your laptop, link to your cellphone and generate a map centered on any postcode or London street name. Alternatively, ask a passer-by.

Local Information

County Web **http://www.countyweb.co.uk**
UK-wide local directory for business, sports, attractions, towns and weather arranged by county.

DETR – Local Government **http://www.local.doe.gov.uk/**
Responsible for the roads, environment and local government finances – though this site makes it hard to fathom this out.

Electronic Yellow Pages **http://www.eyp.co.uk**
Find a local plumber or order a pizza. You could even splash out and do both.

Scoot **http://www.scoot.co.uk**
Bookmark immediately. A brilliantly useful guide to everything you

need in your local area. Derived from the Yellow Pages, it also provides local cinema listings and restaurant guides.

Tagish's Directory of UK Local Government Websites **http://www.tagish.co.uk/tagish/links/localgov.htm**
Listing of every local government office in the UK and a link to the right website.

Town Pages **http://www.townpages.co.uk**
Find your local library, swimming pool and civic dump. There's a more comprehensive listings site at **http://src.doc.ic.ac.uk/all-uk.html**, but it's a little rough on design and navigation.

Villages online **http://www.rural.co.uk/uk/regional/villages.htm**
Thatched cottage idyll brought up to date. Enterprising villages using the net for community resources and information.

Yellow Pages **http://www.yell.co.uk**
The Internet version of that big yellow book by the phone. Much like Scoot but not as jolly.

Reference

Internet Public Library **http://www.ipl.org**
Stroll through the aisles, pick up your favourite book and download the full text for free. A sometimes odd selection of books – probably down to copyright laws.

refdesk.com **http://www.refdesk.com**
Check the weather, solve a crossword, do your sums – an impressive collection of links to tools and sites that'll help you out.

Reference.com **http://www.reference.com**
Good haystack to start looking for your needle – lets you search newsgroups, mailing lists and websites in one fell swoop.

33//RELIGION AND BELIEFS

In an age of disbelief, the Internet is helping spread the word to non-believers. Although developed as a military science project, it's interesting to note that all the major religious movements have jumped on board as a way of promoting and spreading the good word and keeping in touch with their devoted followers, many of whom have their own sites (although these are hardly shrines – more glitzy information centres). In an afternoon, you can check the ancient scriptures of the Dharma, see your local parish service broadcast by web-cam or take a more active role and be ordained as a priest.

The main sites have embraced the web with impressive enthusiasm. For many webbers, it might even be easier to hit a religious site and catch up on the news and teachings than it ever would be to visit a church. If you are a devout believer, you'll be impressed with the depth of all of the major sites. And lapsed visitors will find the multimedia effects give a new twist to the story.

Unusually, the state of the websites gives away just as much as the teachings of each faith. The Catholic sites are generally plain, simple and, well, Catholic. Compare this to the enthusiastic colour-splashed designs for the Anglican faith. And while the Buddhist sites rival top portals with their clear designs and flood of information, minority movements flourish in the shade. With a free website and a half-decent message, you'll reach a wider audience than any prophet could.

There might appear to be a danger that religion is trivialised by the crackpot loonies trotting out unworkable ideals. Sure, there are plenty of oddities – we've included a few here but the seriously odd we've popped into the Weird Stuff chapter – but they simply reinforce the strength of the established sites.

Religious Sites

Ashtead Parish **http://dspace.dial.pipex.com/ashtead.parish/**
Impressive amateur site from a small local church in Kent delivers the parish magazine of the future. Transcripts of the sermons, audio clips of speeches and masses of local and parish news.

Asiatica Association **http://www.asiatica.org**
A good collection of Hindu and Indian religious journals but aimed at academics.

BuddhaNet – Buddhism **http://www.buddhanet.net/**
Watch the battle for the top Buddhism portal site develop between this and its two equally good rivals: **http://www.dharmanet.org/** and **http://www.edharma.com/**.

Buddhist Society **http://www.buddsoc.org.uk**
An introduction to the Dharma and its concepts.

Catholic Church in England & Wales **http://www.tasc.ac.uk/cc/**
Catholic design and content but plenty of information on your local diocese and an email address for the bishop.

Church of England **http://www.church-of-england.org**
Concentrates on the big picture but search through this trendy website and you'll find local parish information.

Cult Information Centre **http://www.xenu.net/cic/**
UK charity that helps with advice and support warning people about cults and their high-pressure tactics.

Cults 'R Us – Killer Cults **http://www.mayhem.net/Crime/cults1.html**
Gruesome reviews of the worldwide cults that condone murder in their name.

generationj.com **http://www.generationj.com**
Twentysomething Jews get up to speed on issues in this trendy,

interesting e-zine. The very young should try **http://www.sparksmag.com**.

Hare Krishnas **http://www.islandnet.com/krsna/**
Why the guys with cymbals keep marching down the high street.

Hindu Universe **http://www.hindunet.org**
Teaching, philosophy, art, science – everything that's part of the Hindu way of life – for practising or potential visitors. Also well worth visiting the Hindu Resources Online site at **http://www.hindu.org/**.

Islamic Gateway **http://www.ummah.org.uk**
Magazine-style reports on different aspects of Islam with multimedia samples from the Quran.

IslamiCity **http://www.islamicity.org**
Prayer and live radio broadcasts provide the basis for this site, but there's plenty of news and texts on Islam, the scripts and its history.

Jesuits and the Sciences **http://www.luc.edu/libraries/science/jesuits/**
The life and work of Jesuit priests from the sixteenth century to the present day. Plenty of background information with some wonderful, ancient manuscripts.

Jewish Heritage **http://www.jhom.com**
Educating visitors on Jewish heritage and history.

Knights Templar **http://www.yi.com/home/AntonioMendonca/templars.html**
Apparently, the guardians of the Holy Grail are still around. They've been plotting our future.

Muslim News **http://www.muslimnews.co.uk**
World events and news with an Islamic spin.

Reincarnation **http://www.reincarnation-org.com**
Crackpot ideas about inheriting your own wealth when you're reborn.

The Anglican Domain **http://anglican.org**
Not just C of E, but this worldwide site for Anglicans concentrates on local UK parishes, news, discussion and the chance to create your own site. See also the Church of England site at **http://www.church-of-england.org/**.

The Baptist Union **http://www.baptist.org.uk**
What they believe and what they do.

The Burning Bush **http://www.freepres.org/m_kilskeery.htm**
The Kilskeery Free Presbyterian Church in Co. Tyrone publishes an interesting, if political, monthly e-mag for webbers that's generally full of very real and gloomy news of the troubles.

The Pagan Federation **http://www.paganfed.demon.co.uk**
Take your clothes off, hold hands and dance around as you visit this site. Also worth visiting the much smaller Twisted Tree at **http://ourworld.compuserve.com/homepages/twisted_tree/** or White Dragon at **http://www.whitedragon.demon.co.uk/**.

The Religious Movements Homepage **http://cti.itc.virginia.edu/~jkh8x/soc257/antilinx.html**
Unusually for websites studying religions, this one provides a moderate, balanced view of religious movements on the web and around the world. Mainstream with none of those killer cults (see Cults 'R Us).

TheologyOnLine **http://www.theologyonline.com**
Provides an opportunity for all denominations to discuss religion and theological theories.

Universal Life Church **http://www.ybi.com/ulc/index.html**
Apparently, we are all members of this church, but not all of us have yet realised it. Oh yes, there are also plenty of MLM-style income opportunities for church members.

Vatican: the Holy See **http://www.vatican.va/**
Audio and video messages from the Holy Father. Plenty of archives,

news and a chance to read the official letters from John Paul II to political and religious world leaders.

Zen Unbound **http://members.aol.com/zenunbound/index.html**
Bringing aspects of Zen to real life in this interesting monthly e-zine.

Try these newsgroups

alt.hindu
The Hindu religion (moderated).

alt.pagan
The old religion.

alt.religion.christian
Christianity discussed.

soc.culture.jewish
Jewish culture and religion.

soc.religion.christian.bible-study
Reading and study of the Bible (moderated).

soc.religion.eastern
Eastern religions discussed with care (moderated).

soc.religion.islam
Discussions on Islam (moderated).

talk.religion.misc
Wide-ranging thoughts on religion.

talk.religion.newage
For and against the minority religions.

34//SCIENCE AND DISCOVERY

Since the Internet started off as a science project for the military and developed as a medium to exchange scientific findings, it's no surprise that there are hundreds of thousands of sites dedicated to science and discovery.

Science students are responsible for the greatest range of web pages. Every university has a main site and generally allows its students to create their own site, but most of these sites are transient and disappear when the person graduates.

The universities themselves publish everything from introductory texts to the latest research, mainly for their own student population, but a fantastic resource for any other student. The university sites tend to be rather sparse on design but, in true academic tradition, they pump them full of serious content.

Government and military research labs are just as generous in sharing their research and data. Poke around at the NASA site and you'll find the latest pictures of the galaxy as used by their own scientists. But there's also medical research and projects developed by teams across the world – such as the poor body sliced into thousands of slivers and available as images for medical students or the plain curious.

At the other end of the spectrum, consumer sites repackage the language of science into palatable chunks. These provide a great introduction to any subject, help with homework or a bonus lesson for inquisitive kids. The *New Scientist* probably offers the best range of articles on developments in science – written in a way that's accessible to any reader. And for kids, there are online experiments, tours of museums, virtual buttons to press and test tubes to fill in their quest for answers.

Starting Points

The Last Word **http://www.last-word.com**
Answers to your questions from the team at the *New Scientist*. So why is the sky blue? Great for children with homework – or flummoxed fathers.

Discover Magazine **http://www.discover.com**
Science and technology repackaged into palatable, reader-friendly features.

Tomorrow's World **http://www.bbc.co.uk/tw/**
Auntie charges into the future with the help of the TW team.

Space and Astronomy

Asteroid & Comet Impact **http://impact.arc.nasa.gov/**
Worry yourself silly with the thought that an asteroid or comet could hit the Earth and lead to our total destruction.

Astronomy Magazine **http://www.astronomy.com**
What's in the sky and how to see it.

Bradford Robotic Telescope **http://www.telescope.org**
Not too much on the telescope but a very readable guide to the way that stars, galaxies and suns work.

Earth and moon viewer **http://www.fourmilab.ch/earthview/vplanet.html**
Real pictures of the earth and moon; use the nifty navigators to change your position and see the shadows move.

Johnson Space Center **http://www.jsc.nasa.gov/**
News from the space shuttle and its experiments. For the big picture on space exploration, visit the main NASA site (http://www.nasa.gov).

Mars Exploration **http://mpfwww.jpl.nasa.gov/**
See what the Pathfinder probe saw when it visited Mars.

NASA **http://www.nasa.gov**
Big-budget space exploration clearly explained.

Space Telescope Science Institute **http://oposite.stsci.edu**
See what NASA scientists are watching in the sky with pictures from Hubble and the NASA telescopes.

Star Stuff **http://www.starstuff.com**
Spot Saturn rising and identify planets and galaxies.

This Week's Sky at a Glance **http://www.skypub.com/sights/sights.html**
Don't guess, see for sure what's in the sky tonight.

News and Discovery

National Geographic **http://www.nationalgeographic.com**
High adventure and scientific discovery melded together.

Nature **http://www.nature.com**
Academic magazine that provides a forum for announcements of scientific discoveries. Non-scientists will find the New Scientist site far easier to read.

New Scientist **http://www.newscientist.com**
Clear and impartial scientific coverage; vast range of articles, news and jobs in the sciences.

ScienceDaily **http://www.sciencedaily.com**
The latest discoveries from universities and labs around the world.

Scientific American **http://www.sciam.com**
Well-written articles on the latest scientific discoveries.

SciTech Daily **http://www.scitechdaily.com**
Daily news reporting advances in science with links to journals and papers.

Science

ArchNet **http://archnet.uconn.edu**
Dig up gems from a library of online archaeology resources.

Artificial Life **http://alife.santafe.edu**
Recreating life within a computer. Not to be confused with Artificial Intelligence – something many computers seem to suffer from.

Centre for Alternative Technology **http://www.cat.org.uk**
Eco-friendly use of power – from solar panels to a green washing machine.

Dinosauria **http://www.dinosauria.com**
Prehistoric beasts in all their glory. Particularly popular with little boys of all ages.

Fun Science Gallery **http://www.funsci.com**
Build your own microscope from toilet rolls and similar ideas for building scientific machines and equipment with household objects.

Science Explorer **http://www.exploratorium.edu/science_explorer/**
Chemical reactions in a teacup and other experiments to do at home with household items – simple step-by-steps and clear illustrations.

Science Learning Network **http://www.sln.org**
How the world works; a dozen museums, forums and features to encourage children to investigate.

Science Museum **http://www.nmsi.ac.uk/**
Plenty of buttons to press and levers to pull at this playful site. Guides, pictures and video clips of our scientific milestones.

The Constants and Equations Pages **http://tcaep.co.uk**
Essential if you are studying maths, any of the sciences or

astronomy. All the equations, constants, resources and information you could possibly need.

The Natural History Museum **http://www.nhm.ac.uk/**
School coach trips are banished as you surf past the blue whale and dinosaurs. Visitors can pose questions to the experts in this enjoyable learning experience.

The Why Files **http://whyfiles.news.wisc.edu**
Clear explanations of the science behind news stories and events – from mad cow disease to genetics.

Visible Male **http://www.uchsc.edu/sm/chs/browse/browse_m.html**
First slice your human. Now let anyone view the 1mm sections in gruesome detail. Quite stomach-turning. Oh, there's a female too.

Try these newsgroups

alt.folklore.science
Astonishing scientific tales.

alt.sci.planetary
What's happening with the planets.

sci.aeronautics
Flight and how to do it (moderated).

sci.bio
Biology dissected.

sci.chem
Reactions to chemical science.

sci.space.science
Your thoughts on space research (moderated).

35//SHOPPING

Is this really the future of shopping? Will we all be browsing the virtual aisles and finding the best deals online? It looks likely, since once you've tried the system, you'll find it fast, convenient, fuss-free and cheap. You'll get fantastic range with just about every specialist store and hypermarket just a click away from your armchair. You can't actually touch the products but you can view them from every angle, read the reviews and compare features.

Best of all, you'll find value for money on the Internet. The larger sites are able to offer discounts that astonish old-fashioned shoppers. The bookstores alone slash their prices by half on bestselling titles. And if you are looking for expensive, high-margin items, from designer clothes to consumer electronics, you can – at best – expect to pay just a quarter of the high-street price.

The latest trend in shopping is to buy via online auction. There are dozens of US and UK sites that let you enter your own gear into an auction or buy from other people. It's a great way to pick up a bargain.

In this section, we cover the auctions, shopping malls and bargain-finders. If you're looking for a particular product – like books, music or videos – try the specialist chapters in this book.

Even better, for an in-depth view of hundreds of the best places to shop, take a look at the companion volume to this book – **The Virgin Internet Shopping Guide**.

Top tips for safe shopping

1 Only enter your credit card and personal details on a secure site (that has the closed padlock icon in the bottom line of the browser).

2 Only shop with companies that provide a full contact address and phone number.

3 Try to stick with shops you know or can phone to check that they exist.

4 Ensure that delivery costs to your country are made clear before you order.

5 Keep a note of the transaction number.

6 Request delivery by recorded post or courier – to help trace missing shipments.

7 If a package is damaged, refuse to accept it and call the company.

8 Make sure that you have rights of return on faulty or damaged goods.

9 Ensure that if you're expecting new goods, you receive them rather than a used product.

10 Use the automatic price snoops to find the best price.

Compare Prices

To help you get the best deal, use one of the comparison tools that scours a bunch of online shops for the lowest prices.

Acses **http://www.acses.co.uk**
Helps find the cheapest book, video or CD on the market – a UK site but, oddly, it currently only searches US stores.

Bottom Dollar **http://www.bottomdollar.com**
Brilliant US-based site that lets you compare prices on a great range of products (not just the usual books and CDs). It's as fast and powerful as MySimon but its design is rather less jolly.

Buy.co.uk **http://www.buy.co.uk**
Find the cheapest electricity, gas or other utility – plus a good directory of shops on the web.

BuyBuddy **http://www.buybuddy.com**
Scour the web for the cheapest place to buy books, computers or home goods.

ComputerPrices **http://www.ComputerPrices.co.uk**
Helps you find the cheapest computer kit in the UK. Compare these with US prices at BuyBuddy (**http://www.buybuddy.com**).

Internet Shopper **http://www.internetshopper.com**
Fast searches and neat results. Lets you hunt through a reasonable range of products including books, music, video and software available at US stores. Without the range of MySimon.

MySimon **http://www.mysimon.com**
One of the best from the US. Send dedicated bargain-hunter Simon off to scour the shelves of over 1,200 shops.

MyTaxi **http://www.mytaxi.co.uk**
Impressive UK-specific shopping tool to help find the cheapest book, video or CD – plus a good directory of shops.

ShopGuide **http://www.ShopGuide.co.uk**
The bargain finder's guide to the UK – fast, well designed and easy to use; great for comparing prices of over 90 stores selling books, videos, games and music.

Yahoo! **http://www.yahoo.com**
Lets you search for goods from people that have set up their own Yahoo! store or the major stores on the web. US-based.

Shopping Centres

BarclaySquare **http://www.barclaysquare.co.uk**
Less than a dozen shops tucked under the safe shopping umbrella of Barclays Bank. Notable are InterFlora and NME's CD shop.

ShoppersUniverse **http://www.shoppersuniverse.co.uk**
Neat, simple mall with over two dozen well-known shops. Or visit ShopGuide and find independent sites.

Auctions

Auction Guide **http://www.auctionguide.com**

Going, going, go for it – neat guide to online auctions around the world. For a similar idea, but a different approach, try The Auction Channel (**http://www.theauctionchannel.co.uk**) that combines traditional auction-house sales into one site.

Auction Universe **http://www.auctionuniverse.co.uk**

Flog your gear to other webbers; vast online personal auction site.

Bonhams **http://www.bonhams.com**

One of the few old-style auction houses that lets you bid online; subscribe (for free) and you'll get all the details for the auction.

eBay **http://www.ebay.com**

The mother of all auction sites, with hundreds of thousands of items for sale. Bid from around the world – but check with the vendor on shipping costs.

Ebid **http://www.ebid.co.uk**

Great-looking site, but not much going on – QXL still wins on activity.

E-swap **http://www.eswap.co.uk**

Not a swap-shop but a nice, personal auction site. The busiest sections are the computer and music gear for sale; good but not quite up to QXL.

QXL **http://www.qxl.co.uk**

Buy or sell goodies at the top UK auction site. Unlike the other auction sites, QXL sells gear itself, as well as allowing anyone to sell their belongings in personal auctions.

36//SPORTS

What could be less sporty than sitting in front of a computer looking at a screen and clicking a mouse? Yet the Internet is full of excellent sports sites run by teams, organisations and fans. Maybe it's because spectator sport is one of the most popular leisure activities. The variety of sites gives you a choice – stick to the official zones for slick design and lots of nice pictures, or head off towards the amateur fanzines for their infectious enthusiasm.

Any true fan will revel in the statistical information – results, analysis and archives held in databases all over the web. Head for the vast websites for those all-important reports and results or the fanzines for endless analysis. If you missed a match – be it baseball or billiards – there's a site with a report and the final scores. And commentary. And pictures. And often video clips.

Enough about sportsmen. Use the web to help you train, improve your golfswing, workout, find the sweet-spot on a racket or tie a perfect fly. Or find out about a new sport, what's involved and how and where to learn near your home. The bigger sites include comprehensive databases of courses, pitches, banks and grounds, each rated to help you find the best place to play golf, improve your tennis, fish, ride or kick a ball.

Football Teams

Come on you reds/blues/greens/whatever. Footie Search and Football365 have plenty of links to the smaller clubs, Footballpages has them all – but here are some of the official sites:

Arsenal **http://www.arsenal.co.uk**
Aston Villa **http://www.astonvilla-fc.co.uk**
Bolton Wanderers **http://www.boltonwfc.co.uk**
Chelsea **http://www.chelseafc.co.uk**

Coventry City	**http://www.ccfc.co.uk**
Derby County	**http://www.dcfc.co.uk**
Everton	**http://www.evertonfc.com**
Leeds United	**http://www.lufc.co.uk**
Leicester City	**http://www.lcfc.co.uk**
Liverpool	**http://www.lfconline.co.uk**
Manchester United	**http://www.manutd.com**
Middlesbrough	**http://www.mfc.co.uk**
Newcastle United	**http://www.newcastle-utd.co.uk**
Sheffield Wednesday	**http://www.swfc.co.uk**
Sunderland	**http://www.sunderland-afc.com**
Tottenham Hotspur	**http://www.spurs.co.uk**
West Ham United	**http://www.whufc.co.uk**
Wimbledon	**http://www.wimbledon-fc.co.uk**

Football

Fantasy League **http://www.fantasyleague.com**
Pit your managerial talents against others in a bid to win up to £10K. There are hundreds of small, free (or cheap) enthusiast sites with their own fantasy leagues, but this is one of the best (and most expensive, at up to £25 per season).

FA Premiership **http://www.fa-premier.com**
Official site for the league, but try Unofficial Football Network or Football365 for the smell of the turf.

Football365 **http://www.football365.co.uk**
Footie trivia, stories, results and analysis – all with a larf.

Footballpages **http://www.footballpages.com**
Links to every UK team, in every division, with their official and unofficial fansites.

Footie Search **http://tw-net.winsocket.com/fsearch/**
The place to find your team's official and unofficial sites.

SoccerAge **http://www.soccerage.com**
A world perspective on football with video clips of spectacular GOOOAAALLLSSS!

Soccernet **http://www.soccernet.com**
More gossip and enthusiasm than SoccerAge but without the video clips.

Teamtalk **http://www.teamtalk.com**
Home in on your team and get swamped with news, fixtures, stats, players and betting.

Ultimate Soccer Page **http://www.angelfire.com/sc/englandA/**
Obsessive fan documents every match and result of the national squad ... since 1872!

Unofficial Football Network **http://www.ufn.co.uk**
Transfer talk, unofficial news and speculation are the staple diet for hungry fans.

When Saturday Comes **http://www.dircon.co.uk/wsc/**
Opinionated views and scurrilous gossip with the latest team-talk and results from the team at WSC.

Racing and Betting

Channel 4 Racing **http://www.channel4.com/sport/racing_c4/**
Visit if only to see John McCririck's arm waving as Mr Smooth, Brough Scott, keeps all on a tight reign – not up to the prize-winning TV show but worth a fiver each-way.

Gone to the Dogs **http://www.thedogs.co.uk**
Adopt a dog, see the results and find out how to bet on greyhounds.

Sporting Life **http://www.sporting-life.com**
Who'll win what, when and why. Form heaven.

Sportingbet.com **http://www.sportingbet.com**
Slick site that lets you place bets on almost any sporting event. Based in Alderney, it's also tax-free!

UK Betting **https://www.ukbetting.com**
Not as flash as the Sportbetting site but quicker and easier to use. Unfortunately, you'll be taxed as with a normal bookie.

Sports Guides

Aggressive Skating **http://www.aggressive.com**
Rad baggy-trousered teens should point their inline skates this way.

All England Lawn Tennis **http://www.wimbledon.com**
Tennis at Wimbledon and little else.

Black Belt Search **http://www.blackbeltsearch.com**
Directory of martial arts sites from self-defence schools to Bruce Lee.

Boxing.com **http://www.boxing.com**
Gloves-off commentary about boxing in the US and around the world (in that order) – also includes a live report of a selected big fight.

British Shooting and Fishing **http://www.premier-pages.co.uk/sports/british.htm**
There are hundreds of individual 'I shot a moose'-style sites around, but this provides a central collection of field-sport websites and organisations that cover hunting, shooting, fishing and conservation in the UK.

CNN/SI **http://www.cnnsi.com**
Combine CNN and Sports Illustrated and you have a vast, statistic-rich site with heavy emphasis on US sports, but there is world coverage in here if you look.

CricInfo **http://www.cricinfo.org**
A beautifully mown, level pitch. Bring your own tea to enjoy all the information, results and features you could wish for.

Cricket Unlimited **http://www.cricketunlimited.co.uk**
Combining commentary from the Guardian's team of cricket reporters with facts and reports from Wisden make this hard to beat. On a level wicket with CricInfo.

Cyber/Darts **http://www.cyberdarts.com**
Surprisingly interesting – and very popular – website that provides reports on darts technology and hundreds of events from around the world.

fishing **http://www.fishing.co.uk**
Where to fish and buy your equipment in this magazine-style site.

Freestyle Frisbee **http://www.frisbee.com**
Now you're a web junkie, you'll need to master the basic sport: frisbee.

Golf Today **http://www.golftoday.co.uk**
Golf from a (mostly) European perspective – but still has news from worldwide tournaments and a directory of courses around the world. For similar coverage but with a US accent, try Golf.com at **http://www.golf.com/**.

Horseweb **http://www.horseweb.co.uk**
No frills horsey site that covers horses and tack for sale.

International Table Tennis Federation **http://www.ittf.com**
Whatever you do, don't call it ping-pong.

ITV-F1 **http://www.itv-f1.com**
The official site for Formula 1 racing from the licence-holding official TV station. Yes, it really is official.

Martial Arts Global **http://www.martial-arts.shoto.com**
Improve your karate chop with techniques and lists of schools.

Outdoors OnLine Inc. **http://www.ool.com/homepage.html**
Hunting, shooting and fishing US-style. For a more genteel UK vision, try **http://www.premier-pages.co.uk/sports/british.htm**.

Real Tennis **http://www.real-tennis.com**
Neat site about eccentric rackets game said by enthusiasts to be the best game in the world.

Rugby Football Union **http://www.rfu.com**
Official news on the national squad and its matches.

Scrum.com **http://www.scrum.com**
Rugger talk and play. For the official line, visit the RFU (**http://www.rfu.com**).

Specialized **http://www.specialized.com**
Cool dudes who make cool mountain bikes have a cool site, featuring lots of trails for stump-jumping action around the world – with plenty in the UK.

SportsWeb **http://www.sportsweb.com**
All the major sports, with plenty of local and world news.

The Tennis Server **http://www.tennisserver.com**
How to get ahead in tennis. Loads of features and advice.

The Where to Fish Directory **http://www.where-to-fish.com**
Where you can fish, in Britain and abroad. Over 3,000 pages cover streams, courses, sites and pits. For a specialist guide to fishing in gravel pits, try **http://www.fisheries.co.uk**.

Triathlete **http://www.triathletemag.com**
Just reading the training schedules will make you feel faint. If you compete, there's plenty of fitness and training regimes, plus results.

UK Mountain Bikes Resources **http://www.sussex.ac.uk/Users/nealet/bikes.html**
Lists exactly what the title states.

Try these newsgroups

alt.fishing
Fishing tackled.

alt.sports.baseball.atlanta-braves
Just one of the hundreds of team groups.

alt.sport.darts
Fun with small metal arrows.

rec.autos.sport.f1
What you think of their driving.

rec.running
Rather more than sprinting for the bus.

rec.scuba
Have fun diving.

rec.sport.boxing
Hard-hitting discussions on boxing.

rec.sport.cricket.info
The latest news and scores (moderated).

rec.sport.golf
Pitch-putting ideas.

rec.sport.rugby
Rugger talk.

rec.sport.soccer
Football in all its glory.

37//TRAVEL

Adventure, advice and cheap tickets pretty much sums up this section. Glossy magazines and travellers' tales sit awkwardly together in a heap of inspiration for your next hols. Take their advice, then find out more from the excellent set of guides to cities and countries around the world. Finally, use the virtual travel agents to grab a really good deal.

If you're after a cheap flight, take a quick sniff at the official sites of the airlines to check seating plans and timetables, then hurry on to the bucket shops.

To try and claw back direct ticket sales, some airlines have devised ingenious auctions of tickets. Once you've registered, you're sent an email whenever there's a special deal available. Try the big US carriers such as United (**http://www.ual.com**) or American (**http://www.american.com**).

Many people now use the Internet to book hotels, B&Bs or rented villas. Instead of relying on printed brochures you can take a virtual stroll through the rooms, check the views and pin-point the building on a local map.

Once you've planned and booked your trip, there's plenty more on offer. Language guides help you pick your way through a new language, and you'll never step out of line with advice on business and tipping etiquette in foreign lands.

For lots more about all this, try **The Virgin Internet Travel Guide** – the travelling companion to this book.

Airlines

All the main airlines have their own sites. Many let you buy tickets online, but you'll probably find a cheaper price from one of the main online agents. If nothing else, you can check the flight times and join their frequent flier schemes.

Aer Lingus	**http://www.aerlingus.ie**
Aeroflot	**http://www.aeroflot.org**
Air Canada	**http://www.aircanada.ca**
Air France	**http://www.airfrance.com**
Alitalia	**http://www.italiatour.com**
American Airlines	**http://www.americanair.com**
British Airways	**http://www.british-airways.com**
British Midland	**http://www.iflybritishmidland.com**
Cathay Pacific	**http://www.cathaypacific.com**
Continental	**http://www.flycontinental.com**
Delta	**http://www.delta-air.com**
EasyJet	**http://www.easyjet.co.uk**
El Al	**http://www.elal.co.il**
Go	**http://www.go-fly.com**
Iberia	**http://www.iberia.com**
KLM	**http://www.klmuk.com**
Lufthansa	**http://www.lufthansa.co.uk**
Olympic	**http://www.olympic-airways.gr**
Qantas	**http://www.qantas.com**
Ryanair	**http://www.ryanair.ie**
SAS	**http://www.sas.se**
Singapore Airlines	**http://www.singaporeair.com**
TWA	**http://www.twa.com**
United Airlines	**http://www.ual.co.uk**
Varig	**http://www.varig.com.br**
Virgin	**http://www.fly.virgin.com**

Starting Points

MSN Expedia **http://www.expedia.msn.co.uk**
Microsoft lands in the UK. Everything you need to research destinations and book flights, hotels and cars instantly. Good design with piles of information.

Epicurious Travel **http://travel.epicurious.com**
Great for ideas, daydreaming and planning but not so good for cheap tickets. Combines the style of Conde Nast's Traveller magazine with food, dining and online booking.

Tickets

A2bTravel **http://www.a2btravel.com**
Vying for top slot as best UK travel agent site. Everything your local agent can provide and so very much more. Also worth checking prices at the websites of real agents FlightBookers (**http://www.ebookers.com**) and Trailfinders (**http://www.trailfinders.co.uk**).

Bargain Holidays **http://www.bargainholidays.com**
Jaunty fun in the sun at cut-prices.

Biztravel.com **http://www.biztravel.com**
Maximise your frequent flyer points and make the most of your expense account trips. Great for business users but not always the cheapest tickets.

Cheap Flights **http://www.cheapflights.com**
Automatically scour over 30 agents to find the cheapest deal.

Eurostar **http://www.eurostar.com**
Travel to France and Belgium made very easy.

Lastminute **http://www.lastminute.com**
Don't plan ahead and save a fortune. Great deals on top hotels, restaurants, concerts and flights.

Thomas Cook **http://www.thomascook.co.uk**
Holidays, flights, currency and last-minute bargains from the high-street agent.

Travel Select **http://www.checkin.co.uk**
Simple, efficient travel agent.

Travelocity **http://www.travelocity.co.uk**
Just about the biggest travel agent on the web. Gives you instant access to the same system that's used by the high-street travel agents.

Guides and Resources

1Ski **http://www.1ski.com**
Where to ski and the best deals available for package deals.

Adventure Magazine **http://www.adventure-mag.com**
Row across the Pacific or perhaps do something really adventurous.

Africa Guide **http://www.africaguide.com**
Great gap year fodder. An excellent guide to the 51 countries in Africa that covers medical and travel advice, together with links to local attractions, businesses and sites.

Britannia **http://www.britannia.com**
Central directory of sites that help you plan, book and enjoy travels around the UK.

Christine Columbus **http://www.christinecolumbus.com**
Remember Christopher? Well, Christine packed his bags before he set off – here's her advice and products for women travellers.

FrequentFlier **http://frequentflier.com**
Keep up to date with frequent flyer schemes.

International Student Travel Confederation **http://www.istc.org**
Students sign up and travel the world on cut-price tickets, staying in hotels at rock-bottom prices.

Lonely Planet **http://www.lonelyplanet.co.uk**
Guide books to almost every destination; best for experienced travellers eager to get as much as possible from their trip.

Maps Worldwide **http://www.mapsworldwide.co.uk**
Find your way around any city or country.

Opinionated Traveler **http://www.opinionatedtraveler.com**
Destination guides without the waffle, written by travel pros and journalists.

Railtrack **http://www.railtrack.co.uk**
Clean, simple, efficient – and it works. Much better than nagging National Rail Enquiries, but you should probably do that too.

Rec.Travel Library **http://www.travel-library.com**
Travellers' journals to help plan your next adventure.

Roadnews.com **http://www.roadnews.com**
Nothing to do with cones, but excellent advice on using your laptop when you travel.

Rough Guides **http://www.roughguides.com**
Great guides to countries and cities for independent travellers on tight budgets.

Strolling.com **http://www.strolling.com**
Beat the blisters and relax as you watch online video tours of London, New York, Paris and Dublin.

The Complete Gap Year **http://www.gapyear.co.uk**
Tons of information, ideas and links for students planning a year out.

The EmbassyWeb **http://www.embpage.org**
Your local embassy – whatever your nationality, wherever you are.

The Original Tipping Page **http://www.tipping.org**
How, when and what to tip. Aimed at visitors to the US but helps out around the world.

Travelang **http://www.travlang.com**
Phrases to help you out when you're travelling.

Travelmag **http://www.travelmag.co.uk**
Fascinating features and masses of ideas for hols and adventures.

UK Travel Guide **http://www.ukguide.org**
Welcome to Britain. A guide for visitors to (and residents of) the United Kingdom.

Underbelly **http://www.underbelly.com/index.html**
What to avoid – but, so far, only covers a few cities. Still, it might grow and provide an antidote to some of the glossier sites.

Virtual Tourist **http://www.vtourist.com**
Concise guides to local transport and visitor information for an impressive range of cities and countries.

WebFlyer **http://www.webflyer.com**
Choose your frequent flyer scheme with care, advises Randy. He'll tell you why and plenty more besides.

Accommodation

French Connections **http://www.frenchconnections.co.uk**
Over 400 rather nice homes to rent in France.

Holiday Rentals **http://www.holiday-rentals.co.uk**
Holiday homes to rent around the world.

Infotel **http://www.infotel.co.uk**
Where to stay in the UK – includes, unusually, guesthouses, with prices, location and rating. Online booking is antique but adequate.

International Home Exchange **http://www.homexchange.com**
Swap your semi for a palace.

Leisure Planet **http://www.leisureplanet.com**
See the hotel before you book; a vast collection of over 50,000 hotels, each with a mini slide show, plus area guides.

The Great British Bed and Breakfast **http://www.kgp-publishing.co.uk**

Switch from hotels to homes and save – a guide to the hundreds of B&BS around the UK. Unfortunately, there are no ratings.

Try these newsgroups

rec.travel

Travel the world.

rec.travel.air

Travel the world by plane.

rec.travel.cruises

Travel the world by liner.

rec.travel.europe

Navigating through Europe.

rec.travel.marketplace

Travel and lodging for sale or wanted.

rec.travel.usa-canada

Tour North America.

38//WEIRD WEB

There's a lot of peculiar things out there, from sites devoted to missing socks to academic musings on alien abductions and UFOs. Most oddball sites are put together for fun and should be treated in the same way. Unfortunately, there are cults and deadly serious religions on the net that use high-pressure sales techniques to claim new members (see the section on religion for cults and charities that help rehabilitate).

And then there's sex. The impression given in much of the media is that the Internet is full of pornography. It's hardly 'in your face', but neither is it difficult to find – much like the porn magazines you'll find on the top shelf at the newsagent's, but uncensorable and so pretty much uncensored.

At any one time, there are estimated to be over eight million people visiting porn sites on the net. Since almost all charge for access to their content, this represents a vast revenue. And in many ways, the development of the Internet has been pushed forwards by the demands and investment made by the porn industry in better-quality images, live video and sound-delivery technology – which are now standard for music and film clips on less risqué sites. It's probably also fair to say that the porn industry revolutionised the way e-commerce was handled online by developing ways to process credit card payments.

It's not hard to find unpleasant sites on the net. The real trick is to filter through the dross and find cutting-edge weirdness that's an enjoyable route off the main highway. And if you're looking for newsgroups, many of the 60,000 groups are oddball – but the majority of the weirdness goes on within groups starting with the word 'alt'.

Sex

Apparently, the equivalent of 10 per cent of the US population logs into a porn site every day. So where is it? Well, it's not hard to find – try searching Excite! or Yahoo! as usual ('sex' is always one of the most requested search terms). If you really need help finding a first site, you can always try Yahoo! (in its Business_&_Economy/ Companies/Sex/Virtual Clubs section), or one of these:

http://www.uploaded.co.uk – funny naughty pix from the lad's mag.
http://www.playboy.com – for the interviews, naturally.
http://www.persiankitty.com – famous collection of erotic websites.

Starting Points

Cool Site of the Day **http://www.coolsiteoftheday.com**
Check its Cool Stuff section for a daily – and generally tame – list of what's new in weirdness.

Cruel Site of the Day **http://www.cruel.com**
Vicious take on 'Cool Site' that's far, far better. Play 'Cruelette' to visit a random crazy site, if you dare.

Weird but True **http://munshi.sonoma.edu/jamal/weird.html**
Get into the spirit of this section with thousands of weird (actually, very weird) stories, comments and news mostly from the world of science and doctors.

Weird Mysteries **http://www.europa.com/edge/weird.html**
Crop circles, little green men and pictures of angels make up the majority of this directory of sites about strangeness.

Web-cams

Linking tiny TV cameras to a website – so you get a live view of what the camera sees. Apart from the obvious sex angle, visit one of the thousands of sites to see what other web-heads are doing in the bedroom/beach/road/office.

Allcam **http://www.allcam.com**
Thousands of cams in offices, shops, homes and schools around the world – neatly arranged into sections.

Earthcam **http://www.earthcam.com**
Best selection and range of web-cam sites on the net.

JenniCam **http://www.jennicam.com**
Probably the most famous cam site – for adults only – from the immodest Jennifer.

JustSurfIt **http://www.justsurfit.com**
Bunch of web-cams: babes on the beach at Fort Lauderdale and a nice view of the crowds in Times Square.

Lochness Monster **http://www.lochness.co.uk/livecam/**
Nice views over the Scottish loch as you sit and wait, and wait, and wait.

Ultimate Taxi **http://www.ultimatetaxi.com**
Checker cab rigged out with disco lights, sound system, laptop – and web-cams to capture punters heading home after the party. If you prefer taxi rides without the party atmosphere, try New York Cab Cam (**http://www.ny-taxi.com**) as you sit with a Checker through Manhattan.

Webcam Central **http://www.camcentral.com**
Great place to find cams, not as polished as the others, but plenty of sites listed.

Webcam World **http://www.camworld.com**
Friendly diary-format chat, news and thoughts on web-cams and other craziness.

A Life of Fear and Loathing **http://www.cornboy.com/hst/bio/**
Paranoia in NY city – the life of the mysterious Hunter S. Thompson. With so many thousands of sites about HST, it's no wonder he's so twitchy.

Alien Abductions **http://www.alienabductions.com**
Why haven't the aliens abducted you yet? Take the Abductalizer test to find out – then read tales of survival from those picked up by the little green men.

America Off-line **http://www.aoffl.com**
Anti-AOL site with a bathroom wall of user's graffiti. Academics would call this a reaction to the successful commercialism of AOL. Either way, it's fun.

Annoy **http://www.annoy.com**
Rants designed to annoy. It works.

BabelOnline **http://members.tripod.com/BabelOnline/**
Parts are funny, parts are sex-crazed, parts just weird. But the excellent design and drawings bring a cult following.

Bianca **http://www.bianca.com**
An 'alternative online community' – so a great place to meet weirdos.

Bufora **http://www.bufora.org.uk**
British UFO watchers tune in and contemplate if there's life in the sky tonight.

Bureau of Missing Socks **http://www.jagat.com/joel/socks.html**
Y2K sock problems, masses of chat and tempting offers to film you with or without socks.

Computer Underground Uplinks **http://www.cybercom.com/~bsamedi/hack.html**
What the Internet used to be about and how to be a cyber-punk.

An impressive collection of how-tos and manifestos on hacking secure websites, free software and conquering the world.

Conspire **http://www.conspire.com**
It's not so much who's watching as how many people.

Cult of the Dead Cow **http://www.cultdeadcow.com**
Sure to offend everyone within the first page. From then on, it's hacking, weirdness, and mad short stories. So a great place to visit.

Dead People Server **http://www.dpsinfo.com**
Is he or she still alive? Thousands of well-known names rated as alive or dead – with all the official details. So, did Bing Crosby die on a Spanish golf course? – yes, in October 1977.

Fortean Times **http://www.forteantimes.com**
Driver killed by low-flying cow and other tales from mid-America (and around the world). A cult read for anyone into the stranger side of life.

Ghosts **http://www.ghosts.org**
More ghost sightings and paranormal activity than you can concoct from a ouija board.

Headball **http://www.braincraft.com/headball1.html**
If it's all getting too much for you, have a go on this interactive game of smacking a couple of heads around the screen.

Miss America **http://www.missamerica.org**
A big warm welcome for Honey – she wants to help children and travel the world. Thunderous applause.

National Enquirer **http://www.nationalenquirer.com**
Online version of scurrilous US magazine.

Nerve Magazine **http://www.nervemag.com**
Thoughtful hedonists tell tall tales about sexy encounters. Amusing with very little real naughtiness.

Oceania **http://oceania.org**
Big plans to build a new country in the middle of the ocean where everyone's free to think and do. Weird? Maybe not.

Piercing Mildred **http://www.mildred.com**
Seriously weird online game to create the freak of the week with the most holes in his or her body.

Salon.com **http://www.salonmagazine.com**
Fab political e-zine with commentary from celebs and columns on everything worth knowing. And not to be confused with the haircare site **http://www.salon.net**.

Sin City **http://www.sincity.com**
Home to Penn and Teller. The big guy and little chap provide weird (funny) articles and weird (weird) tricks. Well worth a visit.

Steamshovel Press **http://www.umsl.edu/~skthoma/**
Whooaah, hold on one minute and let's take a hard look at the evidence. Yep, it was a conspiracy.

Suck **http://www.suck.com**
Seminal daily e-zine with short pithy commentary on life.

Superbad **http://www.superbad.com**
Psychedelic colours, strange tales and silliness. The site design, by the way, is cutting edge and award winning.

Supreme Being **http://www.supremebeing.com**
Mighty God or madman? One confused man's philosophies on life and his (not too offensive) music.

Talk City **http://www.talkcity.com**
Stand in a crowded party and have dozens of strangers talk to you all at the same time?

TheConfessor.com **http://www.theconfessor.com**
'I did it for money' admissions from confused visitors who need to get it off their chests.

The Death Clock **http://www.deathclock.com**
Personalised report on how long you've got till that reaper-fellow visits.

The Kiss **http://www.thekiss.com**
I was sitting watching a movie with my best friend when her brother kissed me – like, wow. The sticky business of first and best kisses.

The Weird, Wild and Wonderful on the WWW **http://www.links.net/www/**
Lists just what the title suggests. A great place to start delving.

Urban Legends Archive **http://www.urbanlegends.com**
'I ate grandma's ashes' and other urban myths from the alt.folklore.urban newsgroup, with intelligent comment from experts.

Virtual Drawing! **http://www.virtualdrawing.com**
Draw something with the zippy Java thing, then email it to a friend who gets to edit your sketch. Pointless demo of the hi-tech features of your browser.

Web Vengeance **http://www.segasoft.com/web-vengeance/**
When the web really gets to you, download this gizmo that lets you shoot your hated sites to pieces.

Weird Web **http://www.weirdweb.com**
Offensive comic strips, assorted silly words and weird facts.

Ya-hooka! **http://www.yahooka.com**
Marijuana news and features – plus lawsuits from guess who.

39//FAQS – FREQUENTLY ASKED QUESTIONS

As you start to use the Internet you're bound to come across questions, worries and problems. Many of these are dealt with in the relevant chapter in the main part of the book; for example, if you want to know how to publish your own web page, look to Chapter 8.

In this section, we've covered some of the most commonly asked questions and their answers.

//THE CONNECTION

***Q* Why can't I connect?**
A You've checked your modem's plugged in and switched on? Make sure that you have typed in the correct user name and password and are dialling the right telephone number.

***Q* Why does my modem keep dialling?**
A Whenever you start a bit of Internet software (your web browser or email program), it automatically tries to connect to the Internet. If it can't connect, or the number's busy, it will redial a few times (normally five times).

***Q* Why do I keep getting disconnected?**
A It's likely that the idle timeout feature is cutting in. This will automatically disconnect you if the computer has not been used for a few minutes. Typically, this happens if you dash off to make a cup of tea or, more likely, you are reading a page without updating or browsing. Open the Control Panel and open the Internet/ Connections icon; now change the 'Disconnect if idle for xx minutes' setting. It's also worth changing the same setting in the modem driver: in the Control Panel, open the Modems icon and click on the Properties button. The other cause could be that you

have a Call Waiting feature or that someone else in the house is trying to make an outgoing call when you're online.

***Q* When I connect to the Internet, the Dialer program tells me I've connected at 115Kbps – is this possible?**

A Your computer is transferring information to the modem at 115.2Kbps, the maximum speed possible with a standard computer, but the modem has connected to the Internet at the best speed it can negotiate. If the line's bad, the modem adjusts its speed down to ensure that the data doesn't get scrambled.

***Q* Will my free ISP account last forever?**

A It should do – but most free ISPs check that you've used your account on a regular basis. If you don't use the service for 90 days, they will probably cancel your account and you'll have to re-register.

***Q* How do I cancel my account?**

A Check your contract with the ISP. Some will require a month's notice, others won't. Visit your ISP's main website and check the email address for the admin department. Send them an email telling them you want to cancel your account – and ask for an email to acknowledge this.

***Q* What's the best time to go online?**

A Depends what's important to you. The cheapest time (in telephone costs) is evenings and weekends. The busiest time (and so the time when the web is slowest) is evenings and weekends. For top speed, connect when the US is asleep.

//BROWSING

***Q* Why does my web browser keep crashing?**

A It shouldn't. This probably means that you're not using the latest version of the browser. As new ways of enhancing web pages are developed, older browsers can find it hard to manage and simply stop working. Visit **http://www.microsoft.com** or **http://www.netscape.com** to download the latest version of your browser.

Q Why isn't a web page there any more?

A The website might have been closed down or, more likely, the designer has redesigned the site and reorganised the way the pages are stored and given them new names. If a page doesn't work, visit the main site's home page.

Q What does 'Error 404 not found' mean?

A It means that the address of a web page does not exist. Either you typed in the wrong address or the site has been redesigned and the names of the web pages have been changed.

Q Do all web page addresses start with the letters 'www'?

A No. You'll often see addresses that look very odd but will still work fine. The way addresses are created is slowly changing, so you can expect to see more addresses that are just names.

Q What's a secure connection? How can I get one?

A Secure connections are set up by the web server (not by your web browser) – you can tell you've got a secure connection when the tiny closed padlock icon is displayed at the bottom of the screen.

Q I saved some images from a website to my hard disk. How can I view these GIF and JPEG format files on my PC?

A The simplest method is to use your web browser as the viewer. Start your browser (choose not to connect and to work offline) then start Windows Explorer. Click and drag one of the images from Explorer on to the browser and you'll see it displayed. The alternative is to use a paint program that's better than Paint installed with Windows. Try Paintshop Pro (**http://www.jasc.com**) or search **http://www.filez.com** for a wide selection.

Q What's a plug-in?

A A plug-in is a special bit of software that adds a new feature to your web browser. For example, if you want to view video or animation in your browser, it needs to have a plug-in that supports this. If you visit a site that uses snazzy multimedia tricks and you don't have the right plug-in, you'll be told and given the chance to download the file required.

***Q* I want to use bitmap images I created on my PC on my own web page. How can I do this?**
A You can, generally, only use GIF and JPEG format graphics files on a web page. You'll need to use an image editor program to convert your BMP format files to either GIF or JPEG. Try Paintshop Pro (http://www.jasc.com) or search **http://www.filez.com**.

***Q* I have downloaded a file that ends in the ZIP extension. When I double-click to run it, nothing happens. How do I open it?**
A A ZIP file contains a compressed version of the original file(s) that have been squeezed down to save space and time when downloading. To unzip your file, you'll need an unzip program. The best known is WinZip from **http://www.winzip.com**.

***Q* When I try to save a page with the File/Save As option in my browser, it just saves the text and layout – not the graphics. How do I get the lot?**
A You need to use an offline browser that will grab all the associated files and store them on your hard disk. Try WebWhacker (http://www.webwhacker.com).

***Q* I have visited a few sites that play music samples and I would like to save these to my hard disk to play back later. How do I do this?**
A Most music is stored in the WAV, MIDI, MP3 or RealAudio file formats. To download and save any of these files, right-click on the link that plays the file and select Save Link As.

***Q* Should I accept 'cookies'?**
A Yes, they are normally perfectly harmless. Most big sites use a cookie (it's a little file on your hard disk that lets a website store

information on your machine) to store your name or preferences or the last time that you visited the site.

***Q* How can I be sure to download a file as quickly as possible?**
A If you are downloading a file from a commercial site, such as CNET, you'll be given a list of various sites that store this file. You could choose the nearest geographic site, but use lateral thinking and pick a site in the world where it's still night-time – the traffic will be much lighter and your download should fly.

***Q* Can I catch a virus by looking at a web page?**
A Viewing images, entering information in a form or just viewing text on a web page is perfectly harmless. That means 99 per cent of all websites are fine. Sometimes, you'll visit a website that uses snazzy multimedia or other trickery. You might be warned that your web browser needs to download a plug-in or Java or ActiveX applet (the name for a little program). These applets are normally developed to provide extra functions – such as shopping carts, multimedia or special effects. However, it is possible to write nasty little applets that trash the files on your computer. To avoid this, don't accept plug-in downloads from sites where you don't know the company.

***Q* Can I stop my kids viewing porn online?**
A Yes, almost totally. Use one of the parental control programs such as NetNanny (**http://www.netnanny.com**) or CyberSitter (**http://www.cybersitter.com**) or, if you're on AOL, click on their Parental Control page. However, the best advice is to move the computer to the sitting room, where everyone can see it and make sure you're in the room when they browse. They'll be too embarrassed to try.

//EMAIL

***Q* Why does an email get returned as 'undeliverable'?**
A You've typed in the wrong email address when you created the

message. Check with your friend that you have their correct address – it should be in two parts: their name or nickname, an '@' symbol and their company or ISP name. For example, 'simon @virgin-pub.co.uk'. Some addresses have full stops or underscore '_' symbols – type this in as well.

***Q* What can I do about junk mail?**

A Unsolicited junk mail – called spam – is the bane of life with email. Dumb companies send out millions of messages and think it'll improve their image. Many ISPs now have anti-spam systems in place that automatically recognise known culprits and reject any mail received from them. You don't have to do anything – but check with your ISP to see if they have this feature. If you keep getting junk mail from a particular address, you can create a new filter (or rule) in your email program that automatically deletes any message from this person as soon as it's received.

***Q* I've joined a mailing list but now I want to get off. Unfortunately, I've deleted the original instructions that tell me how to unsubscribe from the list. What can I do?**

A Visit the **http://www.liszt.com** site and search for your list. Under the description, it should give you instructions about how to subscribe and unsubscribe to the list. If not, see if there is an admin email contact and send them an email.

***Q* Can anyone else read the emails I send?**

A Email messages are sent in plain text form – as you typed it out. As the email passes across the Internet, malicious system managers could, in theory, read it. However, with hundreds of millions of mail messages zipping around the net every day, it's unlikely. If you want to make quite sure that the head of IT in the company isn't peeking at private post, scramble the contents of your messages. The most secure system around is called PGP (**http://www.pgp.com**), although most email programs have some form of encryption built in.

Q What do I do if someone's harassing me by email?
A Tread carefully. If it's an unknown nut, it might be better not to reply (this can wind them up even more); change your email address – get a free account – and tell your ISP that you've been getting this type of email. They are in a better position to try and track down the sender and automatically block any further email.

//NEWSGROUPS AND CHAT

Q Where can I find the newsgroups that my ISP doesn't handle?
A Visit Deja (**http://www.deja.com**) to read what's been said in all the newsgroups, or visit Jammed (**http://www.jammed.com**) for a list of news servers that will let anyone access all the newsgroups.

Q Will I get junk mail if I post a message to a newsgroup?
A Some unscrupulous companies comb the newsgroups to pick up the email addresses of users, then sell these on as mailing lists, so you may well get junk mail. If your ISP provides you with more than one email address (most do), reserve one for your newsgroup activity and ditch any unwanted mail received on that address.

Q I posted a message a few days ago, but it's gone. What's happened?
A It's 'expired' – been removed from the newsgroup. So many messages are posted every day that your ISP's computer has to delete messages after a few days to save space.

Q How can I search for old newsgroup messages?
A You need to use one of the archive sites, such as Deja (**http://www.deja.com**), which stores copies of messages from all newsgroups.

Q Can I write a test message before diving in?
A Yes, but use the alt.test newsgroup – don't write test messages to a normal newsgroup or you'll get a lot of rude replies.

Q I want to try IRC (Internet relay chat) but how do I find a server that lets me use this?
A Ask your ISP – they should have an IRC server. Alternatively, when you install your IRC software, it will have a list of IRC servers that you can use or you can search Liszt (**http://www.liszt.com**) for a server near you.

//SHOPPING

Q Aren't I playing into the hands of thieves by paying with a credit card at an online store?
A No. Even VISA and MasterCard both say it's perfectly safe – so long as you shop sensibly. In fact, it's easier for a thief to pinch your card details when you pay at a restaurant or in a shop or by phone!

Q I've found a site that stocks something I want to buy – how do I know it's safe to proceed?
A The top rules for buying online are: (1) Only type in your credit card details if you're on a secure server (little closed padlock in the bottom corner of your browser). (2) Do you know the company name? If not, check further to find out the registered address and contact number – no contact phone number, no sale! (3) Check the policies on returns and guarantees.

Q Can I buy from any online shop?
A No. Many shops will sell only to people who live in that country. This means that only US residents can buy from the majority of the US-based shops. All the shops listed in the main directory will ship around the world.

Q Is there anything that I cannot buy online?
A In theory, no – there's a shop for everything, however weird! In practice, you are more likely to hit incompatibilities or customs problems. For example, US videotapes won't work in the UK and, if you want to order a banana tree from California, customs in the UK won't allow it into the country for fear of spreading disease.

***Q* Are warranties and guarantees the same for items bought on the net?**
A Yes, unless it's otherwise specified. The only exception is to (normally electronic) products you've bought from outside your country. For example, if you live in the UK and buy a computer in the US, it's very unlikely the warranty will be honoured.

***Q* I'm trying to find the best range of shops that sell cigar cutters – what's the best strategy?**
A. Forget about using one search engine at a time. Instead, use a metasearcher like DogPile (**http://www.dogpile.com**) to automatically search a dozen of the top engines at the same time. It'll return a neat list of sites that cover cigar cutters, as indexed by AltaVista, Excite!, InfoSeek, Lycos and Yahoo!

***Q* How do I find the cheapest prices?**
A The US is the land of the bargain-finding website. The best site is MySimon (**http://www.mysimon.com**). It will scan dozens of online shops for a particular product and then list the cheapest suppliers. In the UK, there's ShopGuide (**http://www.shopguide.co.uk**) and MyTaxi (**http://www.mytaxi.co.uk**) – but these are limited to searching for the cheapest books, videos and CDs.

//GLOSSARY

address (email) Unique name that identifies a person and lets you send them a mail message.

address (website) The unique location of a site on the web. Sometimes called a URL (uniform resource locator).

address book A list of names and their email addresses. Your email program provides this feature to let you manage your contacts.

ADSL (asymmetric digital subscriber lines) New system of transferring information over a standard telephone cable at very high speeds – several thousand times faster than a modem.

alias An alternative name you use in either chat or email (or both).

anti-virus program Special software that detects and removes viruses from programs and documents. You should run an anti-virus program on any file you download from the Internet or receive via email.

applet A small program that's downloaded from a website and runs within your web browser. Some online shops implement their shopping cart system using an applet.

attachment A file sent with an email message.

authentication Method of identifying a company as being who or what it claims to be. This is usually done through a system of certificates (issued by independent companies such as VeriSign – **http://www.verisign.com** – and Thwate – **http://www.thwate.com**).

authoring Creating a web page.

backbone The high-speed communication lines that link up the ISPs around the world and provides the foundation of the Internet. As more people go online, the traffic over the backbone increases and things start to get sluggish.

bit A basic storage unit used in computers; a bit can only be one of two values '1' or '0'. Data is stored in a computer as a combination of bits (eight, see 'byte'). Bits are normally used when specifying the transmission speed of a modem (for example, 56Kbps means 56,000 bits sent every second).

body The main text part of an email message.

bookmark A way of storing the address of an interesting website in your web browser. When you want to revisit the site, don't bother typing in the address, just click on the bookmark entry. Microsoft calls this feature 'Favorites'.

bounce An email message returned to the sender because it was sent to an invalid address.

bps Bits per second.

broken link A hyperlink that doesn't work when you click on it. You'll see the 'error 404' or 'Error, page not found' warning messages.

browser Special software that you need to view a web page and navigate through the web. The two main browsers are Netscape Navigator and Microsoft Internet Explorer.

byte A basic unit for storing data in a computer; a byte is made up of eight separate bits and can store numbers between 0 and 1024. Your computer's memory and hard disk storage capacity is normally measured in bytes – in a document, one byte would be used to store one character. Compare this with 'bit'.

cache Way of (temporarily) storing the last few web pages you have visited so that next time you visit the page, you save time and avoid downloading the images again. This is a feature of your web browser and controlled automatically.

CGI (common gateway interface) An advanced feature of website programming that allows a web page to send information to a program running on the server. For example, if a web page has a search feature, the search term you enter on the web page is sent to the search program using CGI. See also 'Perl'.

chat System that lets you type out messages that are seen instantly by other users, unlike newsgroups (where you pin up a message in a forum). See also instant messaging and IRC.

client Your computer. Compare this with 'server'.

compression Special way of squeezing a file so that it's smaller and so takes less time to download. Compressed filenames normally end with the letters 'ZIP' – you'll need special software to decompress the file before you can use it.

cookie A tiny scrap of information stored on your computer by a website.

Dial-up A connection to the Internet that is not permanent: you need to dial a number to make the connection (just like using a normal phone). If you get an account with an ISP, it's usually a dial-up account – this means you can get online using a modem.

digital certificate See 'certificate'.

directory A website that contains a list of other websites, normally organised into sections and often with a search feature. Yahoo!

(**http://www.yahoo.co.uk**) is one of the best-known directories that lists half a million websites.

domain name The unique name that identifies one website or computer on the Internet. For example, the domain name 'microsoft.com' identifies the server provided by Microsoft.

domain name system (DNS) A method of converting the domain name to the IP address (a series of numbers) that's actually used to locate the computer.

download To transfer a file from a distant computer on to your own, via the Internet.

email (electronic mail) Way of sending text messages, files and video clips to another user on the Internet. But you'll need to know their unique email address.

emoticons See smiley.

encryption Way of scrambling a message or contents of a file so that only the intended recipient can unscramble it and read it. When you visit a secure website it uses an encryption system to ensure that any information you type in is scrambled as it is transferred over the Internet.

e-wallet Feature of new web browsers that lets you enter a range of different ways of paying for your shopping. You might include your credit card and e-cash, then open your e-wallet when you visit a shop. It's one future method of managing your spending on the net.

FAQ Frequently asked question.

filter Special feature of email software that lets you define the way in which incoming messages are automatically managed and moved into folders according to key words in the message.

firewall Special security system (normally installed in a company) that lets users in the company access the Internet but prevents outside hackers gaining access to the company's computers.

folder In an email program, this refers to a container for your email messages or, on a hard disk, it's a container for files.

forward Feature of email software that lets you send a message you've received on to another user.

freeware Software that can be used on a permanent basis without charge.

FTP (file transfer protocol) Protocol used to transfer files between computers over the Internet.

Gateway A link between two different systems. For example, an email gateway can be used to resend an email message to a fax machine or pager.

GIF A common graphics file format used to store images on a web page.

gopher An older system that allowed users to navigate the Internet – it's now almost entirely replaced by the web and you're very unlikely to see it in action – unless you get caught up on an academic server.

Hayes AT The set of commands used to control almost all modems. Visit modem manufacturer Hayes' site (**http://www.hayes.com**) for more information.

header The part of an email message that contains the recipient's address, sender's name, subject of the message and any delivery options.

home page The first page you see when you visit a website, before proceeding to other documents and links. The home page is normally stored in a file called 'index.html'. If you visit **http://www.microsoft.com**, you are actually viewing the Microsoft home page on its website.

HTML (hypertext markup language) The set of codes that used to layout and format a web page. These codes let you add links, define text styles, use colours and insert images into a page.

HTTP (hypertext transfer protocol) The series of commands (protocol) used by a web browser to ask an Internet server for a particular web page. You'll see this at the start of most web addresses (though you don't have to type it in) to identify this address as a web page rather than a file (which uses a sister protocol, FTP).

hyperlink/hypertext A way of connecting web pages together across the web. One word or image in a page can be linked to any other page on the site or any other site on the web. When the user clicks on the link, they jump immediately to the referenced page.

IE (Internet Explorer) Microsoft's web browser software.

IMAP A new standard that's set to replace both POP 3 and SMTP over the next few years.

instant messaging A facility that lets you know the moment a friend has connected to the Internet and is available for a natter. When you type in a message, it is sent instantly to the other user. You'll need special software, but it's free (Netscape and AOL users have this built-in).

Internet (or net) The millions of computers that are linked together around the world so that each can communicate. The Internet is public, so any user can visit any other computer linked to the Internet. See Chapter 1 for a full definition and history of the net.

Internet service provider (ISP) A company that provides a doorway on to the Internet for you, the user.

intranet A mini, private Internet within a company. Employees can browse their company information in just the same way as you would on an Internet using a web browser.

IP (Internet protocol) The key to the way computers on the Internet can locate each other and communicate. An IP address is a string of numbers that identifies each of the main server computers on the Internet. To make it easier for users to manage an IP address, it's translated into a friendlier text form, called a domain name.

ISDN A high-speed digital version of your standard old phone line. You'll get a speedy connection to the Internet using an ISDN link, but you need a special modem (called a Terminal Adapter) and an ISP that provides ISDN access for its users. ISDN, however, is being overtaken by the new cable modem and ADSL technology.

ISP See Internet service provider.

JavaScript Special programming language that lets web page designers enhance the basic effects provided by HTML.

JPEG A file format used to store the graphic images displayed on a web page; JPEG files are usually used for photographic images, GIF files are better for simple images with fewer colours.

Kbps Kilobits per second, i.e. 1,000 bits of information sent every second – used to measure the speed of a modem or other communication devices. See also 'bit'.

keyword Word that you type into a search engine to find information.

link See 'hyperlink'.

mailbox Special area at your ISP where your incoming mail messages are temporarily stored until you connect to the net and download and read the mail.

mailing list A list of email addresses of like-minded users who want to share information, news and views on the subject. Any email message sent to the list is immediately distributed to everyone who has subscribed to the list.

mail server A computer on the Internet that deals with your email: storing your incoming mail until you login and read it and passing on the email messages you send to the right address. Your ISP will provide you with the address of its mail server. You'll need to configure your email software to look at this address for your new mail.

MIME (multipurpose Internet multimedia extensions) A way of sending a file within an email message. In the old days, you would have to encode any file attachment before sending it over the net. Now, MIME is the standard used to painlessly and automatically send files between users.

modem A special device that connects your computer to a telephone line and allows you to dial and connect to an ISP and so gain access to the Internet. A modem works by converting your computer's data into sound signals that can be sent along a phone line. New communication systems (like ISDN, ADSL and cable modems) do away with this conversion and send information in its native digital format to provide much higher transfer speeds.

moderated A newsgroup, chat system or mailing list that is monitored by someone who ensures that the messages are decent or to do with the subject.

name server A special computer on the Internet that converts a domain name to its IP address. See DNS.

Netscape Navigator One of the most popular web browsers on the market – get a free copy from **http://www.netscape.com**.

newsgroup A public discussion forum that lets anyone discuss a particular subject, hobby or interest. There are over 60,000 newsgroups that, collectively, are called Usenet.

news reader Special software you need to access, read and post messages to a newsgroup – web browsers from Microsoft and Netscape have a news reader built in.

offline Not connected to the Internet.

online Connected to the Internet, so incurring telephone charges.

Perl A very popular programming language that's used to add advanced features (such as a shopping cart or search engine) to your web site.

PGP (pretty good privacy) A way of encrypting an email (or file) so that only the intended recipient can decrypt it and read the message – used by some small shopping sites to enable customers to safely send in their credit card details.

plug-in Special program that works in conjunction with your web browser to provide an extra feature (often multimedia, video or animation) – if you need a plug-in to view a particular web page, you'll be told and given the chance to download the file automatically.

PoP (point of presence) A telephone number (provided by your ISP) that your modem dials to connect to their computer and so to the Internet. Make sure that your ISP provides PoPs in your local area and that these are local numbers.

POP 3 A method of transferring email messages over the Internet. The POP3 standard is normally used to retrieve your messages and the SMTP standard is used to send the mail.

post office See mail server.

protocol A set of rules that defines the way something happens. For example, the POP3 system of sending mail is a protocol that defines the commands used to actually transfer the message.

public domain Something (either a text or program) that is freely available to anyone to view or try. The copyright still remains with the original author, so you can't copy it, resell it or change it without their permission.

secure site A shopping site that provides a system (almost always the SSL standard) to ensure that there is a secure channel between the site and your browser – anything you type in (such as your credit card details) cannot be unscrambled or read by a hacker. You can tell you are at a secure website because your web browser displays a tiny closed padlock icon in the bottom status bar.

SET (secure electronic transmission) New rival to the established SSL standard that provides a secure way of sending your payment details over the net to a shop.

shopping cart/basket An electronic equivalent of the wire basket you use in your supermarket. Lets you add items as you browse a shopping site, then move to the checkout to pay.

signature Few lines of text that are automatically added to any email you write or newsgroup message that you post. Your signature could just include your name or provide contact details or company name and slogan.

smiley A facial expression made up of keyboard characters, often added to email or newsgroup postings to add expression or feeling. For example :-) means happy, funny or a joke.

SMTP Simple mail transfer protocol. See POP3.

snail mail The old-fashioned method of sending a letter via the Post Office.

spam Unwanted email – normally sent in bulk to advertise something.

SSL (secure sockets layer) A way of scrambling the data between your web browser and the website so that no hacker and eavesdropper can read the information you are sending. Normally used on a web page that asks you to enter a credit card number or personal details. Your browser will indicate a secure, SSL page by displaying a tiny closed padlock icon in the bottom line of the windows. Don't shop without this!

TCP/IP (Transmission Control Protocol/Internet Protocol) The rules that describe how all information is sent over the Internet and how it finds its way to the right destination. Read the history of the Internet in Chapter 1 for a full description.

UART (Universal Asynchronous Receiver/Transmitter) A special chip in your computer responsible for sending and receiving data in a serial form – which means anything sent via a modem.

URL (uniform resource locator) The correct name for the full address of a web page. For example, 'microsoft.com' is a domain name, 'http://www.microsoft.com' is the website address for Microsoft and 'http://www.microsoft.com/index.html' is the URL to the site's home page.

Usenet The collective name for the mass of over 60,000 newsgroups on the Internet.

UUencoding An older method of converting files into a special format before attaching them to an email message. Thankfully, you don't need to do this any more – it's usually done automatically.

web browser A software program that lets you view a web page and navigate around the web.

web page A single, individual page within a website. Each web page is stored in a separate file; the file contains HTML commands that describe the text, its layout, formatting and links.

web server A computer that stores a website (generally, web servers store hundreds of separate websites or, in the case of mammoth sites from the BBC or CNN, the website is big enough to deserve its own web server.

website A collection of web pages produced by one person or company and about a particular subject.

Winsock Software that lets your computer communicate with the Internet via a standard dial-up connection; Windows includes a Winsock utility that's configured automatically – you shouldn't need to do anything!

WWW (World Wide Web) (or W3 or web) The collective name for the millions of individual websites on the Internet.

//INDEX

//A

//B

//C

//T

//U

//V

//W